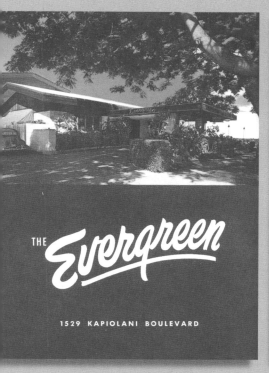

THE *Evergreen*

1529 KAPIOLANI BOULEVARD

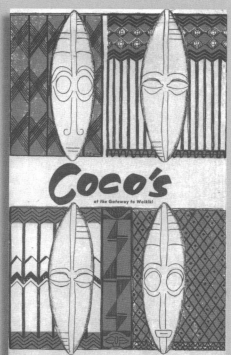

Coco's

at the Gateway to Waikiki

Elliott's

STEWART'S WAIKIKI RESTAURANT (that famous Drugstore Restaurant)

Elliott's Chuckwagon

1015 Kapiolani Blvd.

Free Transportation to and from
Your Waikiki Hotel. Phone 581161

Aloha Grill

LIQUORS   FINE FOODS

1165 BETHEL STREET   PHONE 5-6363

hob nob

coffee house and cocktail lounge

ALEXANDER YOUNG HOTEL . . . IN THE CENTER OF DOWNTOWN HONOLULU

Kapiolani Drive Inn

ALA MOANA AND JOHN ENA ROAD
HONOLULU, HAWAII

We always welcome the opportunity to
serve you and give you the kind of service
that will make you want to come back.

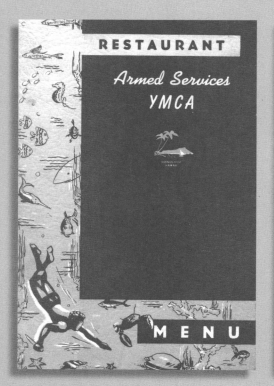

RESTAURANT

Armed Services
YMCA

HONOLULU
HAWAII

MENU

The *Jolly Roger*

KAU KAU

Cuisine & Culture in the Hawaiian Islands

KAU KAU

Cuisine & Culture in the Hawaiian Islands

Hi Uncle,
I hope you enjoy
going back to
the old days!
Jo

To George,
I love your
work!

Arnold Hiura

Aloha,
Arnold Hiura
9/13/10

WATERMARK
PUBLISHING

ISBN 978-0-9796769-3-2

Library of Congress Control Number: 2009937462

SPAM® is a registered trademark of Hormel Foods, LLC and
used with permission here.

Design and production
Gonzalez Design

Watermark Publishing
1088 Bishop St., Suite 310
Honolulu, Hawai'i 96813
Telephone 1-808-587-7766
Toll-free 1-866-900-BOOK
sales@bookshawaii.net
www.bookshawaii.net

Printed in China

To my wife, Eloise,
who worked as hard on this book as I did,
and to our parents, who flavored everything
we ever ate with love....

Toshika and Satomi Hiura
Larry and Ruby Nakama

ACKNOWLEDGMENTS

Researching and writing this book has taken several years and has been a fascinating journey that has taken me to the islands of Kaua'i, Maui, Hawai'i and O'ahu. The process of transforming a concept like this into a reality is a challenging one. *Kau Kau* would not be possible without the support of aio chairman Duane Kurisu, Watermark publisher and editor George Engebretson, copy editor Frederika Bain, designer Leo Gonzalez and photographer and good friend Shuzo Uemoto. Special thanks to all of them.

Chicken long rice

I would also like to thank the following people (in alphabetical order) for their time, interest, knowledge and support in putting this book together: Goro Arakawa, Tom Asano (Kulana Foods), Hiroshi Azeka, Anthony Chang, Rodney Chin (Hawaiian Commercial & Sugar), Karleen Chinen (the *Hawaii Herald*), Chef Sam Choy, Stephan & Saori Doi, Ernest & Marian De Luz, Kathleen Ka'iulani de Silva (HECO), Lance Duyao (Big Island Candies), John & Hilma Fujimoto, Masa Fujita, Glen Fukumoto (UH College of Tropical Agriculture & Human Resources), Ronald & Kay Fukumoto, Frank Gonzales (Kapi'olani Community College), Elmer Guzman (The Poke Stop), Rachel Haili (Haili's Lunchwagon), Rodney & Karol Haraguchi (Haraguchi Farm), Lyndsey Haraguchi-Nakayama (Hanalei Taro & Juice Co.), Clark & Jackie Hashimoto (Hashimoto Persimmon), Glenn & Gail Hayashi, Chuck Hazama, Charles & Helen Higa (Zippy's Restaurants), Andrea Hiura, Alyssa Hiura, Milton & Carol Hiura, Sherrie Ann Holi (Big Island Candies), Allan & Irma Ikawa (Big Island Candies), Larry Ikeda, Karen Ishizuka & Robert Nakamura, Raina Itagaki, Joey Itagaki, John & Asako Iwamoto, Ed Ka'ahea, Arthur Kaneshiro, Masina Kauha, Owen Kawakami, Joe & Rachel Kim, Richard Kim (Joe Kim's Kim Chee), Karen Konishi, Gaylord Kubota (Alexander & Baldwin Sugar Museum), Gail Miyashiro (Cafe 100), Derek Kurisu (KTA Super Stores), Jozette Montalvo (Hawaiian Commercial & Sugar), Audrey Muromoto, Ikuko Muto, Stephanie Nagata, Lloyd & Sue Nakama, Myles Nakashima (Pukalani Superette), Stephanie Sayuri Ohigashi, Stanley Okamoto, Randy & Joan Okumura, Terron & Dee Oshiro, Tyson Oshiro, Monty and Phyllis Richards (Kahuā Ranch), John Richards (Kahuā Ranch), Tim Richards (Kahuā Ranch), Lois Shimabukuro-Miyake (Ka Lei Eggs), Chef Russell Siu, Tiki Suan, Yuki Lei Sugimura, Barry Taniguchi (KTA Superstores), Charles and Lynne Toma (Sam Sato's, Inc.), Kirk Toma (Sam Sato's, Inc.), Rene Tomita, Augustine & Petra Torres, Ronald & Jackie Torres (Jackie's Diner), Nora Uchida (Two Ladies Kitchen), Ira Uradomo (M. Uradomo Farms), Karen Watanabe (HECO), Chef Alan Wong, Chef Roy Yamaguchi, Glenn Yamanoha, Milton Yamasaki (Mealani Research Center) and George Yoshida.

CONTENTS

INTRODUCTION

Food is hot these days—and I don't mean burn-your-tongue hot or so-spicy-you-sweat hot. I mean food is everywhere-you-turn hot. This is true throughout the nation and around the globe. Why, we even have an entire television network dedicated to food. And nowhere is food more talked about, appreciated and central to daily life than in Hawai'i.

In the more than three years I spent researching and writing *Kau Kau: Cuisine & Culture in the Hawaiian Islands*, I thumbed through shelves of books devoted to food at local bookstores.

Poi

What's more, I found more than 100 titles relating to Hawai'i's food and cooking for sale on a Hawai'i-based Web site, more than 300 books on Amazon.com and more than 700,000 sources via a Google search. The Internet is abuzz with dozens of heavily trafficked food-related sites and blogs packed with photos, recipes, reviews and stories about food in Hawai'i.

Our foodmania is stoked by local newspapers, magazines, radio programs and television stations. We can wake up on weekday mornings to television reporters sampling delectable dishes at popular local eateries or hosting chefs in their studio kitchens. A pantheon of celebrity chefs has brought further attention and acclaim to Hawai'i. Thanks to knowledgeable food writers and reporters, Hawai'i's rich food heritage and ever-changing food trends are often in the spotlight.

So why add one more book to the galaxy of good stuff already out there? Who am I to think I might have anything of note to add to this subject? I'm not a chef, or even a respectable foodie—I'm just another guy on the street, an Everyman who eats where you eat, shops where you shop and cooks what you cook. I'm the guy behind you in line at the market, lunchwagon or shave ice stand, someone who subscribes to the notion that there really are at least a million stories in the naked city—and we should share more of them.

Non-expert that I am, I begin with an admission. For most of my life I thought that "kau kau" was actually a Hawaiian word meaning "food" or "to eat." I'm pretty sure many others believe the same. After all, when someone bellowed, "Kau kau time!" it was the equivalent of saying, "Chow time!" or "Come and get it!" I was well into my adulthood when I was enlightened to the fact that "kau kau" was not Hawaiian in origin but was very likely a local pidgin English word derived from the term "chow chow," which is Chinese for "food."

Aha, mo' bettah! I reasoned. How appropriate that a local term as widely used as "kau kau" was actually a product of Hawai'i's multiethnic history. Nothing, after all, is more multiethnic than the food of Hawai'i. To illustrate, imagine playing a word-association game in which someone says, "local food," or "Hawai'i food," and you say whatever springs to mind. Among the responses:

"Plate lunch!"
"Poi!"
"Pineapple!"
"Potluck!"
"Stew!"
"Zippy's!"
"Kalbi!"
"Loco moco!"
"Saimin!"
"Hekka!"
"Rainbow Drive-In!"
"Portuguese sausage, eggs and rice!"
"Laulau!"
"Oxtail soup!"

Whether your favorite food is a traditional ethnic dish prepared at home or a culinary masterpiece served at one of Hawai'i's many fine restaurants, it is safe to say that our food choices are among the most diverse in the world, the product of many cultural and historical influences. This book looks at what we eat in Hawai'i—and offers some suggestions as to *why* we eat what we do.

Besides the fact that it tastes good, of course, some of these key reasons include:

- **Place**. Hawai'i is a special place. As we are located in the middle of the Pacific, the sea plays a big part of our food culture. Hawaiian culture and foodways form the basis for all that came after, including whalers, traders and missionaries, followed by wave upon wave of immigrant groups from around the world.
- **Preservation**. Preserving food has always been a big concern. Given the Islands' isolation, until fairly recently imported foods came on long ocean voyages from faraway places. Many of them were salted, dried, smoked, pickled or canned, the better to survive the trip. Keeping food edible once it was here in this hot, humid tropical climate also relied heavily on these techniques.
- **Diversity**. Modern Hawai'i is a society with no majority ethnic group. This fact and the values of

the host culture allowed different immigrant groups to retain that which is unique to each of their cultures.

- **Community**. Living, working and playing in close proximity with one another, people from different backgrounds shared what they held in common with each other. What evolved was a local culture that featured its own values and way of living—including clothing, language and food.
- **Scarcity**. A lack of material wealth was one thing that most local people had in common with one another, and nothing affected Hawai'i's foodways more than economic necessity. Regardless of their background, people had to grow, catch, gather, make do, adapt, stretch and share to survive.

Today, we often ask each other, "What you like eat?" In the not-too-distant past, the more common question would have been "What get for eat?" This book tries to establish some guideposts in the transition from one way of viewing food to the other.

In this transition period of a mere one or two generations, Honolulu has grown from a series of small, quiet communities where

everyone knew each other to a crowded, fast-paced modern city. Like many baby boomers, I can close my eyes and imagine the sound of shoes on solid sidewalks giving way to the crunch of bare feet on the dirt and gravel roads of rural Hawai'i. When I do, I am suddenly haunted by the sweet perfume of rose apples in my nose, the tartness of green guavas in my mouth and the sticky juice of mountain apples on my chin.

If you, too, can relate to this journey, I encourage you to try the little food features in these pages called Kau Kau Connections. These personal, relatively quick and easy recipes and activities offer some fun ways to reconnect to old memories or make new ones.

Haupia

This is the heart of *Kau Kau: Cuisine & Culture in the Hawaiian Islands*: a look at the evolution of local food and society in Hawai'i— and how they interact—as told from my own experiences, those of the many people I've interviewed and the many sources I've researched. It is a sometimes kapakahi, slightly skewed and biased, perspective on the foods of Hawai'i, our reasons for eating them, and what it might say about who we are and where we may be headed.

CHAPTER ONE

Life on an Island
The Roots of Hawai'i's Cuisine

The food of Hawai'i is most commonly described as being a reflection of its multiethnic population, a smorgasbord of exotic delicacies brought to the table by various ethnic groups as each came to call the Islands home. While this familiar axiom is largely true, it is also interesting to explore in greater detail why people eat what they eat in Hawai'i and the important role that food has played in the process of forging a common cultural identity called "local."

Any engineer will tell you that the most important component in creating any sort of structure is a strong foundation. This is also true—perhaps even more so—in the case of social structures. Hawai'i's diverse, multicultural society is built upon a foundation established by the first people to discover and settle this chain of islands more than 1,500 years ago. These people, skilled navigators from the South Pacific, not only managed to find these islands in the vastness of the North Pacific, but they also brought with them many of the basic foodstuffs that sustained their society for centuries and are still identified as the traditional food of Hawai'i today.

>>> >>> >>> >>> >>> >>> >>>
Traditional Hawaiian methods of food production—pounding poi at Wai'āhole, O'ahu ca. 1922—can still be found today, primarily as demonstrations offered by the visitor industry. Opposite: A turn-of-the-20th-century hukilau.

⋙ ⋙ ⋙ ⋙ ⋙ ⋙ ⋙

A Windward Oʻahu family ca. 1910 assembles the children, family dog and guitar to pose for a pre-lūʻau photo

This was important, for no matter how beautiful the Islands were, they offered the first Polynesian settlers fish, limu (seaweed) and shellfish from the sea; birds, eggs and some edible ferns on land; but no taro, rice or bananas—nothing substantial that could sustain them.

Hawaiians understood that life on a small group of islands some 2,000 miles from the nearest human settlement required special care and consideration. In a sense, these islands were not so different than the canoes that had sustained them over their long and daring voyages. In both cases, the basic necessities of food and fresh water were limited and had to be managed carefully in order for their occupants to survive.

For centuries, Hawaiians relied

on an agrarian economy organized by land divisions known as ahupua'a. Ideally, each pie-shaped region extended from mountaintop to the sea, which allowed for food and other natural resources to be shared from the lowlands to the higher elevations and established a sense of interdependence and responsibility amongst those who had to rely on the bounty of such a limited land area. Fish, shellfish, seaweed and salt from the ocean were offered for taro, sweet potato, yams, arrowroot, breadfruit and fruits from lowland and midland farms and rivers, which were offered for the wood, stone, ferns, herbs and other plants that thrived in the uplands.

Taro, usually pounded into poi, formed the staple of the Hawaiian diet, sometimes augmented by sweet potatoes, yams, breadfruit and bananas. The Hawaiians developed irrigation systems and terraced farms.

Under their careful stewardship, the sea provided a wide variety of fish and other edible sea products such as limu, 'opihi (limpets), crabs, lobsters, turtles and he'e (octopus).

Hawaiians were expert fishermen who employed a variety of methods to catch fish. Hook and line, fish traps, nets and fishponds were all skillfully utilized. Hawaiian fishhooks were made from bones, shell or wood and came in many different shapes and sizes depending on the type of fish they were intended for. Fishing line was made from strong plant fibers and sinkers out of stone. Hawaiians also designed lures, such as special shell lures, that they used to catch octopus.

Other means of catching fish included spears, fish traps and various types of nets. One method of spear fishing utilized torches at night to see in the shallows close to shore and along the reefs. Hawaiians were

skilled at net fishing, with specialized nets designed for use either from shore or from canoes.

Finally, Hawaiians developed an ingenious system of aquaculture to ensure that they would have access to a food supply no matter the weather or how their other fishing efforts fared. Large fishponds were constructed with rocks along the coastline. Sluices enabled small fish to enter from the open ocean and kept larger fish from leaving. 'Ama'ama (mullet) and awa (milkfish) were the main fish raised, although other fish were caught and released into fishponds, including manini (convict tang), āholehole (Hawaiian flagtail) and moi (Pacific threadfin), amongst others.

Meat was derived from domesticated pigs, dogs and chickens, while certain wild birds were also hunted for meat. To conserve their limited resources, Hawaiians established seasons for gathering scarce food and

A tableau at the now-defunct Hawaiian Wax Museum depicts Queen Ka'ahumanu breaking the taboo against women dining with men—and effectively ending the ancient kapu system. Left: a variety of traditional Hawaiian poi pounders.

⋙ ⋙ ⋙ ⋙ ⋙ ⋙ ⋙

In Big Island artist Dietrich Varez' block print Ulu from Kanehunamoku, *paddlers return in a sailing canoe brimming with 'ulu (breadfruit) from the mythical floating island of Kānehunamoku, reputed to lie offshore of Hana, Maui.*

ADRIFT ON AN ISLAND

When you voyage … you begin to see the canoe as nothing more than a tiny island surrounded by the sea. We have everything aboard the canoe that we need to survive as long as we marshal those resources well….
— Master navigator
Chad Baybayan

Beginning in the 1970s, the voyaging canoe *Hōkūle'a* changed the way the world viewed the people of the Hawaiian Islands—as well as how the people of Hawai'i saw themselves. Through its history-making ocean voyages, the *Hōkūle'a* and its crew not only proved that ancient Polynesians could have sailed thousands of miles

from the South Pacific to discover Hawai'i more than 1,500 years ago, but also that they were so skilled that they were able to continue to travel back and forth after settlement.

Looking at the *Hōkūle'a*, which is modeled after the remains of ancient traditional Polynesian canoes, one of the most striking things about the remarkable vessel is its size. The *Hōkūle'a* measures 62 feet in length and approximately 14 feet wide—a mere speck in the immense Pacific Ocean and limitless boundaries of sky. Aside from a series of compact sleeping niches incorporated into each hull, the actual living space aboard the canoe is almost entirely limited to a deck measuring roughly 40 feet long by 10 feet wide straddling the twin hulls. Four hundred square feet—hardly more than a good-sized living room—is a tiny space to accommodate 12 to 15 people and their provisions for voyages that lasted over a month and spanned thousands of miles of landless sea.

For the original settlers to have survived their journeys aboard such a vessel is an amazing revelation, considering the amount of drinking water and food they would have needed to stock. According to legendary waterman and writer Tommy Holmes, fresh water was carried in gourds and sections of bamboo, and drinking coconuts also provided potable liquid. Fresh food could only be consumed in the initial stages of the journey, and crews grabbed any opportunity to gather rainwater and catch fresh fish, turtles and sharks. The bulk of the provisions, however, needed to be stored and carefully managed to ensure survival. Preserving food by drying, salting and fermenting allowed the voyagers to store food for long periods without spoiling.

Even more impressive, those who would become known as Hawaiians also brought many of our most familiar and important food items to Hawai'i aboard their canoes. These included kalo (taro), kō (sugarcane), mai'a (banana), niu (coconut), 'uala (sweet potato), 'ulu (breadfruit), 'ohe (bamboo), kī (ti plant), uhi (yam), 'awa (kava), kukui (candlenut), pia (arrowroot) and 'ōhi'a 'ai (mountain apple).

These early settlers also brought pigs, dogs and chickens. These animals, along with rats that had inadvertently been stowed away on the canoes, could have been used as food in an extreme emergency, but many survived to be used as breeding stock after making landfall. Much of the food was consumed raw—especially fish and seafood—while some food was cooked aboard the canoe on a hearth lined with stone, coral and sand. Coconut husks and shells served as fuel.

No matter how expertly they navigated and how well they managed their resources, however, success hinged on yet another key factor. One of the greatest challenges to successfully executing long ocean voyages, *Hōkūle'a* crewmembers report, was the mental and emotional condition of its participants. Cramped quarters, limited food and water, raging storms and days spent hopelessly adrift in the doldrums could easily let uncertainty, fear, tension and worse destroy the cohesiveness of life on board.

Once you go on the canoe, because it's so small, you try to make it like one family.
—*Hōkūle'a* crewmember Snake Ah Hee

A big part of maintaining a positive and stable atmosphere under often trying conditions, it turns out, was the powerful social impact of sharing food. In the stark and threatening context of a seemingly endless sea, it was easy to appreciate the fact that food was life and, by extension, that the act of sharing food was to share the very essence of life.

Mealtime is one of the few times during the day that the entire crew is together on deck. On long monotonous days, meals are a highlight.
—Polynesian Voyaging Society

Voyagers may have viewed their canoe as an island, their refuge against a sometimes cruel and powerful ocean. Equally important was their ability to view their islands as canoes. For islands, after all, are finite landmasses where survival also means having to share, where coexistence means treating others as family, and where one of life's most enjoyable and anticipated activities is to share a meal with those with whom one shares the journey of life.

꙳꙳꙳ ꙳꙳꙳ ꙳꙳꙳ ꙳꙳꙳ ꙳꙳꙳ ꙳꙳꙳ ꙳꙳꙳

In the late 19th century, Honolulu Harbor was crowded with whalers and other merchant vessels.

for hunting game.

Hawaiians prepared their foods simply, eating them raw, dried, fermented, broiled, roasted, boiled or steamed. To protect certain foods from burning, Hawaiians wrapped them in ti leaves, as in the case of laulau. If a large quantity of food was to be prepared, an imu (earthen oven) was dug. Stones heated by a wood fire were covered with leaves to protect the food. Fish, taro, sweet potatoes, chickens and breadfruit could be wrapped up and placed inside the imu. To roast or kālua a pig, hot rocks were also placed inside the pig to cook it thoroughly.

Sea salt was used, along with drying and fermentation, as a food preservative, but it was also impor-

tant as a seasoning. Other popular forms of seasoning included limu kohu (a type of seaweed) and 'inamona (roasted and ground kukui nut).

Whalers, Merchants and Missionaries

After centuries of isolation, the arrival of British explorer Captain James Cook in 1778 swiftly and irrevocably changed the Hawaiian Islands. Cook is credited as being one of the first sea captains to identify the lack of fresh fruits and vegetables as the cause of scurvy, so he was always searching for sources of fresh food, and Hawai'i was one such source. As news of Cook's expedition spread throughout the world, Hawai'i's strategic position in the middle of

A SALTY STORY, THE OLD HAWAIIAN WAY

Just off the Kaumuali'i Highway, some 17 miles from the town of Līhu'e, Kaua'i, lie the ancient salt ponds of Hanapēpē. There are no fences, no guards or fancy signage to point out the significance of this place to the uninitiated. The only notable sign in the vicinity belongs to the Salt Pond Beach Park nearby. A few intrepid tourists in easy-to-identify rental vehicles can be seen cruising slowly by—armed with their off-the-beaten-path guidebooks, squinting, pointing and wondering if this is indeed the famed cultural landmark they have been searching for.

Perhaps this is how it should be, since the salt ponds at Hanapēpē are one of those extremely rare archaeological sites still being maintained and used for their original purpose—producing what might arguably be the most highly prized sea salt in the Hawaiian Islands, and beyond.

Because the area is situated on State land, only those of Hawaiian ancestry are permitted to create and cultivate their own salt plots, under a rather loosely held set of rules that has survived the test of time. Due to the limitations of land and wells, the governing body established to oversee the salt ponds currently bars new plots from being added. Non-Hawaiians, like lifelong Hanapēpē resident

Masa Fujita, are allowed to practice the art of salt-making here by formally partnering with a Hawaiian holder of an existing plot.

For centuries, humans have been coaxing out precious salt crystals here at Hanapēpē, where a perfect confluence of land, sea and fresh spring water from the highlands greets the omnipresent West Kaua'i sun.

Forget any notion you might have of simply collecting the salt left by evaporated seawater. It takes a time-tested blend of science and art to produce this magnificent salt. First of all, unpredictable Mother Nature reigns over the process, flooding the entire area under several feet of water during the rainy season. As it dries under the hot summer sun, "salt season" might usually run from June through August, but it varies from year to year depending on the weather, Fujita explains. After the floodwaters finally recede, the wells and salt beds have to be painstakingly cleaned and rebuilt each year before the process of salt-making can begin anew.

There is something organic and primal about the salt ponds at Hanapēpē. The smooth, red clay is wet and slippery near the mouths of each well. Just a few feet away, the land is cracked and dry—literally hot enough to fry an egg. A primeval blend of seawater, which enters the underground wells from the ocean several hundred yards away, and fresh water oozes up from the deep wells that feed every salt plot. The presence of tiny brine shrimp indicates that the salinity of

the water is perfect for salt-making, and, according to Fujita, the shrimp are also believed to help reduce the level of algae in the wells.

The well water is pumped into an intermediary well, known as a pūnāwai, and into the salt beds themselves. As the water evaporates from the shallow salt beds, they are refilled with the water from the pūnāwai, itself grown slightly saltier. In about two weeks' time, the first batch of salt is ready to be carefully raked, collected in a bamboo colander, rinsed clean in the pūnāwai and taken home to use. Subsequent batches, fed from the more slowly evaporating pūnāwai water, usually take about seven to eight days to mature, depending on the rate of evaporation determined by the sun and wind.

Fujita's patient nature is evident as he demonstrates the gentle strokes required to collect the pure white crystals from each bed, being careful not to disturb the dirt floor from which they appear to have miraculously sprung. Fujita estimates that each 3-by-8-foot bed, properly tended, might yield from one to two 4-gallon buckets of salt per season, depending on the weather.

There is no mistaking the unique flavor of this salt. Many consider it to be the perfect condiment or seasoning. Because the seawater is filtered through rocks, sand and soil before it blends with fresh water in the wells, the finished salt is milder and more flavorful than salt that is either mined or collected directly from tidal pools,

Fujita explains. There is no "burn" or harshness to it on one's tongue or in one's food—just an ideal flavor that enhances any dish: meat, fish, poultry or vegetables.

This white sea salt, called pa'akai, is not the same as 'alaea salt, which contains a reddish-brown clay, Fujita says. He collects his 'alaea from a secret location up mauka, in the highlands, then blends it with the pa'akai. The 'alaea salt is used more as a condiment than in cooking, he points out. Both types are reputed to have medicinal value.

Salt from the ponds at Hanapēpē cannot be sold, which only serves to push its value beyond mere legendary status. It can only be acquired as a gift from its maker, carefully presented in Ziploc bags to lucky relatives, neighbors and VIPs, who in turn hoard and dole it out like salt junkies. Made by hand, it connects us with our past. All natural, it connects us with the land.

⋙ ⋙ ⋙ ⋙ ⋙ ⋙ ⋙

Masa Fujita tends his traditionally cultivated salt beds near Hanapēpē, Kaua'i.

CONNECTION

GRAINS OF SALT

To take something with a grain of salt means to accept it with some reservations. The metaphor behind this popular saying comes from the fact that food—any food—is more palatable with a little salt.

Salt is universal. Since time immemorial civilizations around the world have recognized the value of salt. Its power to preserve, cleanse and purify—as well as to flavor food—made it one of the most valuable natural elements on earth. Roman soldiers, for example, were paid in part with an allowance of salt ("salarium"), which led to the current term "salary." Romans were also fond of adding salt to their greens, which explains why we call them "salads."

In Russia, it is a customary sign of respect to greet an honored guest with a loaf of bread and a small bowl of salt. Sharing bread and salt thus became synonymous with hospitality, the Russian term for which, "khlebosol' stvo," is formed by two words: "khleb" (bread) and "sol" (salt).

Flavoring a food staple—usually a filling, high-carbohydrate starch—with salt or some type of salty food is the basis on which our local food culture is built. Throughout this book, we will see this principle play out and evolve from past to present.

This concept is clearly articulated in the old Hawaiian saying found in *'Ōlelo No'eau: Hawaiian Proverbs & Poetical Sayings*: "I komo ka 'ai i ka pa'akai—It is the salt that makes the poi go in."

In Japan an onigiri or omusubi (rice ball), simply seasoned and preserved with salt and wrapped in a leaf, was the original take-out meal.

This is a very simple, yet important, Kau Kau Connection. First, make sure you're hungry. Exercise, eat very lightly or skip a meal altogether. Hunger—even mild hunger pangs—is a rare sensation for many people these days. Then, gather the following ingredients:

Poi or rice
Hawaiian salt (pure white—pa'akai—or reddish—
'alaea)
Optional (anything salty):
lomilomi salmon, sweet Maui onion, seasoned nori (seaweed) or ume (pickled plums)

If you're going for the poi, sprinkle the salt on it. Close your eyes and eat. You can try adding lomilomi salmon on top of the poi or dipping sliced Maui onion into the Hawaiian salt and then eating it with poi.

If you chose rice rather than poi, you can mix salt into a small bowl of warm water, then wet your hands liberally in the salty water as you form a rice ball. Otherwise, you can wet your hands first, sprinkle salt on your wet hands and then form a rice ball.

Do not make the ball round. Triangular shape is best.

Stick an ume in the middle of the rice ball; a few drops of ume juice on the rice is good, too. Wrap the rice ball in nori sheets or sprinkle it with furikake nori.

Finally, whether eating poi or rice, close your eyes, chew slowly, and try to savor every morsel. This Kau Kau Connection aims to reconnect our busy, modern selves with our simpler, more soulful past, through the medium of food.

the Pacific soon made it a popular destination for explorers, traders and whalers. Missionaries came as well, to spread the word of their God.

For the most part, Hawaiians were warm and welcoming to the newcomers—sometimes to the detriment of their own way of life. Soon sailing ships from around the world crowded Hawai'i's harbors, bringing goods to supply the burgeoning foreign population and restocking their own larders with fresh food and water to complete their trans-Pacific journeys.

The impact of these outside influences on Hawai'i was pervasive. One area of influence was the introduction of new foods. Cook himself left goats, a breed of English pigs, and melon, pumpkin and onion seeds. Another famed explorer, Captain George Vancouver, probably made an even bigger impact by introducing cattle to Hawai'i in 1793.

The whaling ships and merchant vessels that plied the Pacific were far from being bastions of fine dining, however. On the contrary, food on board these ships was downright terrible—especially what was fed to the common crewmembers. Not a whole lot larger than the canoes on which the Hōkūle'a was patterned, the sailing vessels were only about 100 feet long. There was not much room on board the ships of this era for crews that numbered from 25 to 50 men,

Workers prepare an imu on the grounds of Honolulu's Catholic mission in the summer of 1893.

not to mention the equipment and workspace needed to carry out whaling operations, and enough food and water to sustain the hungry sailors for months at a time.

Fresh fruits and vegetables were only available at the very beginning of a voyage, resulting in illness and death to thousands of sailors due to scurvy, a disease caused by the lack of vitamin C. Their primary diet over the long sea voyages was based on "salt horse" (heavily salted beef, pork or horse meat), salted fish, beans, potatoes and "hardtack" (hard, dry crackers). Even these hardy foods could and would often rot or spoil, however, due to moisture, weevils and

vermin, forcing whalers to eat whatever they could catch, including fish, seals, sea birds, sea turtles, dolphins and whales, in order to survive.

Missionaries began arriving in 1820 with a very different purpose in mind than the whalers that preceded them: to convert the native population to Christianity. To achieve their singular purpose, missionaries had to teach, clothe, clean and feed the Hawaiians by their own strict standards. To accomplish this, they tried to bring as much of what they felt they needed from New England as possible, whether it was suited to the Islands or not, including woolen clothing, the practice of building

MISSIONARY MEMORIES

Missionary recipes are rare and, if available, much more simply written than those of today. Meat, fish, poultry and vegetables were simply prepared—usually they were boiled or roasted with only a few other ingredients—and the directions hardly needed to be written down. According to Barbara Moir of the Lyman Museum, recipes preserved from that time tend to be for baked goods, which utilized more ingredients that needed to be added with some precision in order for the dish to succeed. Even these, however, typically assume that the person using them already knew how to cook and were written without a lot of detail, such as how long a dish should be baked or how hot the oven should be. This is also the case because one could not control heat with any great precision in wood- or coal-burning ovens.

The following Spice Cake and Pumpkin Pie recipes are presented in the style of Hawai'i's missionary women. The Dried-Apple Pie and Ginger Cake recall missionary-era foods but are presented in more modern terms.

Pumpkins were grown in Hawai'i in the 1800s and were treasured for making pies by the women eager to recreate familiar tastes from their childhood. Dried apples and other fruits were sent to missionary wives from their families in New England, or were bartered from visiting ships, and these were also made into pies. Spices, too, were traded for or sent by families far away and were very highly prized commodities. Spice cake was very typical of that era among New Englanders and missionary wives; Moir notes that Ginger Cake seems to have been a favorite of the Lyman family, whose descendants still live in Hawai'i today.

1800s Dried-Apple Pie
Makes one 9" pie

¾ lb.	dried apples
4 c.	apple cider, or water mixed with lemon juice to taste
¼ c.	sugar
3 Tbsp.	cornstarch or arrowroot
½ tsp.	cinnamon, ground
¼ tsp.	nutmeg, ground

Crust
½ lb.	lard
½ tsp.	salt
½ c.	boiling water
3 c.	sifted flour
2 Tbsp.	butter
1 Tbsp.	milk

In a large saucepan, combine dried apples and cider, adding water if necessary to just cover the apples. Cover pan, bring cider to a boil and simmer the apples, stirring occasionally, for 20 to 30 minutes, or until soft but not mushy. Drain apples, reserving ¼ cup of the cider. Set apples aside to cool.

In a bowl whisk sugar, cornstarch, cinnamon and nutmeg together. Add apples and toss the mixture to coat. Stir in reserved ¼ cup cider.

Combine crust ingredients and set aside to cool enough to handle. Turn oven to 400°F. Knead dough together just enough to make it cohere—don't overwork it, or it will be tough. Divide into 2 slightly unequal balls. Roll out on lightly floured board or cloth. Roll the larger portion into a 10" round and fit it into a pie dish. Moisten the edge with water. Roll the other piece into a 9" round and reserve for the top crust.

Spoon the apple mixture into the bottom crust and dot with small pieces of butter. Lay the top crust loosely over the filling and pinch the edges together. Brush the top with milk. Use a knife to cut slits in the top crust to allow steam to escape. Bake 15 minutes, then turn heat to 350°F and bake 30 minutes more.

Spice Cake
(As it originally appeared in an 1887 newspaper from Royalton, Vermont, home of missionary Sarah Lyman of Hilo.)

One and one-half cupfuls of buttermilk
One and one-half cupfuls of brown sugar
One-fourth cupful of butter
One teaspoonful of soda,
one teaspoonful each of cinnamon, cloves, and allspice, and
Two and one-half to three cupfuls of flour, according to the richness of the buttermilk.

Pumpkin Pie

Halve the pumpkin, take out the seeds.

Rinse the pumpkin and cut it into small strips. Stew them, over a moderate fire, in just sufficient water to prevent their burning.

When stewed soft, drain off the water and let the pumpkin steam in the pot over a slow fire, for fifteen or twenty minutes, taking care that it does not burn.

Take it from the fire, and when cool, strain the pumpkin through a sieve.

If you wish to have the pies very rich, to a quart of the stewed pumpkin add two quarts of milk and twelve eggs. If you like them plain, to a quart of the pumpkin add one quart of milk and three eggs. The thicker the pie is with pumpkin, the less will be the number of eggs required for them.

Sweeten the pumpkin with sugar, and very little molasses—the sugar and eggs should be beaten together. Ginger, the grated rind of a lemon, or nutmeg is good spice for the pies.

Pumpkin pies require a very hot oven. The rim of the pies is apt to be burnt before the inside is baked sufficiently. On this account, it is a good plan to heat the pumpkin mixture scalding hot when prepared for pies, before turning it into the pie plates. The more eggs in the pies, the less time will be required to bake them.

1800s Ginger Cake

½ c.	butter
½ c.	sugar
2	eggs, separated, whites beaten stiff
1 c.	molasses
2½ c.	flour
1 tsp.	salt
1 tsp.	cinnamon
1 tsp.	ground cloves
1 tsp.	ground ginger
2 tsp.	baking soda
1 c.	boiling water

Preheat oven to 350°F. In a large bowl, cream butter and sugar. Add egg yolks, one at a time, mixing well. Stir in molasses.

In a separate bowl, sift flour, salt and spices together. Dissolve soda in boiling water in another small bowl; add this to creamed mixture alternately with flour mixture, stirring well after each addition. Fold in stiffly beaten egg whites. Pour into a loaf pan and bake 45 minutes.

CONNECTION

HAWAIIAN HARDTACK: THE SALOON PILOT

Saloon Pilot crackers may very well be one of Hawai'i's most beloved nostalgia foods of all time, cutting across ethnic, economic and geographic backgrounds. These hard, nearly tasteless crackers—refugees from 19th-century sailing ships—appear on the surface to be extremely unlikely candidates for the Hawai'i Kau Kau Hall of Fame, yet everyone seems to harbor some warm personal memory of them.

The origin of Saloon Pilot crackers dates back to "hardtack"—a simple product made of flour, water and salt. Baked thoroughly—sometimes twice—hardtack was a nearly indestructible food suitable for long sea voyages. Also known as ship's biscuit, sea biscuit, pilot bread or navy bread, it was barely breakable with the teeth, so sailors preferred to consume their hardtack by first crushing it with a solid object like a rifle butt or rock and then softening the pieces with coffee or bacon grease. Sugar would be added if it were available. Mixing the crushed hardtack with condensed milk created an even greater treat called "milk toast."

Hardtack made its way to Hawai'i aboard the vast and varied armada of whaling and merchant ships that arrived here in the 1800s. In 1851, a Scottish baker with the last name of Love arrived in Honolulu with his wife and three sons. He decided to stay and opened Love's Bakery in 1853, building his business by catering to the needs of whaling ships, including supplying them with hardtack. Love later developed the Saloon Pilot cracker by adding shortening to the hardtack recipe, making it far easier to chew. Another Love's outlet opened in Hilo in the 1920s (left).

Those of us who grew up in Hilo were particularly fond of the Saloon Pilot and Sweet Creme crackers baked by Hilo Macaroni Factory, which was founded in 1908 as the Hilo Seimen Gaisha. The recipe for the Hilo Macaroni version of the Saloon Pilot cracker was given to the company's founder by a baker aboard a World War I German ship that was detained in Hilo Harbor. Hilo Macaroni Factory closed in 2003, however, and today Diamond Bakery (founded in 1921) on O'ahu is the only remaining producer of Saloon Pilots.

When was the last time you had a Saloon Pilot cracker? This is a very simple Kau Kau Connection. Just try a box of Saloon Pilot crackers in one these traditional ways:

- When we were small, my brother and sister and I used to crumble Saloon Pilots into a cup of hot cocoa and let it get nice and soft.
- We'd mash them in a bowl, sprinkle it with sugar and pour milk over it. This was dessert.
- My dad liked to eat them with sweet condensed milk on top.
- Saloon Pilot Crackers are great with butter and guava jelly.
- Put Saloon Pilot crackers in a bowl and fill it with beef stew.
- My grandfather soaked his Saloon Pilot crackers in a bowl, filling it with coffee, cream and sugar. Then he added butter on top.

Paniolo herd cattle toward transport steamships waiting offshore on the Big Island's Kōhala Coast, ca. 1930s.

wood-framed homes, and their New England cuisine.

In general, missionary food was based on traditional English cooking, with Native American ingredients such as corn, pumpkins and cranberries added. Central to this menu were stews, soups, boiled meats and vegetables, casseroles and puddings. In New England, the missionaries had had access to fish, especially cod, which they salted for use during the harsh winters. Salted pork was also very common and was used in stews or cooked with baked beans. Other familiar English fare—such as roasted meats, smoked ham, bacon, baked pastries, butter and cheese—was also popular.

It would be impossible to imagine the sense of isolation experienced by missionary wives as they struggled to maintain the traditions of New England cookery here in the Hawaiian Islands. The voyage from Boston to Hawai'i around Cape Horn was 18,000 nautical miles (20,714 miles) and took five months. Their determination to feed their families food from their homeland was but one way to bridge the vast distance and to nurture their families in this strangest of places.

Foods such as corn, flour, butter, cheese, molasses, potatoes, salt pork, dried beef, salt cod, corned beef and dried apples shipped from New England were highly coveted in Hawai'i—even if they arrived in the Islands damp with seawater and contaminated by mold, insects and rats. But in order to survive, missionaries

SALT COD, SALT SALMON AND SALTED BUTTERFISH

There was always plenty of salt and fish in Hawai'i, of course, and Hawaiians had their own means of salting and drying the bounty they harvested from the sea, including akule (big-eyed scad), 'ōpelu (mackerel scad) and aku (skipjack tuna). Several types of salted fish imported from outside the Islands, however, still managed to make a big impact on the local diet.

Like a number of other important foods, salt fish sailed into Hawai'i on the ships of whalers, traders and missionaries. Bacalhau, the Portuguese name for dried salted codfish, was a staple aboard European sailing ships for centuries, as well as an important food item for New England missionaries. Because of its long seafaring history, bacalhau made from cod caught in the North Atlantic also sailed its way around the world and into the cuisine of many other places, including Puerto Rico, the Philippines and other Pacific islands.

Bacalhau was just one of those foods that was perfectly suited for Hawai'i. As durable as wood or leather, it needed no refrigeration; it was amenable to a wide range of seasonings, ingredients and cooking styles; supplies of it were ample; and, best of all, it was affordable. Plantation workers of all different ethnic backgrounds came to use bacalhau in their everyday cooking. After soaking (often overnight), rinsing and/or boiling it to soften it and extract some of the salt, bacalhau was added to greens, potatoes, garden vegetables, soups and stews. It imparted a lot of flavor to any dish and, with lots of rice, made for a cheap and filling meal.

In addition to bacalhau, salt salmon and salted butterfish were also very popular. Supplies of these fish came mainly from the Pacific Northwest and Alaska and were shipped to all parts of the world. In the days before canning technology was developed, American fishermen caught and produced salt salmon in Alaska before the United States purchased it from Russia.

An interesting footnote to what could be called the great butterfish mystery is provided by marine scientist and writer Susan Scott, who explains in her *Ocean Watch* column that the "butterfish" popular in Hawai'i is neither a true butterfish nor "black cod" as is commonly assumed. It is actually sablefish but is called "black cod" because of its color and shape, Scott explains. Sablefish are only found in cold waters of the Pacific Ocean from California to Alaska, across the Bering Sea to Siberia and down the Kamchatka coast to Japan.

The three types of salted fish were sometimes substituted for each other, depending on availability. Salt salmon was prepared in various ways—often in combination with vegetables—but two of its most famous uses were and still are in laulau and as lomilomi salmon. Salted butterfish was more commonly used in laulau than salt salmon. Hawaiians did prepare and steam laulau in underground imu prior to the introduction of salt salmon or butterfish, but they quickly came to prefer the flavor that was imparted by the fatty fish, which then became a traditional ingredient in making laulau.

The sad irony is that today bacalhau and salted butterfish—which were so commonplace at a time when people had very little money or access to food—are now very hard to find and expensive to buy.

Lomilomi Salmon

1 lb.	salt salmon
1	large onion, finely diced
4-5	large ripe tomatoes, mashed or diced
2-3	ice cubes, crushed

Scale salmon, rinse and soak in water for 3 hours. Drain.

Pull meat away from skin or scrape it off with spoon. Shred or cut meat in small pieces. Add onion and tomato and chill.

Just before serving, add crushed ice.

had to also adapt to what was to be had in the Islands. Beef, for example, was available thanks to Captain Vancouver, along with the milk and butter that cows could supply. Fish, chicken, coconuts, taro and bananas became important parts of the missionaries' diet, along with sweet potatoes, onions, lettuce, cabbage, beans, melons, grapes, squash, tomatoes and other vegetables they could grow in backyard gardens.

In spite of the Islands' bounty, however, missionary life was not easy for those who found it difficult to adjust to a different diet, as a journal entry written by missionary Sarah Lyman reminds us: "No eggs, no fish and no melons," she writes. "We are destitute of both fish and pork for the school, and we have over 60 boys. We made our supper tonight (as we not infrequently do) entirely of taro. We have it fried in the morning, toasted at noon, and roasted at night."

The impact of the newcomers, including missionaries, on the native culture extended well beyond their numbers because they wielded considerable influence over Hawaiian royalty. Westerners soon exerted control over the political, economic, religious and social interests of the Islands and dramatically transformed everything from land ownership to what people wore and ate. King David Kalākaua built 'Iolani Palace in the manner of European palaces,

complete with fine carpets from England, furniture from Boston and dishes from Europe and China. His guests were served champagne from France and different wines to accompany each course at his lavish dinner parties. The King's menu included such exotic delicacies as turtle soup, sweetbreads, oysters, sirloin of beef, fresh asparagus, turkey, pigeon pie, cheesecake and fine French pastries.

Today, the imprint of the early explorers, merchant seamen, whalers and missionaries who made their way to the Islands in the late 18th to mid-19th centuries can be found in our local food culture, in such foods as salt beef (as in salt meat and watercress); beef jerky (a favorite omiyage, or food gift, brought back from Las Vegas); salt salmon (as in lomilomi salmon); hardtack (as in Saloon Pilot crackers); or beef stew with potatoes and carrots (here usually eaten over rice or with a bowl of poi).

Food was just a part of the broader transformation wrought by the newcomers from abroad, who shook up the very core of the Hawaiians' traditional worldview and religious beliefs. In 1819, following the death of his father, King Kamehameha the Great, King Kamehameha II broke an important kapu (taboo) by eating and drinking with women. Some important Hawaiian taboos barred women from eating or preparing certain foods, others

Kahuā Ranch Beef Stew

3 lbs.	boneless stew beef
	Salt and pepper, to taste
	Water to cover meat
1	medium onion, roughly diced
1 lb.	carrots, cubed
1 lb.	potatoes, peeled and cubed
3	stalks celery, cut in 1" pieces
1 Tbsp.	flour
¼ c.	water

Brown meat, adding salt and pepper, then cover with water. Add onion. Cook about 2 hours until meat is tender.

Add carrots and cook 30 minutes more. Add potatoes and cook another 30 minutes. Add celery and cook an additional 15 minutes.

Mix flour and water and pour slowly into stew; cook until raw floury taste disappears. Serve over hot rice.

CONNECTION

A paniolo strikes a jaunty pose at 'Ulupalakua Ranch in 1942.

THE PANIOLO LEGACY

Here's a tasty Kau Kau Connection—something to reflect on the food legacy left by Hawai'i's paniolo. To begin with, have you ever wondered why beef jerky can be found at every supermarket, convenience store and gas station in Hawai'i? Or why locals flock to buy beef jerky at gift shops in Las Vegas—even if none of those bags of jerky are actually made in the state of Nevada? The next time you enjoy a bag of beef jerky, remember the days when "jerking" beef was one of the best and tastiest ways to preserve it.

If you want to go a little further, savor the real deal—get some pipikaula from your favorite neighborhood market (Ft. Ruger Market, M.S. Tanabe Superette, Tamashiro Market or Marujyu Market on O'ahu; Takamiya Market or Pukalani Superette on Maui; KTA on the Big Island; Big Save on Kaua'i; etc.). Equally enlightening would be a trip to a Hawaiian food emporium, such as Helena's Hawaiian Food, Ono's Hawaiian Food, People's Cafe or Highway Inn, to enjoy some salt meat and watercress, pipikaula or both.

Or you could try cook 'em yourself. Here is a recipe for salt meat and watercress. If you're buying in the Islands, the watercress you use will probably come from Sumida Farm in 'Aiea, that tranquil little green patch right next to Pearlridge Center, which has been producing the spicy greens since 1928—another connection with Hawai'i's food history.

Salt Meat and Watercress

3 lbs.	salt meat (see note below)
6 qts.	water
1	thumb-sized piece ginger, crushed
1	bunch watercress, trimmed

Rinse salt from meat. Cut into bite-sized pieces. Cover meat with water and bring to a boil. Lower heat and simmer 30 minutes. Drain and rinse. Repeat process, then taste meat. If it is too salty, repeat a third time.

Add fresh water to the pot, then add meat and ginger. Bring to a boil again; lower heat and simmer 1 hour.

Rinse watercress in warm, salted water. Cut in 2" pieces. Add to meat after an hour, first the stems and a little later the leaves.

Note: To make salt meat, rub a brisket of beef with coarse Hawaiian salt. Then put a layer of salt in a crock, lay meat on it, and completely cover and surround with salt. Five pounds of brisket will take approximately 3¾ cups of Hawaiian salt. Cover crock and refrigerate 5 to 6 days to cure. Salt crystals will liquefy as they absorb liquid from the meat. If desired, discard this liquid and replenish the salt after 3 days.

If you want to try some traditional beef stew, just follow in the footsteps of a couple of modern-day paniolo. Marian De Luz grew up in a ranching family, the Adrians, so she is no stranger to the lifestyle. Today, as the matriarch of the De Luz family ranch, she can routinely handle dinner for 15 to 30 hungry cowboys on any given day, serving up such traditional paniolo favorites as roast beef and gravy or beef stew, along with salad, bread and dessert. Other tasty dishes include local-style chicken hekka, homemade Portuguese sausage and vinha d'alhos (Portuguese-style vinegared meat).

Phyllis Richards has fulfilled a similar role at Kahuā Ranch for over 40 years. A former nurse, she is known for her healthy as well as tasty cooking—whether she is feeding the entire Richards clan a family dinner or 50 hungry ranch hands a working cowboy lunch. A classic Kahuā Ranch cowboy lunch may be comprised of beef stew (recipe pg. 19), a big pot of rice, potato salad, coleslaw with pineapple, Kahuā cake and Kahuā Ranch iced tea.

forbade them from eating with men. Breaking these taboos was punishable by death. Thus, when Queen Ka'ahumanu chose to dramatize her acceptance of Christianity and the end of the ancient kapu system, she did so by eating foods that women had previously been forbidden to eat—doing so in the company of men.

Chiefess Kapi'olani is said to have demonstrated her defiance of the fire goddess Pele in 1824 by traveling to the volcano and eating 'ōhelo berries, which were sacred to Pele and kapu to women. In relatively swift order, heiau (sacred temples) were destroyed and images of gods were burned, leading to the demise of the ancient kapu system. Instead, Western customs, food and fashion became the order of the day.

This shift in belief system was followed by equally drastic changes in land ownership and government. In 1848, the Great Mahele implemented a system of land division based on the foreign concept of private property. Private land ownership was an unfamiliar concept to the Hawaiian people, who since ancient times had related to the land in a more holistic and communal manner, living and working under the ahupua'a system.

Thousands of acres of land fell under the ownership and control of the non-Hawaiian population, who led the shift in Hawai'i's food production from a subsistence economy to one geared for export and profit. The

Phyllis and Herbert "Monty" Richards at home at Kahuā Ranch; Monty's uncle, Atherton Richards, co-founded the sprawling ranch in 1928.

Hawaiians' traditional diet was transformed, along with their agrarian way of life, as eager capitalists seized the economic opportunities they saw in large-scale plantation-based agriculture. Over time, commercial production of sugarcane, pineapple, coffee, macadamia nuts and papaya took over the prime agricultural lands, as the next chapter will discuss.

Home on the Range

The introduction of cattle and subsequent establishment of large ranches also left a lasting imprint, introducing beef to the Hawaiian diet and establishing the proud tradition of the Hawaiian cowboy, or paniolo. Foreign-introduced goats, sheep and cattle all wreaked their share of havoc

on Hawai'i's natural landscape, but of these animals, it was the pipi (cattle) that had the most profound impact not just on the diets of the people of Hawai'i but on their culture and lifestyle as well.

Ranching offered a totally unique way of life for Hawaiians and later immigrants who were drawn to its ruggedly independent mode of existence. Compared to the strictly controlled practices of the sugar plantations, for example, many of the tasks required of the paniolo required them to operate for days or even weeks away from ranch owners, supervisors and even their own families. The Spanish vaqueros that set the standard for the paniolo were a colorful lot, introducing the guitar

▷▷▷ ▷▷▷ ▷▷▷ ▷▷▷ ▷▷▷ ▷▷▷ ▷▷▷

Birds on a wire: A rancher shows off the results of a pheasant hunt in Upcountry Maui.

to Hawai'i—which in time led to the birth of Hawaiian kī hō'alu, the "slack key" style of guitar. Later, the Portuguese, who demonstrated a strong affinity for the ranching and dairy industry, introduced the 'ukulele to the musical melting pot.

Ranching involved a high level of self-sufficiency when it came to food. In a life history interview with "Hall of Fame" cowboy Frank Silva,

the paniolo recalled, "We raised everything—chickens, turkeys, ducks, rabbits, goats and pigs." Cowboys also used to hunt wild pigs for food, and often followed the practice of capturing and castrating young pigs (laho'ole), which they would then raise in pens until they were ready for market.

His family grew all their own vegetables, Silva said, milked their

own cows and made their own butter. They had five acres of coffee trees. People even grew grapes and made their own wine, along with 'ōkolehao from the ti plant and pineapple or pānini (cactus) swipe. "Anything that ferments you could make swipe," Silva noted, "even sweet potato." Still others brewed their own beer—"Real good beer," he recalled.

Rather than the Island diet's ubiquitous rice, bread was the main food staple in the Silva household. "My mother used to bake bread in a stone oven. Hawaiians just loved homemade bread." His father used to sell them for five cents a loaf—"great big loaves," Silva said.

But ranching was about cattle, and, in the days before refrigeration, meat that was salted, dried or smoked to keep it from spoiling became an important part of the local diet. Fresh meat had to be enjoyed immediately after the animal was slaughtered. At such times, families would usually prepare a big pot of pipi stew with potatoes, carrots and onions. Fresh meat was also enjoyed pūlehu style—broiled—over hot coals. Before rice, the stew or pūlehu meat was eaten with poi. And, at such times, it was natural to share food with one's neighbors. "If you killed an animal you give the neighbors," a native of Kawaihae recalled. "If you went hunting and caught a pig, you give the neighbors. Those days no more freezers like now—so we shared

Portuguese Bean Soup
Serves 12

2 lbs.	Portuguese sausage, cut in ¼" pieces
1 lb.	ham hock
1	onion, sliced
2 qts.	water
2	carrots, diced
3	potatoes, diced
1	small cabbage, chopped
1 can	tomato sauce (8 oz.)
2 cans	red kidney beans, including liquid (15 oz. each)

Put sausage, ham hock and onion into a large pot; add water. Cover and cook over low heat for 1 hour. Remove meat from ham hock, reserving bone for another use, if desired. Return meat to soup and add carrots, potatoes, cabbage and tomato sauce; cover and continue cooking for 1½ hours more, stirring occasionally. Stir in beans, including liquid, and cook a few more minutes, adding more water if necessary.

everything with our neighbors and they shared theirs with us."

In an interesting variation of the traditional ahupua'a system, it became common practice for fishermen along the coast to share or trade their fish with cowboys and ranchers and bring meat home for their families. This practice of sharing is still an important cultural practice today, and in some ways echoes the tradi-tion commonly expressed by omiyage (gift-giving).

As ranch life developed, people of all ethnic backgrounds left the sugar plantations and became part of Hawai'i's ranching industry. Today, many multigenerational families perpetuate the Islands' ranching legacy through their values as well as their food traditions.

Economic boom times in Hawai'i also brought to light one of the saddest and most disturbing legacies of the newly arrived European and American visitors and settlers: the near extinction of the Native Hawaiian population. Previously isolated from the rest of the world, thousands of Hawaiians succumbed to diseases introduced by Westerners, including smallpox, measles, Hansen's disease, whooping cough, influenza and gonorrhea. Some historians estimate that as many as 300,000 people populated the Hawaiian Islands at the time of Cook's arrival. By 1850, the total population of the Islands had dwindled to 84,000—including 1,500 foreigners. By 1860, the population had fallen to 70,000. By 1920, there were fewer than 24,000 pure Hawaiians.

The decimation of the Hawaiian people, coupled with the unbridled demand for sugar and pineapple, created a serious labor shortage in Hawai'i. To address the issue, foreign businessmen backed by the Hawaiian government looked to recruit and import the workers they needed from abroad. This development was to be the next big thing impacting the Hawaiian Islands. ◐

⋙ ⋙ ⋙ ⋙ ⋙ ⋙ ⋙

Meat on the hoof: Big Island cattle bound for market are loaded into a launch for shipment to O'ahu aboard the S.S. Honolulu.

The Story of the Lū'au

With reference to traditional Hawaiian food, the first thing that comes to mind for many people is a lū'au—a large banquet or feast at which foods such as poke, kālua pig, laulau, poi, sweet potatoes, lomilomi salmon, chicken long rice, squid lū'au and haupia are served. The term "lū'au" actually refers to the young taro leaves that are cooked with coconut milk and he'e (octopus, often called squid)—a popular dish served at these gatherings.

In ancient Hawai'i, feasts were usually called "pā'ina" (meal, dinner) or "'aha'aina" (gathering for a meal), not "lū'au." These festivities were held on auspicious occasions, such as to celebrate a successful harvest, victory in battle or completion of a canoe or home.

Under the ancient kapu system, however, these gatherings were not for everyone. Men and women were not allowed to dine together, for example, and commoners and women were forbidden to eat certain foods, such as pork. It was not until 1819 that King Kamehameha II and Queen Ka'ahumanu abandoned these kapu.

A *Honolulu Advertiser* report on a Restoration Day feast in 1847 that fed 10,000 people offers some idea of the grand scale that some of these celebrations might attain:

Kamehameha III arrived from town in a carriage drawn by four gray horses and purchased from Tahiti's Queen Pomare, who received it as a gift from Queen Victoria. This was the scene at the summer retreat of Kamehameha's Kaniakapupu, Sound of Land Snails, deep in the jungle-like shadows of Nuuanu Valley.

The menu included: two hundred seventy-one hogs, 482 large calabashes of poi, 602 chickens, 3 oxen, 2 barrels of salt pork, two of bread, 3125 salt fish, 1820 fresh fish, 12½ barrels of luau and cabbage, 4 barrels of onions, 18 bunches of bananas, 55 pineapples, 10 barrels of potatoes, 55 ducks, 2245 coconuts, 1000 heads of taro and 180 squid.

32. **POI AND FISH (A Hawaiian Dish.)**
PUBLISHED BY THE ISLAND CURIO STORE HONOLULU

As far as actually calling a large feast a lū'au, cultural authorities Mary Kawena Pukui and Samuel H. Elbert trace the use of the term for that purpose back to 1856, in the *Pacific Commercial Advertiser*.

Today, lū'au are held to celebrate children's first birthdays, graduations, weddings and anniversaries and other notable events. Family-style lū'au are very personal and can range from very simple to very elaborate. A great deal of effort is often invested in obtaining hard-to-get ingredients such as 'opihi (limpets) and 'a'ama (rock crab). Other ethnic dishes such as sashimi, sushi, lumpia and kalbi are included to augment core Hawaiian dishes such as kālua pig, laulau, lomilomi salmon, poi, chicken long rice, squid lū'au, ake (raw liver), sweet potatoes and haupia.

Commercial lū'au, which try to combine some of the classic Hawaiian dishes with other selections that might appeal to non-native diners, are popular with visitors and locals alike, and are offered at a number of resort properties as well as at private venues. The menu of one very popular lū'au company on O'ahu includes kālua pig, chicken long rice, Island fish, teriyaki beef, fried chicken, tossed green salad, poi, lomilomi salmon, rice, pineapple coleslaw, three bean salad, dinner rolls, haupia, fresh pineapple, vanilla coconut cake, chocolate cake, coffee and hot tea.

Here are some recipes essential for creating your own lū'au:

Laulau
Makes 6 laulau

18	ti leaves
6 pcs.	belly pork (1" by 2½" each)
6 pcs.	salted butterfish or salmon (2" by 2" each)
24	taro leaves

Remove stiff rib from underside of ti leaf. Crisscross three ti leaves and place four taro leaves in the center. Put pieces of pork and butterfish on taro leaves; fold ti leaves around them to create a bundle. Wrap ti leaves tightly with string. Steam 3 to 4 hours. Serve hot.

Variation: May use boned chicken thighs instead of pork.

Haupia for a Crowd
Makes four 8" by 12" trays

4 lbs.	fresh coconut, grated
6 qts.	water
1 box	cornstarch (Kingsford Brand)
2½ c.	water
1¾ c.	sugar

In a large pot, combine grated coconut with 6 quarts water and bring to a boil, then allow to cool. Line a large bowl with a double thickness of cheesecloth larger than the bowl. Turn coconut mixture into the bowl, then gather cheesecloth together and squeeze to yield 6 quarts of milk.

In a small bowl, blend cornstarch with 2½ cups water. In the top of a large double boiler, combine coconut milk, sugar and cornstarch mixture, stirring constantly with a wire whisk as water comes to a boil in the lower pot. Continue stirring until coconut milk mixture comes to a smooth gel-like consistency. Pour into 8" by 12" trays. Refrigerate overnight.

Poi Cocktail
Poi "cocktails," common in 1920s and '30s cookbooks, were the white settlers' idea of something the whole family could drink at a lū'au.

Fresh poi
Milk
Sugar, to taste
Cinnamon or nutmeg, a sprinkle

Pasteurize the poi for children by heating it in the top of a double boiler for 30 minutes. While poi is warm, put 2 Tbsp. into a glass. Fill glass with milk. Stir with a fork. Add sugar and spice.

148 Luau, Hawaiian Feast.

"Lawalu" Fish
Visitors to the Hawaiian Islands in the 1930s were encouraged by local souvenir cookbooks to recreate their lū'au experience when they returned home, using Mainland ingredients. This dish would have been served with "a small dish of condiments, consisting of chopped walnuts, chili pepper, green onions, salted dried fish, and rock salt" and eaten wearing "a lei, a wreath of fresh flowers or colored paper."

6	medium-sized fish, cut in half, *or*
3-4 lbs.	halibut or swordfish, cut in 12 pieces
	Salt, to taste
2	green peppers, cut in 12 pieces
12	corn husks, stems and leaves kept intact when removed from corn

Season fish with salt. Place fish and a small piece of pepper in each husk. Place in saucepan with an inch of water. Steam 3 hours, adding more water if necessary. Serve in husks.

Kulolo, Something Good
This enthusiastic 1898 recipe is reprinted as it originally appeared in an O'ahu church's fundraising cookbook.

Six cups taro flour, 4 cups cocoanut milk, 4 tablespoonfuls sugar; grate fine the meat of 2 cocoanuts and mix all together well; put in a deep dish well buttered, and bake 1 hour in a moderate oven; eaten warm or cold it is excellent and cannot be beat!

CHAPTER TWO

From Distant Shores
Food and Folkways from across the Sea

Y ou might call it a "perfect storm" of historical circumstances that led to the widespread commercial cultivation of sugar in Hawai'i, which in turn profoundly shaped the future of the Islands. The Civil War had devastated the Deep South, the country's major producer of sugar. Meanwhile, demand for sugar spiked because of the Gold Rush and the massive movement of people westward across the American continent. As newly established cities along the West Coast swelled in population, their residents demanded sugar and other food supplies, which in turn proved to be a boon for agricultural products from Hawai'i. In addition to sugar, Irish and sweet potatoes, onions, pumpkins, oranges and coffee were grown in Hawai'i for export to West Coast markets. Molasses, a by-product of the sugar-refining process, was also exported.

Eager to turn a profit, sugar planters desperately needed to find new sources of cheap labor to meet the growing demand. And with the Hawaiian population nearly decimated, plantation owners looked abroad to import laborers from China, Japan and Okinawa, Korea, Portugal, Puerto Rico, the Philippines and other countries.

James Dole pioneered the large-scale production of pineapple in central O'ahu in 1901; a period postcard depicts an early pine plantation. Opposite: Bound for work in the sugarcane fields, Chinese laborers sail to Hawai'i aboard the S.S America Maru in 1901.

97. Pineapple Plantation. Hawaiian Islands.

>>> >>> >>> >>> >>> >>> >>>

Hawaiians roast a pig, 1912. Fish, taro, sweet potatoes, chicken, bread-fruit and other foodstuffs could also be wrapped for roasting in the imu.

Economic forces, driven largely by the sugar industry's need for labor, brought many people from distant lands to Hawai'i. The major immigrant groups arrived primarily to work in the burgeoning sugar industry. The pineapple industry did little, if any, active recruitment of workers from overseas. Instead, they were successful in luring workers away from sugar plantations by offering slightly better wages and conditions.

Many other groups settled in Hawai'i, arriving in smaller numbers from countries such as Germany, Greece, Scotland, Ireland, Norway and Russia. Some African Americans from the American South came as well. Post-plantation-era immigration has also had a big impact on Hawai'i's ethnic mix, including people from Thailand, Vietnam, Cambodia, Samoa, Tonga and Micronesia.

Each ethnic group that came craved familiar foods from their homelands, trying to bring or recreate many of their own food traditions in Hawai'i. Ingredients needed to prepare the various ethnic foods had to be imported, made or grown locally, or substituted for with something that was available here. First to arrive, enterprising Chinese established restaurants, rice mills and noodle shops. They were followed by Japanese, the largest ethnic immigrant group to arrive in Hawai'i, who established import companies as well as dozens

of local companies manufacturing such essential foodstuffs as tofu, shoyu, mochi and sake.

Any Island resident should have no problem naming at least two or three of the most popular dishes identified with each of the major ethnic groups in Hawai'i. Distinguishing the precise origins of different ethnic dishes can sometimes get hazy, however. The Chinese, for example, so influenced the cuisine of other Asian cultures that such originally Chinese foods as noodles, tofu and soy sauce are integral to many Asian food cultures, brought over with only minor variations. Overlapping food

traditions can make it very difficult to say which ethnic group should be credited with bringing what to Hawai'i—especially when one starts to consider the histories of the places from which they came.

Although the Philippines and Puerto Rico are on opposite sides of the world, for example, their foods bear some strong similarities—the result of centuries of Spanish colonial rule over both localities. Both Filipinos and Puerto Ricans prepare similar versions of lechon—whole roasted pig with a beautifully glazed, crunchy skin—not to mention other local favorites such as adobo, chorizo

THE PEOPLING OF HAWAI'I

Pre-
1778 Although there is no scholarly consensus, many historians believe that the Hawaiian Islands were originally settled over 1,500 years ago by people from the South Pacific. They also note that a second wave of immigrants began arriving from Tahiti in about the 12th or 13th century. Hawai'i's pre-contact population is believed to have peaked at about 300,000.

1778 British explorer Captain James Cook arrives in Hawai'i, followed by whalers, traders and American missionaries. The impact of these newcomers is immense. Hawaiians have no natural immunities to resist diseases introduced by outsiders. Ravaged by diseases and stripped of their land and traditions, the Hawaiian population dwindles to less than 50,000 by the early 1800s.

1848 The Great Māhele, or Division of Land, clears the way for foreigners to acquire and own land in Hawai'i.

1850 The Masters and Servants Act paves the way for the contract-labor system and allows for importation of workers from other countries.

1850 Gold Rush spurs demand for Hawaiian sugar.

1852 First Chinese contract laborers arrive. Between 1852 and 1898, approximately 50,000 Chinese laborers arrive to work on Hawai'i's sugar plantations.

1861 The American Civil War cuts off sugar supplies from the South, further increasing demand for Hawaiian sugar.

1868 First 148 Japanese laborers, known as "gannen-mono," arrive in Hawai'i.

1876 Reciprocity Treaty grants Hawai'i the right to export unrefined sugar to the U.S. duty free. American businessmen begin mass cultivation of sugar and pineapple to fill the booming demand on the U.S. continent.

1878 First Portuguese arrive. By 1884, they number 9,471.

1885 Government-contracted labor (kanyaku imin) begin arriving in large numbers from Japan. By 1901, Japanese account for 69 percent of Hawai'i's plantation work force.

1887 "Bayonet Constitution" in Hawai'i proclaimed by sugar planters; King Kalākaua is stripped of his powers.

1893 The Hawaiian monarchy is overthrown by Americans.

1894 Private companies take over the recruitment of Japanese laborers. Between 1894 and 1900, 57,000 Japanese arrive in Hawai'i.

1898 Hawai'i is annexed by the United States.

1900 Hawai'i is made a Territory of the U.S. Contract labor is prohibited by U.S. law.

1900 Puerto Ricans arrive. By 1920, 2,095 Puerto Ricans are employed on Hawai'i's sugar plantations.

1900 First Okinawan immigrants arrive on S.S. China. They are counted together with the Japanese immigration figures.

1903 Korean immigrants arrive aboard the S.S. Gaelic. Some 7,843 Koreans arrive between 1903 and 1905, when the Korean government halts emigration.

1906 The first 15 Filipino laborers arrive in Honolulu aboard the S.S. Doric and are assigned to the Olaa plantation on the Big Island. By 1916, 18,144 Filipinos have arrived.

1907 Executive order stops migration of Japanese laborers from Hawai'i, Mexico and Canada.

1907 A shipload of 2,250 Spaniards arrives to work on the plantations.

1908 "Gentlemen's Agreement" restricts Japanese immigration to the U.S.

1924 U.S. Congress prohibits further immigration from Japan. Between 1885 to 1924, a total of approximately 200,000 Japanese immigrate to Hawai'i, most of them to work on sugar plantations.

➤➤➤ ➤➤➤ ➤➤➤ ➤➤➤ ➤➤➤ ➤➤➤ ➤➤➤

Chinese passengers traveling in steerage share a shipboard meal aboard the S.S. China *in 1901.*

and chicharrones. And while Puerto Ricans arrived in Hawai'i before Filipinos, Filipinos (275,000) far outnumber Puerto Ricans (30,000) here, so many local versions of certain foods common to both places tend to be identified as Filipino rather than Puerto Rican in origin. Spanish occupation of the Philippines also helps to explain the tradition of outstanding Filipino bakeries in Hawai'i putting out fragrant pan de sal and sweet, buttery ensemadas on a daily basis.

History also explains why the Japanese word for bread is also "pan," which is derived from the Portuguese, who landed in the port city of Nagasaki in the mid-1500s. The Portuguese influence can also be traced in numerous other food-related Japanese words, including jabon (pomelo), tempura and bobora (pumpkin). The world, it seems, was already shrinking rather quickly centuries ago. So, although ethnicity does play a big part in the evolution of kau kau in Hawai'i, funky food riddles abound at almost every turn.

Perhaps one way of appreciating the richness of the unique ethnic overlays that exist in Hawai'i is to try to organize foods by type into roughly three general ethnic groups, which, according to the 2000 U.S. Census, make up the majority of Hawai'i's population:

1) Hawaiian/Polynesian: Hawaiians, Samoans, Tongans and other Pacific Islanders: 113,539 (9.4 percent)

2) Caucasian: Americans, English and Europeans (including Portuguese): 294,102 (24.3 percent)

3) Asian: Chinese, Japanese, Koreans and Filipinos: 503,868 (41.6 percent)

The 2000 Census also counted 259,343 (21.4 percent) of the population as "Mixed (Two or more races)."

Hawaiian and Polynesian Food

It is important to appreciate that Hawaiian food and culture form the basis for everything that came after in the Islands. European and Asian cuisine can be found throughout the world, but only in Hawai'i are they so uniquely intertwined with Hawaiian food and with other ethnic cuisines. Like the kalo (taro) that symbolizes the very soul of Hawaiian culture, Hawaiian food keeps all who partake of it firmly rooted to this land. And, with its raw fish, 'opihi, limu, 'a'ama crab and wana seasoned by the sea, it reminds us that we share life on a small chain of islands—surrounded by a vast ocean.

Variations of the basic Hawaiian diet can be found throughout Polynesia, including Samoa, Tonga and Tahiti. With few exceptions, meals are built around a starchy staple such as taro, sweet potatoes, yams, breadfruit or bananas. Hawaiians prefer poi produced from taro, but types of poi are also made from breadfruit, known as poi 'ulu (Hawai'i), bananas with coconut milk (Samoa) or bananas and taro (Tahiti).

Lū'au (taro leaves) are an important part of the Hawaiian diet. Samoans prepare their lū'au by wrapping taro leaves, onions and coconut milk in whole taro leaves and then cooking the bundles in an umu (underground oven), which is also the traditional means of cooking food in Tonga, Hawai'i (imu) and Tahiti (hima'a).

Poi is accompanied by 'īna'i, or food-that-is-eaten-with-poi, often harvested from the sea. Hawaiians were skilled fishermen who carefully managed the ocean's resources as a

》》 》》 》》 》》 》》 》》 》》

More than one way to catch a fish: by net (opposite), spear, hand-held torch or, more recently, with a kerosene-fed mounted torch (this page).

▶▶▶ ▶▶▶ ▶▶▶ ▶▶▶ ▶▶▶ ▶▶▶ ▶▶▶

Hawaiians lay out a picnic in an O'ahu banana patch. Below: A water buffalo supplies the power in a rice field in this postcard view ca. 1910.

sustainable source of food. Besides fish, the Hawaiian diet included octopus, lobsters, crabs, limu (seaweed), shellfish and other sea creatures. They also consumed sugarcane, ferns, herbs and a variety of fruits. Dogs, chickens, birds and pigs were sources of meat, although pigs were usually reserved for special occasions.

Seasonings tended to be simple—mainly salt, which along with drying and fermentation was also an important means of preserving food. Kukui nuts, coconut milk, limu and ferns were also used to flavor food, much of which was eaten raw, or simply cooked by steaming or roasting.

Similarities link many Pacific Island cultures, such as the popularity of a dish made of raw fish marinated in lime or lemon juice, coconut milk, salt, onions and tomatoes. Samoans call this dish "oka"; Tongans

call it "'ota" and the Tokelauans "ika mata." It is also found in the Philippines, where it is called "kinilaw."

Thus, while various Pacific Island groups have immigrated to Hawai'i over time, many of their foods already appear familiar to locals because of their similarities to Hawaiian food.

Caucasian Influences

The introduction of Western food to Hawai'i by sailors, whalers, merchants and missionaries is discussed in greater detail elsewhere in this book. For the same reasons as in Hawai'i, Western food items such as salt beef, canned meat such as SPAM™ and corned beef, canned fish like tuna, sardines and salmon, and "ship's biscuits," known in Hawai'i as Saloon Pilot crackers, gained popularity throughout the Pacific.

Sailors hailed from different countries, so variations of foods such bread, wine, stew and sausages arrived in Hawai'i via multiple sources. This was true of bacalhau, the Portuguese name for codfish. Heavily salted bacalhau was a staple on long sea voyages and first arrived in the Islands on sailing ships well before the Portuguese immigrated as settlers.

It would be an understatement to say that the influence of

Caucasians in Hawai'i far outstripped their numbers. As merchants, missionaries and teachers, they controlled wealth, religion and values. Becoming "advisors" to the Hawaiian royalty, they dictated how Hawaiians were governed, the structures they lived in, how they dressed and entertained themselves and what they ate. Influential families intermarried extensively amongst themselves and with the Hawaiian royal class, thereby influencing everything either directly or by setting the example at the top.

Eventually, five Caucasian-run corporations known as the "Big Five" came to wield inordinate control over the Islands via their ownership of banks, supply houses, transportation companies and the plantations that led to the importation of wave upon wave of immigrant laborers to the Islands.

The Portuguese were one Caucasian immigrant group that often lived—and ate—in different

Cultivating Rice Field with Water Buffalo, Hawaiian Islands.

Far left: Members of the city's business elite dine in style at 'Iolani Palace. Left: A Palace menu features Turtle Soup a la Reine; a fish course of mullet, kumu, crabs and anchovies; and entrées of duck, pigeon, goose, turkey and veal.

ways from other European new-comers. Brought to Hawai'i by the plantations to serve as mid-level intermediaries between management and labor—as lunas (supervisors) in the cane fields, for instance—they imported a hearty, spicy cuisine that quickly found a place in the general Island diet. Portuguese bean soup remains a popular local staple today.

Food customs in Hawai'i were strongly influenced by events in American history. The Civil War and Gold Rush fueled trade with the continental U.S., bringing goods to Hawai'i and providing a ready market for Hawai'i sugar and other food products.

World War II brought over a million American military personnel and civilian war workers to Hawai'i, far outnumbering the local population. They introduced foods such as hamburgers, hot dogs and canned rations, including SPAM™.

Hawai'i residents soon found themselves caught up in the prosperity of postwar America. Influenced by radio and television, local people embraced the pursuit of the "American Dream"—including their houses, cars, appliances, clothing and food.

The people of Hawai'i have long been familiar with the foods of the United States and Europe. As the Islands evolved from a port of call

for sailing ships crossing the Pacific to an outpost of American capitalism to the world-famous visitor destination that they are today, the people of Hawai'i have naturally incorporated the foodways of both West and East into their daily diet.

Asian Flavors

The next group to overlay its culture over Hawai'i society hailed from Asia, led by the Chinese, who made a tremendous impact on the food in Hawai'i. By 1884, more than 25,000 Chinese had come to Hawai'i to work in the sugarcane fields. There were only slightly more than 40,000

THE KAU KAU 100: AN ETHNIC POTLUCK PRIMER

The following items aren't so esoteric that only hardcore foodies can appreciate them, nor so easy that only first-time visitors would find them a challenge. Rather, they're at the level that most residents should know in order to navigate the local food scene—a Hawai'i potluck primer.

Adobo Filipino dish of pork or chicken simmered in a vinegar and garlic marinade

'Ahi Hawaiian name for yellowfin tuna ("maguro" in Japanese), great grilled or as sashimi or poke

Aku Hawaiian name for skipjack tuna ("katsuo" in Japanese); can be eaten as poke or sashimi, but is usually fried, or salted and dried

Akule Hawaiian name for big-eye scad ("aji" in Japanese), salted and dried, or pan-fried whole

'A'ama Crab Thin-shelled Hawaiian rock crab, salted and eaten raw

Andagi Round, cake-like Okinawan doughnut

Arare Seasoned Japanese rice crackers ("kakimochi" or "mochi crunch")

Azuki Red beans, cooked and sweetened with sugar, used in many Japanese desserts ("an" in Japanese)

Bacalhau Portuguese term for salted codfish, a durable staple on the plantations

Bagoong Pungent, salty shrimp or fish paste used as a seasoning in Filipino food

Bi Bim Bap A popular Korean dish of vegetables and pieces of meat, fish or chicken served over rice, topped with an egg and hot sauce

Bi Bim Kook Soo Korean dish of thinly sliced vegetables over cold noodles

Bittermelon A bitter, spiny gourd used in many Asian dishes

Black Bean Sauce Chinese black beans fermented with ginger, garlic, rice wine and other ingredients, used to flavor many types of foods

Bulgogi (also Pulgogi) Korean barbecued beef

Char Siu Sweet Chinese barbecued or roasted pork

Chicharrones Deep-fried pork rinds

Chicken Long Rice Chinese long rice prepared in chicken stock with shredded chicken, garnished with green onions

Chili Pepper Water Hawaiian red chili peppers soaked in vinegar and water and used like Tabasco sauce as a condiment or seasoning ("karai water")

Chow Fun Wide, flat Chinese rice noodles stir-fried with meat and vegetables

Chow Mein Thin Chinese wheat or egg noodles stir-fried with chicken, meat and vegetables, your basic plate-lunch "fried noodles"

Crack Seed Chinese snack made of dried fruits mixed with salt, sugar and seasonings

Dim Sum Bite-sized Chinese dumplings stuffed with different meats and vegetables, then steamed, baked or fried

Dinuguan Filipino dish made of pork cooked in pork blood and vinegar

Furikake Japanese seasoning made of dried seaweed, salt, sesame seeds and bonito flakes

Gandule Beans Puerto Rican pigeon peas, often cooked with rice

Gau Sticky, sweet Chinese rice cake

Gisantes Filipino dish of pork, tomatoes and peas

Halo Halo Filipino dessert made with coconut milk, ice and fruit

Haupia Hawaiian coconut milk pudding

Hekka Stir-fry dish of plantation origin made of chicken, vegetables and long rice noodles

Ika Japanese term for cuttlefish; usually seasoned, dried and eaten as a snack

Imu A Hawaiian underground "oven," heated with hot rocks, used to roast a whole kālua pig and other foods; central to any lū'au

'Inamona Kukui nut meat, roasted, grated and mixed with salt to season a variety of Hawaiian dishes—especially poke

Jai A Chinese vegetarian dish especially popular around Chinese New Year ("monk's food")

Jook A bland Chinese rice soup ("congee")

Jun Meat or fish marinated in a Korean sauce, then dipped in flour and egg, then fried

Kalbi Korean barbecued short ribs marinated in shoyu and sesame sauce

Kālua Pig Hawaiian roast pig, traditionally baked in an imu

Kamaboko Japanese fish cake

Kim Chee Korean dish of pickled and fermented vegetables, often seasoned with chili peppers

Kochu Jang Korean chili pepper sauce

Kombu (or Konbu) Japanese term for kelp ("dashima" in Korean or "haidai" in Chinese)

Kook Soo Korean noodles in broth with meat and vegetables

Kūlolo Sweet Hawaiian pudding made of taro and coconut milk

Laulau Pork or chicken, salted butterfish or salmon, wrapped in taro leaves, then in ti leaves, and steamed

Lechon Filipino- or Puerto Rican-style whole roast pig ("lechon baboy" or "lechon asado")

Li Hing Mui Chinese preserved plum flavored with sugar, salt, licorice and other seasonings; also ground to a powder and used to season a wide range of snack foods

Loco Moco Local meal of rice topped with a hamburger patty, fried egg and gravy

Lomilomi Salmon Hawaiian dish made with diced tomatoes, onions and salted salmon

Lumpia Deep-fried Filipino appetizer similar to spring rolls

Lup Cheong Sweet, oily Chinese sausage

Lychee Chinese fruit with sweet, smooth flesh

Malasadas Portuguese sweet fried pastry rolled in sugar

Manapua Chinese bao, baked or steamed buns filled with char siu pork or other meats

Mandoo Stuffed Korean dumplings, similar to Chinese won ton

Manju Sweet Japanese bean-paste buns

Mapo Dofu Spicy Szechuan dish made with ground pork, black beans and tofu ("mabo tofu" in Japanese)

Miso Thick fermented soybean paste used in Japanese cooking

Musubi Japanese rice ball ("onigiri")

Namasu Japanese dish of vegetables in a vinegar sauce

Nishime Japanese dish of vegetables with pork or chicken

Nori Japanese seasoned seaweed

Ogo Japanese term for a type of seaweed

Okazu Japanese term for any food to be eaten with rice; okazu-ya are small take-out food stores that sell various dishes ala carte

'Opihi Hawaiian term for limpet, usually eaten raw (with salt)

Pancit General term for Filipino egg or rice noodles

Pao Doce Portuguese sweet bread

Pasteles Puerto Rican favorite made with taro and mashed green bananas and seasoned pork, wrapped in banana leaves

Patis Fish sauce used to flavor many Filipino dishes

Pho Vietnamese rice noodles in beef or chicken broth

Pinakbet Filipino dish of pork cooked with okra, string beans, eggplant and tomatoes, flavored with shrimp paste

Pipikaula Hawaiian dried, spiced beef, similar to beef jerky

Poi Hawaiian staple food made by cooking the taro corm and then pounding it with water into a paste

Poke Hawaiian dish made with cubed raw fish and various ingredients such as onions, limu, Hawaiian salt, shoyu, red chili peppers, sugar and 'inamona (kukui nut meat)

Ramen Japanese wheat noodles in broth topped with meats and vegetables

Saimin Noodle soup unique to Hawai'i

Sari Sari Filipino shrimp stew with vegetables

Sashimi Japanese term for thin slices of raw fish

Senbei Japanese tea cookies

Shoyu Japanese word for soy sauce

Siu Mai Chinese steamed dumplings filled with ground pork ("pork hash," or "shumai" in Japanese)

Soba Slender Japanese buckwheat noodles

Somen Thin Japanese rice noodles

Squid Lū'au Hawaiian dish made of octopus cooked with lū'au (taro) leaves and coconut milk

Taegu Spicy Korean dried codfish

Tako Japanese word for octopus ("he'e" in Hawaiian)

Takuan Japanese pickled turnip

Tempura Japanese vegetables, meat or seafood quick-fried in a light batter

Teriyaki Japanese sweetened shoyu sauce or marinade used to flavor a variety of foods

Tofu Soybean curd of Chinese origin, popular in Japan and other Asian countries

Tonkatsu Breaded, deep-fried Japanese pork cutlet

Udon Thick Japanese wheat noodles

Ume Salty, sour pickled Japanese plum

Unagi Japanese fresh water eel, usually basted in teriyaki sauce and broiled

Vinha D'Alhos Portuguese fish or pork in vinegar and garlic

Warabi Japanese term for fiddlehead fern ("hō'i'o" in Hawaiian)

Wasabi Known as Japanese horseradish but green and hotter

Won Ton Chinese dumplings, often served in a soup

Yakitori Grilled Japanese-style chicken skewered on a stick

Hawaiians and just over 6,000 people of European descent in the Islands in 1890, so the Chinese came to constitute more than a third of the existing population at that time.

Chinese immigrants were eager to leave the plantations to pursue other occupations as soon as their labor contracts were fulfilled. Some established rice farms to meet the growing local demand for rice and to export to the continental United States, which saw rice supplies produced in the South, along with sugar, cut off by the Civil War. Between 1889 and 1910, rice was second only to sugar as the largest agricultural crop in Hawai'i, with an annual output of almost 42 million pounds.

Chinese also began manufacturing noodles and other Asian staples locally—not only to satisfy the Chinese community, but to fill the needs of the growing Japanese and Korean populations as well.

The Chinese freely intermarried with Hawaiians, even merging their names to form such unique Chinese-Hawaiian family names as Apana and Auwae in the process. They did the same with food, accounting for delicacies like manapua, which is believed to have derived its name from the Hawaiian expression "mea 'ono pua'a," which translates as "pork pastry or cake."

As Chinese moved off the plantations, Japanese were recruited in large numbers to work in the booming sugar industry. More than 60,000 Japanese immigrants arrived between 1885 and 1900, mainly from Hiroshima, Yamaguchi, Fukuoka and Kumamoto prefectures. Immigrants from Okinawa began arriving in 1900, bringing their unique culture, language and foods. In total, some 200,000 Japanese arrived between 1885 and 1924, comprising up to 40 percent of Hawai'i's total population.

Combining industriousness with sheer numbers, Japanese became a dominant force in the Islands' sugar and pineapple industries, as well as other trades. By 1914, Japanese produced over 80 percent of Hawai'i's coffee. They took over much of the

---

Lechon Kawali
Serves 4

1½ to 2 lbs. pork belly
           Water sufficient to boil pork
5 cloves   garlic, crushed
1 tsp.   salt
1 Tbsp.   black peppercorns *or*
½ Tbsp.   ground black pepper
           Vegetable oil for frying

Slice pork into 1" pieces. Bring a pot of water to a boil and add pork with seasonings. Reduce heat and simmer 1 hour. Remove meat, drain and allow to air dry. Heat oil and deep-fry pork until it is crisp and skin blisters. Serve with lechon liver sauce.

Lechon Liver Sauce

4 oz.   chicken livers
¼ c.   cider vinegar
½ c.   breadcrumbs
1½ Tbsp.   minced garlic
½ c.   minced onion
            Pinch salt and pepper
1½ Tbsp.   brown sugar
½ c.   water

Broil livers until half-cooked. Press through a mesh strainer. Combine strained liver with remaining ingredients. Simmer 20 minutes over medium heat. Makes about 1½ cups.

rice farming from the Chinese; became independent farmers of fruits, vegetables, poultry and hogs; and transformed Hawai'i's commercial fishing industry with ideas and innovations brought with them from Japan. Wooden-hulled sampans, or "aku boats"—modeled after highly efficient Japanese fishing boats and adapted to ocean conditions found in Hawai'i—formed the core of the modern fishing industry for decades.

By 1930, Japanese operated nearly half of all Honolulu's retail establishments. In many local Japanese restaurants, saimin stands and okazu-ya, the flavors of Japan were modified to fit the tastes of the people in Hawai'i, becoming an integral part of food culture in Hawai'i. By the 1940s, people of Okinawan ancestry had made a huge impact in both hog raising and the restaurant industry. Like the Chinese, the Japanese soon began manufacturing food, including shoyu, sake, tofu, miso and pickles.

Between 1903 and 1905, some 7,000 Koreans arrived, adding their tasty grilled meats and spicy seasonings and side dishes to the local menu. The majority of Koreans in Hawai'i came from Cholla Province located in southwestern South Korea, where kim chee (salted vegetables seasoned with sweet, hot peppers) was eaten on a daily basis. Korean immigrants began making kim chee commercially in Hawai'i in the late 1930s.

A Chinese "kow-kow man" carries food and hot tea to field workers ca. 1912. Opposite: Both Filipinos and Puerto Ricans prepare similar versions of "lechon," roast pork.

In spite of their differences, all of these Asian immigrants came from rice-based food cultures. Each cuisine also relies on soy sauce and features a range of noodle dishes, such as Chinese won ton mein; Okinawan soba; Korean kook soo; Japanese soba, ramen, somen and udon; Filipino pancit; Vietnamese pho and even local-style saimin.

By 1930, 100,000 Filipinos had arrived, bearing a culture and cuisine that integrated Spanish, Asian, Malayan and American influences. Of these, the strongest culinary influences came from Spain, while Chinese immigration to the Philippines in the 1500s can be seen in such dishes as pancit (noodles) and lumpia, which can be described as a Filipino egg roll. Adobo, a dish of Spanish and Mexican influences, was prepared with pork or chicken cooked in a marinade made of vinegar, bay leaves, peppercorn and garlic. Predominant seasonings in Filipino cooking include patis (fish sauce) and bagoong (shrimp sauce), lemongrass, ginger, soy sauce and vinegar.

Growing Diversity

The foods brought to Hawai'i by different ethnic groups were unique, but they shared a number of charac-

CHRISTMAS ON PARKER RANCH

Many children of immigrants gained their first impressions about "American" food from the plantation owners and managers for whom their parents worked. Caucasians were viewed as holding a superior status in the paternalistic hierarchy of the times, whether the subject in question was housing, fashion or food.

Hans L'Orange, who served as manager of Oahu Sugar Company in Waipahu from 1933 to 1957, would visit every school in the area around Christmas, said Goro Arakawa, a longtime Waipahu resident and owner of the general store Arakawa's, which closed in 1995. "A lot of children have memories of looking up from their desks to suddenly find his towering presence filling the doorway of their classrooms," Arakawa recounted. "He would have oranges, apples, candies and nuts." In a 1999 oral history interview, Waipahu oldtimer Edith Valdriz recalled Christmas parties held for plantation workers and their children at Oahu Sugar: "Hans L'Orange would hand out bags of oranges and candies. All us kids would all line up and say thank you."

Children of workers at Parker Ranch in Waimea, Hawai'i, also remember what a special occasion company-sponsored Christmas parties were. Nancy

Piianaia wrote in the *Waimea Gazette*:

Those who attended these early Ranch parties as children will never forget their excitement in the weeks preceding the event. For many, this night was Christmas! They dressed in their best clothes—some even had new shoes for the occasion—and waited anxiously until evening came. Then families gathered and walked to Barbara Hall, for there were no cars in Waimea. Fathers carried large flashlights to light the way, and you could see neighbors making their way down the streets to town. Many families walked two or three miles in the cold, and sometimes wet, night.

There, the children received brown paper bags filled with oranges, apples, hard candy, raisins and walnuts gathered from the orchards at Waiki'i, Piianaia writes. New school supplies—composition books, pencils and pens—from the ranch store were also carefully wrapped for the school-age children and placed under the tree. The adults received gifts as well. After the gifts were distributed, ice cream was served. With the lack of refrigeration, this taste of ice cream was a very special Christmas treat that the kids carried with them throughout the year, she recalls.

Immigrant families quickly began celebrating these new-fangled American holidays—each in their own way—especially as the Hawai'i-born generation of children grew up as American citizens by birth. Many of these family food customs are still carried on today, although their origins may have been lost to memory. From sharing an ice-cold watermelon on the Fourth of July to baking pumpkin pies from scratch on Thanksgiving, the melding of American and other ethnic customs was surely and seamlessly reflected in the foods of the holidays.

During the American New Year, we had another treat when Father brought home a Hoffman ham from our store. Mother would bake it with brown sugar. She had it sliced and served the yummy ham along with a Chinese dumpling (jin dui), made from mochi flour with fillings of coconut, pork or black sugar resembling a round and chewy doughnut.
—J.W. Lau, Journey to the Sandalwood Island: A Family Saga

HAWAIIAN FRUITS.

Pineapples and Bananas, Hawaii.

teristics in common with each other—especially when they are viewed by type or region. This might help to simplify matters some, since it is easy to see how the three general categories of Polynesian, European/American and Asian can encompass a nearly unlimited variety of flavors.

This mindset also makes accepting new dishes introduced by more recent immigrant groups much easier. Thai and Vietnamese foods, with their rice and noodle bases and their range of familiar/unfamiliar vegetables, seasonings and preparations, for example, have established themselves and are rapidly growing in popularity. The number of Korean and Filipino restaurants has also mushroomed, boosted by an influx of recent immigrants from those countries. Similarly, Japanese noodle shops, bakeries, sushi bars and izaka-ya (pubs that serve food) now cater to a sizable population of students, business people and other long-term visitors from Japan.

Local people, already well attuned to the parameters of Asian cooking, seem to welcome the novelty and the adventure of exploring new food offerings. This is true of dishes introduced from different regions of a country. Although Chinese food in Hawai'i used to be largely synonymous with Cantonese cuisine, for example, today locals seek out places offering Mandarin-style dishes such as mu shu pork, Peking duck, Mongolian hot pot, Mongolian beef, beggar's chicken and pot stickers, or Szechuan-style dishes such as kung pao chicken, tea-smoked duck, twice-cooked pork and mapo dofu as well.

One of the broadest—and strongest—connections linking the different food traditions is the sea. Nearly all of the major ethnic groups that settled in Hawai'i share a cultural link to the sea as a source of sustenance. Not only Hawaiians and Pacific Islanders fit this profile; so do the island cultures of Japan, Okinawa, the Philippines and Puerto Rico. The majority of the Portuguese who came to work on the plantations hailed from the islands of Azores and Madeira, and even China and Korea

boast extended coastlines. More than just a food source, these island peoples share what amounts to a common mindset and an identity. All of them thrive in Hawai'i, their palates tuned to the convergence of flavors from days past—perfectly prepared for the diversity of the future. ◙

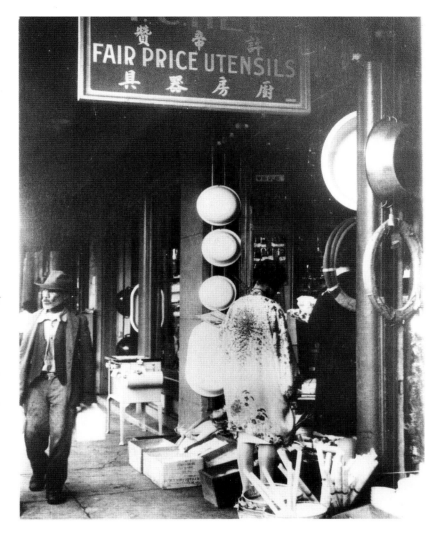

⋙ ⋙ ⋙ ⋙ ⋙ ⋙ ⋙

Consumers browse through a kitchen shop in Honolulu's Chinatown ca. 1900. Above: Produce delivery by horse and wagon.

MANAPUA

Like many favorite local foods, manapua are Chinese in origin. But the Chinese name for these fluffy white buns filled with shredded pork is char siu bao. Their local name results from jamming several Hawaiian words together.

Manapua are deeply embedded in the collective memory of old Hawai'i. In simpler times, they were sold on the streets of many communities by peddlers who were known only as the "manapua man." Carrying their tasty goods in containers hung on each end of a pole, the manapua man canvassed the neighborhoods with the pole slung over his shoulders, calling out, "Manapua, pepeiao, pork hash ..." Pepeiao and pork hash are other popular dim sum treats.

There are many reasons for the manapua's lasting popularity. It easily fulfills two of the primary requisites—good taste and affordability. And, like a SPAM® musubi or hot dog, manapua is a quick and satisfying mini-meal combining a savory portion of meat with a bland starch. It can be just enough to quell one's hunger—or to make a full meal of them, just eat more! One manapua (lots of bun, slightly sweet) along with one or two pork hash (no bun, slightly salty) makes a perfect pairing. These days, many local people take a box of manapua to meetings rather than doughnuts, serve them as an after-game or after-practice snack for their kids' sports teams or take them to tailgate parties and picnics. Manapua are convenient finger food, with no need for plates or forks.

Like everything else local, manapua have evolved over the years. For one thing, they are considerably larger than traditional char siu bao ever were. The texture of the bun is soft and fluffy, yet a little chewy. Manapua were traditionally steamed, but baked manapua are also quite popular today. Besides shredded pork, a wide variety of fillings can now be found, such as kālua pig, lup cheong, chicken, curry chicken, azuki bean and sweet potato. Manapua are even sold in 7-Eleven stores in Hawai'i—including a pepperoni version.

The call of the manapua man no longer echoes through Hawai'i's streets, but their tradition remains alive in the form of street vendors who sell manapua and other snacks from vans parked near beach parks, worksites, playgrounds and schools. People still refer to these motorized vendors as the "manapua man."

Most people prefer purchasing their manapua from a number of well-established shops, however, including Libby's Manapua Shop, Chun Wah Kam, Island Manapua Factory, Royal Kitchen and Char Hung Sut. Most of these famed places are located on O'ahu, which makes boxes of manapua a popular omiyage for people to take to friends and relatives on the other islands.

Few people make their own manapua any more, but here is a recipe for those intrepid souls who would like to try.

Manapua (Char Siu Bao)
Makes 18 buns

Buns
3½ c.	flour, divided
1 Tbsp.	shortening, plus more to grease bowl
¼ c.	sugar, divided
1 pkg.	active dry yeast
1 c.	warm water, divided

Filling
1 tsp.	sesame oil
¾ lb.	char siu, diced
3 Tbsp.	chopped green onions
2½ Tbsp.	sugar
4 tsp.	shoyu
2 tsp.	flour
2 tsp.	cornstarch
¼ c.	water

To make the buns, put 3 cups of flour in a large bowl. Cut in shortening (you can do this with two butter knives). Stir in 2 Tbsp. sugar. In a small bowl, combine the remaining 2 Tbsp. sugar with the yeast and ⅓ cup of warm water. Stir until yeast is dissolved. Add the remaining ½ cup flour; mix well.

Combine flour mixture, yeast mixture, and the remaining ⅔ cup water. Knead on lightly floured board for 5 minutes or until dough is smooth and elastic. Place dough in a greased bowl, cover and let rise until dough has doubled, ½ to 1 hour.

While the dough is rising, make the filling. In a saucepan, heat oil and stir-fry char siu for 30 seconds. Add green onions, sugar and shoyu. In a small bowl, mix flour and cornstarch with water until smooth. Stir into char siu mixture. Cook until mixture thickens; cool.

When dough is risen, punch it down and divide into 18 portions. Oil hands and flatten pieces of dough. Put about 1 Tbsp. char siu filling in center of each piece of dough. Form buns by pulling dough up around filling. Pinch to seal seams. Place on squares of waxed paper and let rest 20 to 30 minutes. Place on rack and steam over boiling water for 15 minutes.

CONNECTION

KAU KAU CONNECTION: HAWAIIAN "BARBECUE"

One clear example of how profoundly local food is infused by Asian tastes is the fact that when you refer to "barbecue" here (as in barbecue meat, barbecue chicken, barbecue burger, etc.) what you're saying, really, is teriyaki, not the sweet, spicy, smoky, reddish-brown stuff that made Kansas City famous. You can get that Mainland-style barbecue here in supermarkets and restaurants, of course, but just be aware of this regional idiosyncrasy when engaged in a dialogue with a person from outside Hawai'i, and vice versa.

In the Islands, some form of local "barbecue" sauce (i.e., teriyaki) might just be the most popular and versatile means of flavoring any combination of meat, poultry, seafood, and vegetables. Many recipes (including classics like beef tomato, chop steak or pork tofu) rely on some combination of shoyu, sugar, ginger and garlic. Therefore, I am proud to share what is possibly one of the all-time, all-around best local-style teriyaki sauces ever created. My father-in-law, Larry Nakama, passed his legendary teriyaki sauce recipe on to his children, and his daughter, Eloise Nakama Hiura, describes it here:

Larry's All-Purpose Teriyaki Sauce

Dad used a one-gallon glass mayonnaise jar to make his teriyaki sauce. He kept the sauce handy and used it in preparing all sorts of dishes until it ran out and he would have to whip up another batch. I recall my first lesson in making the sauce was to learn how to "eyeball" the ingredients and taste the sauce in between to adjust—Dad didn't measure anything.

First, he poured the shoyu in, about ⅔ of the jar. Second, he added the sugar until the mixture rose to fill ¾ of the jar. Third was sherry wine (my sister Joan says other types of wine could be substituted, but I remember Dad specifically sending me to the store for sherry). The sherry raised the mixture about another inch above the previous level. Then he lined the lid with wax paper, covered the jar and shook it to mix the ingredients. Next, he tasted it to see if he needed to adjust the flavor with more shoyu, sugar or sherry.

Finally, Dad poured some oil in a skillet and, while it was heating, peeled and crushed some ginger and cloves of garlic. He would brown the ginger first and scoop it into the jar; then he browned the garlic and poured it in.

Of course, not everyone can get their hands on a gallon-sized glass mayonnaise jar, so—as best as we can tell—here is Dad's recipe translated into measurable form:

8 c.	shoyu
6 c.	sugar
¼ c.	sherry wine
¼ c.	oil
3" piece	ginger, peeled, sliced and crushed
4 cloves	garlic, peeled and crushed

Combine shoyu, sugar and wine. Heat oil in a small frying pan and brown ginger. Add ginger to shoyu mixture, leaving oil in the frying pan. Brown garlic and add to shoyu mixture. Mix well.

This might seem like a lot, but believe me, it is a blessing to have this all-purpose sauce prepared and ready for any situation. You can use it full strength as a marinade for meat, chicken, pork or seafood, or cut it to taste with water (try about three parts sauce to one part water) to stir-fry anything—vegetables, noodles or rice. Using the same three-to-one ratio, you can make my father's 'ono shoyu pork or shoyu chicken. Enjoy!

Larry Nakama passed his recipes—including the one for his legendary teriyaki sauce—along to his children.

THE CHINESE

Chinese immigrants skillfully infused Asian influences into the culinary preferences of both Hawaiians and Caucasians alike. They introduced such Asian staples as rice, noodles, soy sauce and tofu to the Island table and created such local classics as chicken long rice, chop steak and beef tomato in the process.

The Chinese also created a near-monopoly of the restaurant business. Chinese restaurants quickly gained in popularity because they served fast, tasty, affordable food. In Hawai'i, Chinese food usually meant Cantonese cuisine from Guangdong Province in southern China, where most of the immigrants came from. Cantonese cuisine is known for quick stir-fried and deep-fried dishes prepared in woks. Some popular Cantonese dishes include orange chicken, shrimp Canton, beef broccoli, crispy chicken, chow fun, won won soup and duck with plum sauce, now all common sights in the modern local plate lunch.

Honolulu's Chinatown ca. 1900.

Chinese Soup

Soup was a constant and necessary presence on the Chinese table. Simple broths, made from meat bones and vegetables or pickles and designed to aid in digestion, were often served with everyday meals as beverages or poured over the customary last bowl of rice. Light soups were served in small cups throughout banquets as palate cleansers between courses and to signify the end of a series of dishes.

Making soup was a lesson in economy. Inexpensive, tough meats were tenderized by simmering in water. The meat was removed from the water and roughly sliced from the bone, and the meaty bones were returned to the water to continue simmering. Tough vegetables were then blanched in the same broth.

The meat and blanched vegetables could then be stir-fried with other foods such as tofu, mushrooms and onions, while the nutritious broth, rich in protein from the bones and vitamins and minerals from the vegetables, would serve as the beverage for the meal. Nothing was wasted, not even the cooking water.

One classic example of this style of cooking is the Hawaiian lūʻau staple chicken long rice. Some versions are less liquid, like the Samoan sapasui; others are soups, like the sotanghon served in the Philippines and Guam and the Chinese-inflected version presented here.

Anthony Chang's Chinese Soup

8 oz.	long rice noodles (mung bean vermicelli)
3 lbs.	chicken parts or whole chicken
3	cartons low-sodium chicken broth (32 oz. each)
1 Tbsp.	Hawaiian salt
½" piece	fresh ginger root, sliced
1	large, sweet Maui onion, cubed
1 bunch	green onions, thinly sliced
1 head	bok choy, chopped

Set long rice noodles in a bowl and cover with hot tap water. Set aside to soften for 30 minutes.

Combine chicken, chicken broth, salt and ginger into a large pot. Bring to a boil over high heat, then reduce heat to medium-low and simmer until the chicken is tender and no longer pink, about 35 minutes. Remove chicken and set aside. Strain broth into a new pot, discarding solids, and put back on the burner.

Stir onion into the broth and bring to a boil, then reduce heat to medium-low.

Meanwhile, remove the skin and bones from the chicken and discard. Roughly chop the meat and add to broth with noodles, green onion and bok choy; simmer until noodles are tender.

Here is another classic Chinese soup. Watercress is a versatile and popular vegetable, high in vitamins A, B_1, B_2, B_3, B_5, B_6, C, D, E and K, while dried dates contain fiber, iron, niacin, potassium, magnesium, vitamins A and B, calcium, phosphorous and copper. Dates were traditionally used to assist with constipation (because of their mild laxative effect), anemia, fatigue and the prevention of abdominal cancer. This combination of ingredients makes a soup considered to be ideal for relieving a cough or excess heat.

Watercress Soup

	Water
	Bone portion of pork butt, meat attached
3	large dried dates
2-3	bunches fresh watercress

Set two pots of water boiling. Blanch pork in one; remove from water. In the other, combine dates and blanched pork. Boil at least 2 hours. Add watercress and boil at least 30 minutes more, or until watercress becomes soft. Soup may be boiled longer for a richer flavor.

>>> >>> >>> >>> >>> >>> >>>

Launch lūʻau on the Japanese sampan Ryno Maru.

THE JAPANESE

Although the Japanese culture is often described as homogeneous, its food genealogy actually reflects a variety of influences from sources as diverse as China (noodles, tofu, shoyu) and Europe (baked and deep-fried dishes such as tempura). Regardless of its origins, traditional Japanese food is renowned for its fastidious preparation—seen especially in the skill with which fresh seasonal and regional ingredients are incorporated. A formal Japanese meal often involves an assortment of foods artfully presented in individual plates and bowls.

In Hawaiʻi, Japanese food—like many other things—is a less formal adaptation of the original. Having arrived in larger numbers than other ethnic groups, Japanese in Hawaiʻi were able to import many of their favorite Japanese foods, and they had a large enough population to produce their own goods in Hawaiʻi, including such popular items as shoyu, sake, miso, and tofu and its soy by-products okara (soybean pulp) and aburage (fried bean curd).

One key aspect of Japanese food that never changed, however, is the prominence of rice in the diet. Linked to sacred deities, rice is the focus of most Japanese meals. All other side dishes—known as okazu—are meant to accompany the rice. Japanese rice is bland and sticky, so okazu were seasoned mainly with salt or shoyu. A simple Japanese meal would consist of rice, one or more okazu dishes, miso soup and tsukemono (pickles).

Sushi was made to celebrate special occasions and, as a result, became a party and potluck staple. Su is the vinegar seasoning used to make sushi rice. While it is easy to focus on the fillings and toppings that are part of most sushi dishes, good sushi really starts with well-seasoned rice. Like many good cooks, my mother depends primarily on experience and feel, but this is her basic sushi su recipe. Don't worry if you end up making extra, she says, for it keeps well and can also be used to make namasu, a popular side dish or appetizer made of thinly sliced, uncooked vegetables and seafood.

Mom's Sushi Su

4 c.   white vinegar
6 c.   sugar
Scant ½ c. salt

Combine ingredients in a non-aluminum saucepan and bring to a boil, making sure the solid ingredients are dissolved. Let cool and store in glass bottle(s). Su will last for months even if left unrefrigerated. In fact, besides flavoring the sushi rice, the su also helps to keep it from spoiling.

Sushi Rice

Cook 4 cups of rice and transfer to a large mixing bowl. My mother uses a big wooden sushi mixing bowl. After rice has cooled some, fold 5 jiggers of su into the rice (1 jigger per cup of rice, plus 1 jigger "for the pot"). A jigger, or shot glass, holds about 1½ ounces. Mom follows this ratio of one jigger per cup of cooked rice "plus one for the pot," making this a very flexible recipe—good for any size meal. However, Mom says she reduces the amount of su that she adds to the rice when making inarizushi, or cone sushi, because the cone itself is seasoned.

Miso Soup

	Fu (gluten cakes)
	Water
3 c.	dashi (see recipe)
½ c.	miso
2 tsp.	raw sugar
1 stalk	green onion, finely chopped

Cover fu with water and set aside to soften.

Put miso in a bowl and add dashi gradually, stirring constantly. Strain through a sieve into a pot. Heat, but do not boil.

Drain fu and squeeze out excess water. Add fu and sugar to miso broth. Remove from heat and add green onion.

Dashi

5" strip	konbu
3 c.	water
1 c.	katsuobushi (shaved dried bonito) *or*
½ c.	iriko
1 tsp.	salt
1 tsp.	shoyu

Rinse konbu and add to water. Bring to a boil. When large bubbles appear, remove konbu. Add katsuobushi or iriko and remove from heat. Let soak for a few minutes. Strain; season broth with salt and shoyu.

A woman carries freshly baked loaves of sweet bread reflecting the shape of the beehive Portuguese oven at rear.

THE PORTUGUESE

The Portuguese became an integral part of plantation society, living and working alongside plantation workers of other nationalities. From 1878 to 1887, nearly 12,000 Portuguese—mainly from the Madeira and Azores islands—arrived to work on Hawai'i's sugar plantations.

Portuguese immigrants preferred bread rather than taro or rice. They were famed as bakers, and the undeniable aroma of pao doce (sweet bread) wafting from traditional Portuguese stone ovens is etched into the memories of many plantation residents. Portuguese were also fond of foods cooked with wine, pickled in vinegar or simmered into soups and stews. Besides the pao doce, Portuguese foods that enjoy great popularity in Hawai'i today include malasadas (a fried pastry rolled in sugar), Portuguese bean soup, Portuguese sausage (linguica) and vinha d'alhos.

Vinha D'Alhos
Serves 6

3 lbs.	boneless pork
1½ c.	vinegar
2 cloves	garlic, crushed
6	Hawaiian red peppers, seeded and chopped
1	bay leaf
2 tsp.	salt
6	whole cloves
¼ tsp.	thyme
⅛ tsp.	sage
2 Tbsp.	salad oil

Cut pork into 2" by 1½" pieces. Combine vinegar, garlic, red peppers, bay leaf, salt, cloves, thyme and sage; pour over pork and let marinate overnight in refrigerator, stirring 2 or 3 times.

Put pork, with marinade, in pot and cook for 20 minutes over medium heat; drain. Heat oil in skillet; add pork and sauté over low heat for 10 to 15 minutes until browned.

Filipino field laborers break for lunch in the canefields.

THE FILIPINOS

More than a simple meeting of East and West, Filipino food represents a complex, multicultural mix of cuisine from different parts of the world. Early trade with China, for example, led to such Philippines favorites as lumpia (egg rolls) and pancit (noodles). By far, however, the greatest influence came from 400 years of Spanish rule. The popular adobo (meat cooked in vinegar) and lechon (roast pork) can be attributed to the Spanish, along with an affinity for cooking with tomatoes, onions and garlic. Toss in the rich tradition of Filipino baked goods like ensemada (cheese buns), pan de sal (hard rolls) and flan (custard deserts), and it is easy to accept the conclusion of some food historians that around 80 percent of Filipino dishes are inspired by the Spanish. Adding yet another layer to the discussion are the considerable cultural variations among the many islands and distinct cultural regions that make up the Philippines.

In contrast with other ethnic groups, early Filipino immigrants were mainly single men who did not cook extensively for themselves. This presented a limited impression of what Filipino cuisine really was. Moving beyond the principal seasonings of bagoong and patis (fish sauce), over time the diversity and subtleties of Filipino food have slowly become more widely recognized and appreciated. Recently, Filipino food—with its heavy emphasis on rice, stews and soupy dishes, and an inspired use of vegetables such as ampalaya (bittermelon), kalabasa (squash), talong (eggplant), mais (corn), patatas (potatoes), onions and tomatoes, in combination with meats and seafood—is gaining in popularity.

Adobo

¼ c.	cider vinegar
¼ c.	shoyu
2 cloves	garlic, crushed
¼ tsp.	cracked peppercorns
¼ tsp.	salt
1 Tbsp.	brown sugar
2	bay leaves
2½ lbs.	chicken or pork butt, cut into 1½" pieces

In a large pot, mix all ingredients except the meat. Add meat, making sure it is covered with sauce. Cover and let marinate for 1 to 3 hours.

Bring to a boil; then lower heat and simmer 30 minutes for chicken or 45 minutes for pork.

THE KOREANS

Like most Asian cuisine, Korean food revolves around rice—and sometimes noodles—accompanied by meat, vegetables and tofu often seasoned with soy sauce, salt, garlic, sesame oil, ginger and a thick chili sauce called gochujang. An array of banchan, or side dishes, are often served in addition to the rice and entrée, and kim chee, a fermented, spicy vegetable dish, is usually a part of every meal.

While chicken, pork and seafood are all important in Korean cuisine, beef dishes are the best known. Grilled (gui) beef dishes such as bulgogi and especially kalbi (see following page) are especially popular, so much so that many Korean restaurants have yakiniku-style grills installed at their tables.

Although the importance of meat in the Korean diet has its roots deep in the country's history, early immigrants to Hawai'i, like many of their counterparts, were not able to eat meat all the time. Only in the latter part of the 20th century has beef become regular table fare.

In Hawai'i, the popularity of Korean food has been sparked in part by new immigrants arriving in the 1970s, following the revision of immigration laws in 1965. While the 1970 census lists about 9,000 residents of Korean descent, by the 2000 census over 41,000 declare themselves of Korean ancestry.

Richard Kim (left) is a third-generation keeper of the flame. In the late 1930s, his grandmother, Theresa Soo Chung Kim, struck upon the idea of making kim chee with the Chinese cabbage that her husband, truck farmer Chin Wah Kim, was unable to sell. They originally sold the spicy, fermented vegetable under the Diamond brand solely on a wholesale basis. It was Richard's father, Joe, who gave the business its familiar Joe Kim's Kim Chee name and began retailing the product locally as well as exporting it to Los Angeles. Today, Richard continues to produce the family's famous kim chee, while also processing vegetables and fruits for wholesalers and restaurants.

Richard learned how to make

Korean-Style Kalbi

Marinade

½ c.	shoyu
⅓ c.	sugar
4 cloves	garlic, finely chopped
1 Tbsp.	finely minced ginger
1 Tbsp.	Ko Choo Jung bean paste
1 tsp.	sesame oil
2 Tbsp.	thinly sliced green onion
1 tsp.	sesame seeds, toasted
4 lbs.	beef short ribs

Combine marinade ingredients in a saucepan and heat until sugar dissolves. Cool sauce. Pour over ribs and marinate overnight, turning meat 2 or 3 times.

For best results, grill meat over charcoal or gas, 2 to 3 minutes on each side.

the family's time-honored kim chee sauce directly from his grandmother when he was about 20 years old. So refined is his skill that he instinctively varies the recipe depending on where the cabbage is grown—making slight variations in salt, garlic and other ingredients. According to Richard, you should taste the sauce once after you make it, adjust it if you need to, taste again to check, and then walk away. It's not good, in other words, to keep adjusting over and over again.

"You—your heart and soul—are the intangible thing that makes it good," he said.

Richard recalls a favorite childhood snack using kim chee: "Coming home from school hungry, my older siblings and I would make peanut butter and jelly kim chee sandwiches for an after-school treat. Guava or strawberry jelly was the best, and our kim chee."

THE PUERTO RICANS

Like Filipino food, Puerto Rican cuisine reflects a strong Spanish influence overlaid on an island culture. The native Taino diet relied on root vegetables such as yucca (cassava), yams and taro, along with beans, rice, tomatoes, garlic and olive oil. Fish and other seafood were also important elements. The Spanish introduced cows and pigs, as well as wheat, chickpeas, cilantro, eggplant, onions, coconut and garlic. African slaves brought plantains and okra and are credited with developing many popular dishes featuring coconut. All these flavors Puerto Rican immigrants brought with them to Hawai'i.

Puerto Rican foods are generally mild in flavor. Their dominant seasoning is sofrito, a paste made from onions, green pepper, garlic and tomatoes sautéed in oil. Sazon, a seasoning salt sprinkled on meats, fish and poultry, as well as in soups and stews, is also frequently used.

The best-known Puerto Rican dish in Hawai'i is the pastele, seasoned pork wrapped in mashed green banana (masa) and spiced with oregano, cumin, cilantro and black olives, then wrapped in banana leaves, resembling a Mexican tamale. Other popular dishes include habichuelas con arroz (beans and rice), arroz con gandules (gandule rice) and ensalada con bacalao (codfish salad).

When Augustine and Petra Torres (left, with their parents' photos) moved from the Big Island to O'ahu years ago, they found themselves far from their agricultural roots, which included growing up on a sugar plantation in Kōhala, picking coffee in Kona and making candies in a macadamia nut factory in Honoka'a. One thing that they did not leave behind, however, was their proud Puerto Rican heritage—especially their love of Puerto Rican food.

Petra learned to cook traditional Puerto Rican dishes from her mother and now passes her knowledge on to her daughter-in-law, Jackie Chong Torres, the owner and chef of Jackie's Diner in Waimalu. In addition to other local favorites, Jackie's is known for its pasteles, yellow rice and bacalhau salad (opposite). Although now widely considered to be the quintessential Puerto Rican dish, pasteles were actually made only two or three times a year for special occasions, such as at Christmas and New Year's, because they were so time-consuming to prepare. Rather than a main dish, they were considered more of a side dish.

When Jackie, who is Korean, asked her mother-in-law to teach her to cook Puerto Rican food, Petra gladly obliged. Today, Petra and Jackie's mother can be found at the diner making pasteles twice a week. First the masa—mashed green bananas—must be prepared. The seasoned pork filling is cooked separately, then the pasteles are assembled and wrapped by hand like tamales in ti or banana leaves. One day of the week is dedicated to "regular" pasteles and the

other day is for spicy ones. They wrap hundreds of pasteles each week, boil them and then freeze them.

If pasteles were not an everyday dish, what did the average Puerto Rican family eat? "We were poor," Augustine said. Spanish rice, also called yellow rice, was the main dish. Banana, taro and breadfruit were important parts of their diet. Augustine and Petra noted that when they visited Puerto Rico they found it rather similar to Hawai'i, with lots of breadfruit, mango and bananas.

"I ate soup—bean soup—almost every day," Augustine recalled. "I still love bean soup." Other "poor man's food" included sardines and onions, and homemade blood sausage made with cow's intestines cleaned out with salt and stuffed with onion, garlic and blood. Sweets included plampinas (a kind of doughnut), fritas (pancakes) and "Johnny Cakes" cooked in a pan and eaten with jelly or honey for breakfast.

Today Petra picks her own gandule beans from a tree in their

backyard and makes her own sofrito seasoning. The Torreses enjoy Puerto Rican food just about every day, as do their children and grandchildren— and now, thanks to Jackie's Diner, the community at large can do so, too.

Bacalhau Salad

There are two types of bacalhau, Petra noted: the dried kind that's not too salty and a heavily salted variety that has to be soaked and/or boiled multiple times in fresh water before it is edible. A single dried filet of bacalhau used to cost 5 to 10 cents on the plantation, she recalled. Today, a filet of the same size costs about $100.

This recipe is more of a rough outline than a by-the-numbers guide:

Once excess salt has been removed from a fillet of bacalhau, boil until very soft. Shred the meat, carefully removing bones.

Add chopped onions, tomato and watercress (optional), seasoning with vegetable oil and a dash of shoyu to taste.

CHAPTER THREE

The Seeds of Local
Lessons from the Plantations

One of the key characteristics of early sugar plantation life was that workers were generally grouped in ethnically segregated camps. Some say this reflected a conscious plantation policy of "divide-and-rule" aimed at keeping workers from unionizing across ethnic lines. Others disagree, calling the establishment of ethnic camps the natural result of having to build additional housing to accommodate groups of workers as they arrived in Hawai'i from different localities at different points in time.

Whatever the reasons behind their development, one indisputable outcome of these segregated camps was that they allowed immigrants to more readily maintain important elements of their ethnic traditions and identity. By living in close quarters with others from the same country, they could communicate in their native languages, wear ethnic costumes for comfort or on special occasions, observe traditional festivals and religious rites, and share foods that were special to their native culture.

≫≫ ≫≫ ≫≫ ≫≫ ≫≫ ≫≫ ≫≫

Yesterday: Kau kau time in the canefields ca. 1920 (opposite). Today: Sugarcane workers break for lunch in a Pu'unēnē field of Hawaiian Commercial & Sugar Co. (below), one of Hawai'i's last remaining plantations.

>>> >>> >>> >>> >>> >>> >>>

A "waterboy" serves thirsty fieldworkers in a Hilo Coast canefield on the Big Island.

People came to accept and respect these differences as a natural part of plantation life. At the same time, living on a plantation also involved participating in a common culture on a daily basis, as all of the ethnic groups intermingled at work, in school and on playing fields. In fact, the lifestyle of this period featured a remarkable level of uniformity in terms of housing, as plantations provided camp after camp of simple cottages to their workers. Those living in close proximity to the mill could mark time by the sound of the plantation whistle at set intervals during the day, from start work time in the morning to curfew whistle at night.

Workers did not wear ethnically distinct costumes to work. On the contrary, with only minor variations they dressed very much alike in hanahana (work) attire sewn from 'āhina (blue denim) and palaka (a woven plaid), along with articles made from other easily obtainable fabrics such as Indian Head cotton or khaki. They reported to work wearing work tabis on their feet, lauhala pāpale (hats) on their heads, kappa (muslin coated in linseed oil) rainwear and bento (lunch) bags slung over their shoulders.

At work, they further bridged their differences by learning to communicate with each other and with their bosses in the unique Hawaiian creole known as pidgin English.

They talked about things they held in common, such as the weather, their children, who attended school and played sports together, and the evil luna (foreman) who pushed them equally to exhaustion all day long.

One of the most important means of binding immigrants from different ethnic backgrounds together into a community was food. Plantation workers packed their meals in sturdy metal lunch pails called kau kau tins or bento tins (sometimes pronounced bento ten). These lunch buckets were usually made of aluminum and featured two sections. The larger bottom portion was used to carry rice, while the removable upper compartment contained the food (meat, fish, vegetables) that accompanied the rice.

At lunch, or kau kau time, workers found as comfortable a spot as possible wherever they happened to be working and stopped to share their lunches. Sitting or squatting in a circle, each worker held his or her own rice container, while placing the upper tray in the circle to share what he or she had brought with others.

This may sound like a simple ritual, but in practice sharing lunch in this manner often involved a complex maze of cultural considerations. There were sure to be times, for example, when a coworker's lunch might look unappetizing—even to the point of appearing inedible. Never-

▶▶▶ ▶▶▶ ▶▶▶ ▶▶▶ ▶▶▶ ▶▶▶ ▶▶▶
Retired Hawaiian Commercial & Sugar Co. truck driver Larry Ikeda visits the mill at Puʻunēnē, Maui.

theless, it would appear impolite if one did not partake of that person's food—at least a token amount.

It is also important to note that these were rather small, intimate groups. At this, the main meal in a long and strenuous workday, workers were aware that others had to have enough to eat and not go hungry. If, for example, a person had brought three pieces of fish for lunch and two of them had been quickly snapped up by coworkers, then it would be unlikely that anyone would take the person's third and last piece. It was also necessary for that person to select something from someone else

in exchange, or else eat just rice and his last piece of fish. Conversely, if no one ate the fish, then that same person would feel constrained from picking from coworkers' lunches.

To avoid any sense of embarrassment or awkwardness, workers were likely to partake modestly of each others' food and to politely compliment each other on the tastiness of the dishes. This practice not only soothed the dynamics of the group; it introduced people to each other's cuisine and familiarized them with each other's culture.

In the bigger picture, it was not so much what each worker brought,

*Early 20th-century
paniolo line up for a
photograph at Upcountry
Maui's Raymond Ranch,
now 'Ulupalakua Ranch.*

for over time the foods that they shared grew more and more generic. Foods such as bacalhau, canned or smoked meat and fish the workers had caught and fried became staples of the plantation diet. More importantly, it was the act of sharing food in itself that helped to forge a tangible bond between people.

This sharing between people of different ethnic backgrounds led to what could be described as a process of natural selection. That is, over time, certain dishes gained broader and broader acceptance and popularity across ethnic lines, while the

more esoteric, exotic or bizarre items either faded from the menu or were relegated to the privacy of people's homes. Rather than a random conglomeration of ethnic delicacies, in other words, Hawai'i's mixed plate today is a representation of those foods that appealed to the broadest base of people over time.

Every ethnic group in Hawai'i has certain foods that its members prepare mainly for themselves and their immediate families. Then there are the dishes that might be taken to office parties, potluck dinners or picnics at the beach. There are

also numerous other food choices that form a spectrum between both extremes, those that are prepared and served depending on the company.

Many of the most popular ethnic dishes in Hawai'i share something in common with others. Meat dishes such as Japanese teriyaki and Korean kalbi and bulgogi, for example, bear strong similarities and are commonly lumped together and referred to as "barbecue meat." Filipino adobo and Portuguese vinha d'alhos both rely on vinegar and garlic as a marinade before cooking.

Noodles are also popular in

almost every culture around the world—especially all forms of Italian pasta. In Hawai'i, noodle dishes can also run the gamut from local-style saimin, macaroni salad and long rice to a variety of Asian noodles such as pancit (Filipino); chow mein or chow fun (Chinese); soba, udon or ramen (Japanese); kook soo (Korean); pho (Vietnamese) and pad thai (Thai).

There are many of these flavor bridges that link the various ethnic groups in Hawai'i together, making the practice of sharing food easier and imbuing local people with an uncanny knack for gauging the food-comfort levels of those around them, in bento lunches shared in the sugar-cane and pineapple fields or at a Fourth of July picnic at the beach.

Today, 'Ulupalakua Ranch's King's Cottage—named for former frequent visitor King David Kalākaua—is the tasting room of Tedeschi Vineyards, which serves up a variety of wines—grape, raspberry, passion fruit and pineapple—on an 18-foot-long bar cut from the trunk of a single mango tree.

How Poor Were You?

Often underplayed is the importance of economics and food preservation in studies of what immigrants and their families ate and why. While some emigrated to Hawai'i for adventure and a fresh start, the majority arrived with the idea of earning enough money to help their families back home—a dream promulgated by labor recruiters who traveled to far parts of the globe on behalf of Hawai'i's sugar planters. Accomplishing that, most laborers intended to return home to join their families upon completing their contracts.

Once here, however, they often found plantation wages so low that they couldn't earn enough to return to their homelands. In fact, many could not avoid incurring a burgeoning debt to the company just for the food and essentials they needed to survive. Frugality—often reaching desperate levels—was a common thread running through the lives of nearly every immigrant family.

TV talk show host Johnny Carson had a running gag going with his studio audiences: He'd bait them with a line like, "It was really cold last night!" and they'd shout back in unison, "How cold was it?" It's hard not to think of Carson when talking to plantation veterans about "before-time"—the old days.

"Beforetime not like nowdays."
"Yeah, no?"
"Yeah, beforetime, we was dirt poor."
"How poor were you?"
"Well, let me tell you. We was so poor dat ...

- "We used to catch grasshoppers and fry them outdoors in sardine cans with oil, sprinkling salt on them before eating them."
- "We used to knock down the bees' nests that hung under the eaves—

A field hand harvests taro in the late 1930s.

Could these otherwise fine, upstanding citizens be stretching the truth just a little? But what they said is true. Plantation people did live off the land, harvesting tree leaves, fern shoots, wild greens and herbs for both food and medicinal purposes. They also cultivated a variety of plants that were technically grasses for the same reason. In his memoir, *Pahoa Yesterday*, Big Island native Hiroo Sato noted, "Fern shoots, for example, were eaten with sardines. The young shoots of weeds such as popolo, ama-ranthus (pigweed) and dandelions were supplemental vegetables."

Poverty, it seems, is a relative thing—for nearly as often as elders describe how poor folks were, they express the opposing sentiment:

We were not poor; we had plenty to eat; we had fruits and vegetables from the land and lots of fish from the ocean—all free! The only thing we never had was money, but we had really good aikane (friends) and kind neighbors—all help each other. These things more important than money.
—Setsu Kyogoku, quoted in *Dear Okaasan*, by Jean Misaki

All the farmers in the valley were poor, that is, below the poverty level in today's terminology, but I can't recall a single family that went on welfare. We helped each other as the need arose. Farm families could always rely on what was available on the farm

the paper wasps. After we burned the nest, we cooked the larvae in a frying pan with shoyu and sugar."

- "The salty Chinese seed or lemon peel came in a small brown paper bag. After we ate all the seed, we would turn the bag inside out and lick all the salt from the bag."

- "We used to chew black tar from the road. No, really. Like gum." (This is believable. The "tar" used to patch roads in the old days would soften in the heat of the day to a chewable consistency.)

- "We only got to drink soda water on special occasions, so we wouldn't just drink it down like kids do nowdays. In order to savor every drop, we'd punch a small hole in the bottle cap with an ice pick or a nail, then we'd drink the soda through that little hole to make it last as long as possible."

- "We used to eat grass! No kidding, we was so poor that my mother used to pick grass and cook 'um. That was our dinner." (Two distinguished civic leaders from Maui shared this story and agreed it was true.)

itself—sweet potatoes, taro, banana, papaya and all kinds of vegetables. In addition, chickens and hogs were raised by the Okinawan families. Hogs were primarily for home consumption and were fed young taro leaves like those used by the Hawaiians for laulau. Since taro was widely grown in Kahaluu, this food supply for the pigs was very easy to obtain throughout the year.
    —Tom Ige, *Boy from Kahaluu: An Autobiography*

The two sentiments are not exclusive of one another, of course. Taken together, the idea that one could have so little money yet not consider oneself "poor" captures the essence of the Hawai'i of days gone by:

It seems the issue of how poor we are is a relative thing—as much a state of mind as it is a matter of dollars and cents. It was, in our past, a matter of sharing a similar fate as one's friends, neighbors and relatives. More than being "thrifty" in our modern way of thinking, the lack of money and material assets made people resourceful, respectful of others who were trying equally hard to survive, and apprecia- tive of those who had so little yet were willing to share so much.
    —Yoshida Matsuo

In his narrative history *Kipu– Huleia: The Social History of a Planta- tion Community, 1910-1950*, William

W.T. Haraguchi Farm grows taro on 50 acres in Hanalei Valley. Left to right: son Whitney, mother Karol, father Rodney, daughter Lyndsey Haraguchi-Nakayama and son-in-law Brad Nakayama. Rodney's great-grandfather star- ted the family business when he bought a rice mill in the valley in 1924.

K. Yamanaka recalled the challenge of feeding one's family on meager wages:

The average worker got paid about $1.00 per day for 8 hours of work. They worked 6 days a week. The plantation provided free medical services, housing, fuel (wood in the forest for bathhouse, kerosene for cook- ing) and water. Also most houses had a large yard for gardening and raising animals. Practically every family raised a large part of the food they consumed. Economic reality dictated that a man earning $1 per day needed food supple- ments to feed a family with 4-8 chil-

dren, thus the need of raising your own food and fishing to provide meat.
    Most economic activities related to meeting the food needs of the family and were not to earn money. The vegetables were consumed by the family or shared with neighbors. Occasionally they were sold to the vegetable man on his Sunday camp visits. Fruits, such as banana, papaya, pear (avocado) and mangoes, were raised for consumption and excess were fed to the pigs that some families raised. Banana was always available and in large supply. Most families raised chicken (Rhode Island red) for eggs and meat for family use.

Because the majority of the immigrant workforce came from Asia, rice became the staple food in the plantation diet. Both the Korean word for cooked rice, "bap," and the Japanese word, "gohan," are also synonymous with "meal." The same holds true of Chinese, Filipino and Southeast Asian cultures as well. Throughout the latter half of the 19th century, taro patches throughout the Islands were converted to rice paddies, and rice remained a major commercial crop in the Islands until local farmers could no longer compete with the influx of cheap rice grown in California's vast agricultural valleys.

It was simple. Everything else could be described as what-could-be-eaten-with-rice—especially anything that could be caught, grown or gathered rather than bought. Fern shoots such as the young shoots of the endemic hāpu'u fern, called "pepe'e" in Hawaiian and "kakuma" in Japanese; and hō'i'o (fiddlehead), called "warabi" by Japanese, along with the tender young shoots of the 'ohe (bamboo or takenoko), and lēkō (watercress) could be grown or gathered in the forests and mountain springs.

Rice kept very well—another one of its selling points—before it was cooked. After cooking, any leftover rice needed to be eaten fairly quickly. Thus the popularity of fried rice:

Fried Rice

3 Tbsp.	oil
½ c.	ham, SPAM™ or any leftover meat, diced
½ c.	vegetables (carrots, green beans, celery, onions, etc.), diced
½ tsp.	salt
1 Tbsp.	shoyu
½ Tbsp	sugar
1 Tbsp.	oyster sauce
3	eggs, beaten
4 c.	cooked rice (yesterday's is better than freshly made, since you don't want it too sticky)
¼ c.	chopped green onion

Heat oil in frying pan. Add meat and vegetables and sauté until cooked. Add salt, shoyu, sugar and oyster sauce; cook 1 minute. Add eggs and cook briefly, then add rice. Continue cooking and stirring until eggs are done and rice is heated and seasoned through. Sprinkle with green onion to serve.

>>> >>> >>> >>> >>> >>> >>>

Mitsuzo Nagasako and his family pose at their Nagasako Candy Store in Lahaina, Maui, ca. 1921. The family later opened the Nagasako Supermarket, an okazu-ya and a mini-mart, all in Lahaina.

Food purchases at the company store were restricted to the bare essentials, such as rice, salt and shoyu. Refined sugar was a luxury, but raw sugar could be obtained if people knew someone who worked at the mill. Generally speaking, dried or heavily salted foods such as bacalhau, salt salmon, smoked meat and salt beef and pork were popular because they kept for long periods without refrigeration in Hawai'i's humid climate. They were also valued because only a little was needed in combination with vegetables from the garden and rice to stretch a family meal.

Children, meanwhile, had very little access to stores of any kind. The average town or camp would be likely to have a mom-and-pop store or two that sold sodas, shave ice, ice cakes, candy bars, pastries, crack seed or other snack items—but not much else. However, purchasing any sort of treat required spending money, which was hard to come by for most families.

With little or no money to spend, children foraged for snacks outdoors, where fruits such as guava, mango, lychee, papaya, mountain apple, rose apple, banana, pohā, poka and liliko'i, waiawī, vi apple, avocado, lemon, orange, tangerine, jabon (pomelo), pineapple, thimbleberry, mulberry, banana, pomegranate, starfruit, peach, plum, lemon and lime (to be preserved as "sour lemon") could be found depending on where they grew

A Maui family business, Hashimoto Persimmon Farm grows and markets fresh fruit and other products at their spread in Kula, Maui. Clark Hashimoto, with wife Jackie and granddaughter Kaylee, still works the same land where his great-grandfather first planted persimmons in 1925.

up. Although firmly prohibited from doing so by plantation policy, they would cut and chew the sweet juice of the sugarcane or pineapple.

Kids knew which fields were mature and where different fruit trees stood. They knew which ones were publicly accessible, which ones were private, and from which they could safely swipe a few with only minimal consequences. Even within a grove of trees, kids knew the nuances of each, such as which ones were sweeter, which ones sour, which ones had smaller seeds and hence more meat. Every variety of mango, banana, papaya or guava tasted or smelled different, or had a different texture.

The following recipes give options for eating the bounty of wild fruits in other ways than straight off the tree:

Pear (Avocado) Bread

On the Big Island, avocados were often called "pears." But whatever they were called, they were plentiful. This was—and is—one of the best ways to eat them.

Cut a ripe avocado (pear) in half and remove the seed, then scoop the meat into a bowl. Break up the avocado with a fork or spoon, stirring in sugar to the proper taste and consistency (sweet and still slightly lumpy). Spread over toasted bread or crackers and serve open-face style.

>>> >>> >>> >>> >>> >>> >>>

The Haliimaile Super Market in Upcountry Maui, shown here in the 1960s, was once the plantation store for Maui Land & Pineapple's Haliimaile Plantation.

Preserved Starfruit

24 to 30	half-ripe medium-size starfruit
4 Tbsp.	rock salt
1½ lbs.	golden brown sugar
1½ tsp.	Chinese five-spice powder
1 tsp.	red food coloring
1½ tsp.	li hing mui powder, to sprinkle on dried, glazed fruit (optional)

Slice starfruit into ¼" slices. Sprinkle with salt and let stand overnight. Drain.
In a large pot, combine starfruit and sugar; mix well. Cook over medium heat about 15 minutes, stirring occasionally. Add Chinese five-spice and coloring and cook 5 minutes more. Cool. Drain excess syrup (quite a lot).
Dry the glazed fruit by one of several methods:

1. Place fruits on cookie sheet lined with two layers of paper towels. Bake at 170°F-200°F until dry.
2. Put slices on a clean screen and set out in the sun for a day (careful of ants!).
3. Use a dehydrator, following its directions.

People not only knew what grew when on the land, they also knew the rivers, where 'o'opu or 'ōpae, crayfish, frogs or hīhīwai were likely to be, lurking in the deep, dark eddies or basking in the sandy shallows. And the ocean, of course, demanded great knowledge of where to cast and which bait to use under varying conditions. Besides the prized 'opihi, limu, wana and even the tiny black pipipi boiled in salt and picked out of the shell with a needle became snacks enjoyed by children.

(akule, 'ōpelu); vinegared or pickled vegetables (kim chee, takuan, pickled onions, cucumbers, cabbage); or canned foods were not only economical; they were dependable, utilitarian and safe from spoilage. They traveled well, which was important because farmers, plantation workers, fishermen and paniolo all had to pack durable lunches and provisions without refrigeration in order to perform their daily tasks. Local fishermen salted, dried or smoked such tasty fish as akule (big-eye scad), 'ōpelu (mackerel scad), aku (skipjack tuna), ahi (yellowfin tuna) and a'u (marlin).

On the plantations, bacalhau was the most popular choice, but others rivaled it. Iriko, for example, are tiny dried anchovies or sardines. Iriko could be boiled to make dashi (broth) for soup or gravy dishes, simmered in shoyu and mirin to make tsukudani (a tasty side dish or accompaniment to rice), or eaten dry as a snack.

Dried ebi (shrimp), katsuoboshi and konbu were all used in similar fashion as iriko. Iriko soaked in shoyu was sometimes used in place of umeboshi in making musubi (rice balls). Katsuobushi also makes for a tasty topping on salads and tofu.

A marvelously multi-cultural suggestion was recently posted online: "Try iriko (Japanese dried anchovy) fried with shoyu and served on rice with poi on da side.

⫸⫸ ⫸⫸ ⫸⫸ ⫸⫸ ⫸⫸ ⫸⫸ ⫸⫸

Some 30 years after the photo opposite was taken, the old building had become the Hali'imaile General Store, the Upcountry Maui restaurant owned and operated by Hawai'i Regional Cuisine pioneer Beverly Gannon—and, here, the backdrop for a wedding photo.

People, in other words, lived close to the land. Their sense of place was defined not by street names, buildings or other manmade constructions, but by the land itself—a far more intimate relationship with the natural world around them.

The Importance of Preserved Foods

The lack of refrigeration in homes across Hawai'i made it essential for families to rely on foods that would keep without spoiling in the heat and humidity of the Islands. Fresh food was enjoyed immediately when available, but the long-term, day-to-day challenge of survival relied on having foods that kept well for days, weeks or even months. As a result, food items such as salt meat; salt pork; salt cod; smoked bacon; smoked meat (wild pig); pipikaula; smoked or dried tako (he'e, or octopus); dried or smoked fish

⫸⫸ ⫸⫸ ⫸⫸ ⫸⫸ ⫸⫸ ⫸⫸ ⫸⫸

Brothers (left to right) Shigeo "Boss" Yokouchi, Noriaki "Spud" Yokouchi and Saburo "Nut" Yokouchi take a break outside their family business, the Yokouchi Bakery, ca. 1955. Today the building at Church and Vineyard Streets still houses a bakery—the Maui Bake Shop.

Winnahz!"

When it came to dried seafood snacks, there was a time when dried abalone was "it" in Hawai'i. Dried abalone was one of the main reasons why no self-respecting boy in Hawai'i would leave his house without his trusty pocketknife. The blade proved surprisingly useful throughout the day—for playing knife games in the dirt, cleaning fingernails, sharpening pencils and peeling mangoes, but also for slicing thin pieces of dry, hard abalone.

Though they are an extreme extravagance today, there was a time when whole dry abalone were displayed in large glass jars tantalizingly positioned on store counters for all to see. At 10 cents apiece, they were surprisingly affordable. The abalone—usually shoved in lint-filled pockets—could be made to last a long time, as each thin slice was chewed and savored like beef jerky.

Where did these prized balls of flavor come from, and why were they so cheap? Most were harvested from the Pacific Ocean off of Baja California. Utilizing harvesting and processing techniques perfected in their native Japan, fishermen were running a successful abalone operation in Baja as early as 1914.

They soaked the abalone meat in a tank of salt water overnight, washed it in seawater the next day and then boiled it in seawater. The abalone were then dried for several days and boiled again in salt water. After drying for about a week, the abalone were boiled a third time and thoroughly dried for a final time. The entire process took about two months. The dried abalone were shipped to San Diego, where they were stored until they could be shipped for sale in China or Japan.

First-class abalone was sold for $200 a ton, second-class abalone for $150 a ton and third-class abalone for $100. Abalone shells were worth more than the meat: First-class shells sold for $250 a ton. Abalone gills and guts were also boiled in shoyu and dried to make tsukudani, which was very popular with the Japanese in Hawai'i.

Dried abalone may be difficult to find nowadays, but other variations on the dried seafood theme abound. Here is a simple, surprisingly tasty recipe:

Wes Yonamine's Dried Aku

Pour a can of Coca Cola into a container. Refill the can with Yamasa brand shoyu and add to the Coke. Add ½" strips of fresh, filleted aku and soak overnight. Remove fish from marinade and blot off excess liquid. Let fish dry in the sun in a dry box until ready, about 12 hours.

Today, Portuguese sausages, called "chourico," are universally popular in Hawai'i for their juicy,

spicy goodness. One of the most popular foods on the plantation, however, was a hard, dry-cured sausage called "chorizo" that was incredibly long lasting. These Spanish-inspired pork sausages are flavored with garlic, salt and paprika, which give them a reddish color and smoky flavor. The paprika and salt, along with the drying process, help to preserve the sausages. The most familiar of these dried chorizo sausages came in big green cans, which are still sold at certain local supermarkets.

Another popular sausage is the Goteborg sausage, a hard, dry sausage of Swedish origin made of coarsely chopped pork and beef. The salami-like sausage has a sweet and salty quality. Some dried sausages are given a light smoking, but Goteborg is cured with spices, then air-dried from 15 days to as long as four or five months.

Like drying, pickling was used to preserve foods, as in the following classic recipes:

Charles and Lynne Toma and son Kirk display their wares at their popular Maui eatery, Sam Sato's in Wailuku. Sam Sato was Lynne's father, who in 1933 founded this Maui institution known for its saimin, dry saimin, baked manju and assorted fruit turnovers.

>>> >>> >>> >>> >>> >>> >>>

A bare-chested Rev. Bino Mamiya takes a turn pounding mochi ca. 1940 at his Hakalau Jodo Mission on the Big Island's Hilo Coast, in the traditional Japanese New Year's activity.

Dorine Tomita's Pickled Mango
Makes 1 gallon

10-11	mangoes, peeled and sliced (about 8 lbs.)
2½ c.	sugar
2 c.	water
1 c.	Japanese (rice wine) vinegar
¼ c.	Hawaiian salt
¼-½ lb.	li hing mui

Boil sugar, water, vinegar and salt together until solid ingredients have dissolved. Cool.

Fill a gallon jar with mango slices, top with li hing mui and pour in cooled vinegar mixture. Mango should be completely covered. Put in refrigerator to pickle, turning bottle occasionally. Mango will begin to pickle in 1 to 2 days, and the flavor will continue to get stronger. Keeps for weeks.

Cabbage Koko

1 small	(or ½ large) cabbage, cut in strips
4"-6"	piece pickled daikon, rinsed, drained and thinly sliced
1 c.	water
¾ c.	sugar
⅓ c.	vinegar
2 tsp.	salt

>>> >>> >>> >>> >>> >>> >>>
At Two Ladies Kitchen in Hilo, the Uchida family specializes in mochi and manju, packaged in carry-out presentations that are ideal for omiyage. The Two Ladies: Nora Uchida (center) and her aunt, Tomi Tokeshi, not pictured.

Mix cabbage and daikon in large container. Combine remaining ingredients in microwave-safe bowl and warm in microwave just enough to dissolve sugar, about 30 to 45 seconds. Do not heat. Pour over cabbage and daikon and stir.

Chill in refrigerator overnight. Stir again next day and serve.

Pickled Onions
Makes 1 quart

2   large Maui onions, sliced

2   Hawaiian chili peppers,
         chopped
¾ c.   white vinegar
2 Tbsp. sugar
1 Tbsp. Hawaiian salt
¾ c.   boiling water

Peel onions and cut off ends; cut in half crosswise, then cut in ½" slices. Pack onions and peppers in a quart-size glass jar with a tight-fitting lid. Add vinegar, sugar and salt. Pour in boiling water and cover jar with lid. When jar is cooled, shake

to dissolve sugar and salt. Let sit at room temperature for 24 hours, then refrigerate.

Drying, smoking, pickling, canning and salting foods meant that highly concentrated flavors became part of the local palate. This worked out well, since a little of such food would go a long way toward flavoring the basic poi, rice, bread or crackers (hardtack or Saloon Pilots) that comprised the bulk of the meal.

Even poi could be dried for

The Kidanis of Lahaina were classic Hawai'i mom-and-pop food entrepreneurs, operating a grocery store, saimin restaurant, ice cream store and potato chip manufacturing business in their Kidani Building on Front Street.

long-term use. Pa'i 'ai, or "hard poi," was made by dehydrating poi to the consistency of a very thick paste, which was then reconstituted, as needed, by adding water. Pa'i 'ai could even be further dried and ground into a powder form, which was also prepared by adding water before eating. Paniolo on the Big Island's Parker Ranch were given pa'i 'ai with pipikaula to take with them on long trips.

In her entertaining blog on food and culture, Leilehua Yuen described how a concoction known as "poi palaoa" could be used as a substitute for poi or to stretch the real thing. This is done by mixing boiled water, which has been allowed to cool slightly, with flour. Water is slowly added, and the blend is stirred until it approximates the consistency of poi. Poi palaoa can either be eaten as is with other Hawaiian food or mixed to stretch the poi.

In *Pahoa Yesterday*, Hiroo Sato recalled a desperate local farmer in the 1920s, who survived by eating only rice and bacalhau, every meal, every day. Not only that, but Sato writes, "He ate the rice by licking the salty taste of the bacalhau. After several days the salty taste was gone and then the bacalhau was eaten."

Preserved foods—salty, smoky, dried—were also good when cooked in combination with vegetables grown or harvested, for they would lend their intense flavor to the bland greens. This provided families with the bulk necessary to feed many people with just a little. Everybody had their means of stretching food, from adding bread or flour to ground meat to dicing up a piece of meat or chicken to be cooked with lots of vegetables, resulting in such Chinese-inspired Island specialties as chop steak or beef tomato. Many people grew up never having had a whole steak, or other large portions of meat such as pork chops or chicken, to eat for themselves. Chinatown resident J.W. Lau recalled:

Once a week Father went to Chinatown and bought 25 cents' worth of pork for soup (ching bo leong soup). Only occasionally like New Year's or one's birthday is about the only time we got to eat chicken and duck or any fancy dishes. As you can see that was the case in our frugal household.

As in the Lau household, one of the surest ways of stretching a limited food supply was via soups and stews. This way, even a small amount of meat or fish would infuse its flavor into a large pot of liquid and vegetables—which would in turn be plentiful enough to feed many people. Classic Japanese miso soup, for example, was most often made by simply adding a dollop of miso to a pot of dashi (soup stock) made by boiling a small amount of iriko or katsuoboshi in water. This miso soup, served

⫸⫸ ⫸⫸ ⫸⫸ ⫸⫸ ⫸⫸ ⫸⫸ ⫸⫸

For more than four decades, Robert and Patsy Yamashita have run the Iwamoto Natto Factory in Pāʻia, Maui, producing the Japanese delicacy natto (fermented soybeans) under the Hama Natto brand.

with rice and pickled vegetables, was the main meal that sustained many Japanese immigrants throughout their lives.

The prevailing question in households across the Islands in plantation days, in short, was not so much "What you like eat?" but "What get for eat?" And what there was to eat very often depended on common ingredients that grew or could be caught in the area, those that were readily available or most affordable and those that would keep

well—bringing the foods different people ate closer than many might imagine.

In total, sugar plantations accounted for the arrival of more than 350,000 workers of various nationalities in Hawaiʻi. While some of these immigrants completed their contracts and returned to their native countries, others pursued opportunities on the continental United States, but the majority chose to start families and set down roots in Hawaiʻi.

Some chose employment in the

pineapple industry, which recruited its workers by offering slightly better pay and housing than the sugar plantations. Besides fieldwork, pineapple canneries also provided a source of employment for women and seasonal work for teens, thereby greatly enhancing a family's opportunities to earn an income. Others left the plantations to start their own businesses and pursue employment in other trades after their labor contracts expired.

Whether it was for economic

⫸⫸ ⫸⫸ ⫸⫸ ⫸⫸ ⫸⫸ ⫸⫸ ⫸⫸

Harry Kaya ran the snack concession at the Iao Theater in Wailuku from the mid-1930s through the mid-'70s. With his dog, Queenie, and his trademark cigar, Kaya was Maui's theater popcorn pioneer.

reasons, or for the opportunities they saw for themselves and their families, or the beauty of the Islands, the majority of immigrants ended up deciding to stay in Hawai'i. In the transition from sojourners to settlers, people from many different lands established families and bore a new generation of children—a generation who were born and raised in the Islands, who attended school together and who shared the same playgrounds, rivers, beaches and parks. They may have eaten their own ethnic fare at home, but they were equally comfortable sharing school lunches and snacks with friends from their communities and eating other foods commonly available to them. Thus were the seeds of local sown—seeds that would soon flourish in the rich volcanic soil of the Islands.

Stone Soup, Island-Style

Many people are familiar with "Stone Soup," the traditional European folktale about a clever traveler who manages to dupe the residents of a town into thinking that he can make soup by placing a magic stone in water. The entire countryside is wracked by famine, so people are secretly hoarding food from each other. Rather than beg for food, the traveler puts on a convincing show by setting up his pot in the middle of town, ceremoniously inserting his stone and pretending to brew his

≫≫ ≫≫ ≫≫ ≫≫ ≫≫ ≫≫ ≫≫
Maui Potato Chips Factory owner Mark Kobayashi displays his Kitch'n Cook'd chips and newspaper stories about his grandfather, Yoshio, who bought the Kahului company in 1956.

"soup." He inhales the aroma, smacks his lips and remarks how delicious the soup is.

The hungry townspeople are slowly convinced by his act, so when the traveler comments how much better the soup would taste with a little cabbage, one of the villagers cautiously retrieves a cabbage he had been hiding and adds it to the pot. Then the wily traveler notes that a soup made with cabbage and salt beef is a meal fit for a king, prompting another person to go get some salt beef to add to the soup. Ultimately, potatoes, carrots, onions and other ingredients are all added to create a delicious meal that is enjoyed by everyone.

Greatly impressed, the villagers offer the traveler a large sum of money for the magic stone, but he refuses to sell it. The next day, he packs up his wagon and continues on his journey. The moral of the story is obvious—once the selfish villagers start to share what they have, there's enough for everyone.

Consider how differently this tale might have unfolded in Hawai'i. Think of people like the late Joe Hamada, who recorded his memories of the times when plantation workers went on strike, leaving everyone without any income. The union would organize hunting and fishing crews,

>>> >>> >>> >>> >>> >>> >>>

The Kawaguchi children lived with their parents, Rikiichi and Shizuko, above their Kawaguchi Fish Market on Lahaina's Front Street. Racks for drying and salting fish stretched around most of the store's interior.

he recalled, and the harvests from everyone's home gardens also went to the communal soup kitchen set up by the public school. "We never went hungry," he said.

Joe also remembered accompanying his father on the long drive to Honolulu at around 2 a.m. to pick up the fish donated by fishermen who supported the striking workers. He remembers that the captain of the *Neptune*, in particular, gave tubs full of tuna that he and his father trucked back to Waipahu, cut up and distributed to every family.

But Joe's most precious memory of the strike was reserved for plantation manager Hans L'Orange, who risked his own welfare by allocating acres of land for the workers to grow food. "You striking against him; he's company man," Joe said with great feeling. "How can he give you land for make kau kau? He's supposed to starve you so you come back to work quick. Not Mr. L'Orange. He give you land. He *give* you...."

Or consider Larry Ikeda, a retired Hawai'i Commercial & Sugar (HC&S) Plantation truck driver on Maui. Life was a struggle for him and his mother after his dad—an independent pineapple grower in Peahi—died when Larry was only six years old. It helped that papaya, banana and avocado "grew wild" in Peahi, he said. And everyone kept vegetable gardens and raised chickens.

But it was not until his mother was finally hired by HC&S and they moved from the relative isolation of Peahi to a camp in Pu'unēnē that their life finally turned for the better. They'd had no real neighbors before, Larry said, but in Pu'unēnē their neighbors were families of Puerto Rican, Portuguese and Filipino descent.

"They felt sorry for my mom," he said. Their Portuguese neighbor gave them freshly baked bread. "Sooo ... 'ono!" Larry remembered, still savoring the taste in his mind. Their Puerto Rican neighbor kept a milking cow and gave them pints of fresh milk. "They were the best neighbors," Larry said. "We shared a lot ... but they never made us feel poor. They

A family business in Makawao, the Pukalani Superette has been selling fresh produce from the surrounding Upcounty Maui bread-basket for more than 50 years.

were my friends."

The act of sharing and giving without making others feel poor is a gift that people today sometimes take for granted in Hawai'i. It is something people just do, just like never going empty-handed to someone's house. It is second nature in the Islands, but there are other places in the world where taking food or drink to someone else's house would be considered an insult to the host.

In an Island version of "Stone Soup," all the traveler would have had to do was show his sincerity, and he would have been offered something to eat as soon as he arrived in town. As the villagers willingly shared their meager supply of food with him, he would have felt guilty about his plan to trick them with the stone, and he would have quietly put the pōhaku back in the riverbed where he had found it. He would have left town the

next day with a sense of gratitude and indebtedness—vowing to return to the village someday and repay the townsfolk for their kindness and generosity.

The real magic, as he would one day realize, lies in one's na'au (gut—the seat of one's soul in Hawaiian) or hara (stomach—one's "center" in Japanese), not in the machinations of one's brain. ◈

Hawaiian Haggis: Balut, Natto and Other Culinary Challenges

Have you ever tried the legendary Filipino delicacy called balut? To prepare it, simply take a fertilized duck or chicken egg and let it incubate for between 14 and 20 days, depending on how far you think you'd like the embryo to develop. (It takes a chicken 21 days to hatch and a duck closer to 30, so plan accordingly.) At the appointed moment, boil the egg. To eat, crack a hole in the egg and suck out the savory soup first. Then crack open the shell, add a dash of salt or other seasonings to taste and consume the contents of the egg—all of them (below).

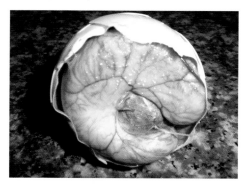

Granted, this is not your everyday snack. (Quick, pass the nachos!) In fact, mention balut to a kamaʻāina and chances are you'll be greeted with nervous laughter (the word itself—bah-loot—does have a certain ring to it.) But before anyone tries to use balut to denigrate Filipino cuisine, they might consider that this dish traces its origins back to China (as so many local dishes do) and is also found throughout Southeast Asia.

Unfortunately, balut is forever doomed to be a poster child for Hawaiʻi's sideshow of freakish foods, sharing the spotlight with international delicacies like haggis—the Scottish specialty made of minced sheep innards mixed with oatmeal, seasoned and stuffed into a sheep's stomach—or surstromming, the Swedish fermented herring that has been crowned by many as the world's smelliest food.

In multiethnic Hawaiʻi, virtually every culture has its share of strange, malodorous—even slightly macabre—foods that others might find downright disgusting. These are the dishes that each group usually enjoys privately at home or in the company of family and close friends.

Island Japanese, for example, don't ballyhoo their natto (opposite)—soybeans fermented to the point of extreme sliminess—or their takuan—pickled turnip, aptly nicknamed "dynamite" by some. And you don't expect to see your Chinese coworker sucking the skin and cartilage off a bony chicken's foot, or exploring the dark, briny depths of a thousand-year-old egg in the company lunchroom.

From the first contact between kanaka maoli and foreign explorers through the pooling of food by immigrants on the plantations, people in Hawaiʻi have developed a keen sense of what foods to share, with whom and in what context. It's as if various ethnic dishes can be placed along a food spectrum ranging from "very appealing" on one end to "very hard to swallow" on the other. The foods with the least amount of downside in terms of flavor, texture and aroma were the ones most commonly shared. These are the foods that have survived the test of time to become the staples of our modern-day mixed plate—the stuff that you are most likely to find at parties, potlucks and on the menus of mainstream local restaurants.

Among them: Korean kalbi, meat jun and mandoo; Portuguese bean soup, sausage and malasadas; Puerto Rican pasteles; Japanese shoyu pork, maki sushi and tempura; Filipino adobo—chicken or pork marinated in a vinegar-based sauce and then fried—pancit (noodles) and lumpia (deep-fried wraps made with a variety of fillings); Chinese chow mein or chow fun noodles and roast pork.

It sounds simple. Some foods are "in" and are widely enjoyed by the general public; others are "out," and are eaten mainly in private. Balut is probably not the best choice to take to that football tailgate party with your old high school buddies.

Reality, however, is rarely so black and white. There is also a large gray area covering the vast middle of this food spectrum—dishes that are not totally mainstreamed to the point of being lunchwagon staples but still have enough of a following that they can be found at certain local restaurants or other private gatherings. Pig's

beneath the sea—usually consumed raw, no less. Besides fish, these include sea urchins, sea cucumbers, sea slugs, octopi, eels, limpets and shellfish, and various types of seaweed.

Several Island ethnic groups also embrace the practice of eating all parts of an animal. Besides the meat, this includes various innards, such as loko (cow or pig intestines) and tripe; organs, such as ake (liver), hearts and gizzards; and assorted body parts, such as feet, tails, tongues and testicles. As a result, such dishes as oxtail soup, oxtail stew, tripe stew and pig's feet soup make popular local meals.

What makes food in Hawai'i so special is the richness of the choices that lie between the two extremes. At the backyard lū'au, guests load up their plates with kālua pig, laulau, lomilomi salmon, chicken long rice and haupia. But then there are those who like poi and those who don't. There are those who like their poi fresh, and those who prefer the tanginess of one- or even two-day-old poi. Finally, there's the table of raw food reserved for the special few who will truly savor it—poke, 'a'ama crab, 'opihi and ake.

Island-style, people seek those connections that bind—in food as well as in other things cultural—allowing each other to choose just how far along the food spectrum they wish to journey.

feet soup and tripe stew fall into this category—as might dinuguang, pork cooked in pig's blood. They may not be for everyone, but they have definitely gone beyond being the status of limited ethnic specialty.

Another reason for this gray area is the degree of cultural overlap in Hawai'i. Take the salty and pungent bagoong, for example. This popular Filipino sauce or paste, made from fermented shrimp or fish, would be a prime candidate for weird food designation in many parts of the country. In Hawai'i, however, bagoong has a close relative in Japanese shiokara, which is also made by salting and fermenting parts of fish, squid or other sea creatures. Both can be compared with the powerfully aromatic Chinese hahm ha, or fermented shrimp sauce, often used in combination with Chinese vegetables such as ong choi, kai choi or choy sum to create mouthwatering dishes. Koreans also have a form of fermented seafood paste called chotkal. Made from anchovies, shrimp or shellfish, it is used to season many dishes, including kim chee. No matter how salty or smelly, it's hard to consider something weird when it looks, smells and tastes so familiar.

Many ethnic groups in Hawai'i also share a love of eating anything from

CHAPTER FOUR

American Pie
World War II and the Postwar Plate

It would be impossible to overstate how profoundly World War II affected Hawai'i—from the day that the bombs rained down on Pearl Harbor on December 7, 1941, to the conclusion of hostilities more than three and a half years later. In many respects, the full impact of the war would not be appreciated until many years after that.

Hawai'i in 1941 was home to a population of just over 400,000 people—a multicultural society comprised of Hawaiians, Caucasians and immigrants from many lands, along with their Island-born children.

A notable feature of this society was that no group held a majority. People of Japanese ancestry formed the largest ethnic group—approximately 37 percent of the total population. Caucasians were the next largest, constituting 24.5 percent of the population, followed by Filipinos (12.4 percent), part-Hawaiians (11.8 percent), Chinese (6.8 percent), and then Koreans, Portuguese (categorized as "Other Caucasian"), Puerto Ricans and others. Census categories determining race and ethnicity in the United States were probably skewed in Hawai'i, in part because of the diverse population and high percentage of people of mixed ancestry.

>>> >>> >>> >>> >>> >>> >>> >>>

Mess halls at Fort DeRussy (below) and Schofield Barracks, early 1900s: More than one million military and civilian defense personnel arrived in the Islands in the 1940s, transforming local mores and tastes. Opposite: By the 1950s, most of the new arrivals were tourists.

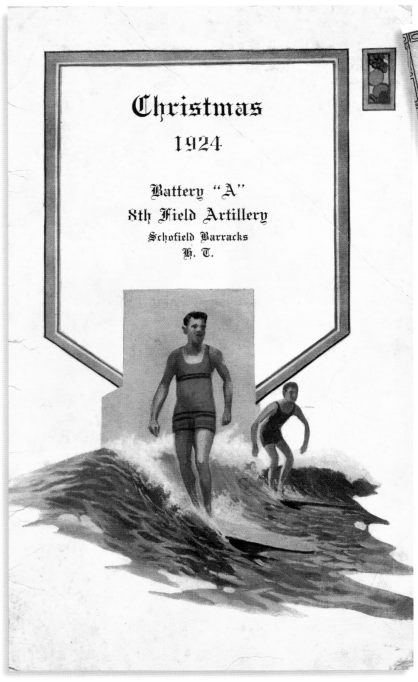

Christmas

1924

Battery "A"
8th Field Artillery
Schofield Barracks
H. T.

Roster of Non-commissioned Staff and Band, 2nd Infantry.

Captain W. R. GIBSON, Commanding.
James H. Mullins, Regimental Sergeant Major
Guy Weaver, Regimental Quartermaster Sergeant.
Lee Cohen, Regimental Commissary Sergeant.
Michael Maher, Color Sergeant.
George B. Stutzman, Color Sergeant.
Ernest W. Ely, Battalion Sergeant Major.
Anthony Potesky, Battalion Sergeant Major.
John T. Linney, Battalion Sergeant Major.

Albert Jacobsen, Chief Musician.
John A. Dapp, Principal Musician.
Guy A. Surber, Drum Major.

Sergeant Dan D. Wood   Corporal Stephen J. Kubeck
Sergeant Louis Miller   Corporal Milton C. Graham
Sergeant Fred Bates   Corporal John D. Kavanaugh
                          Corporal Nelson W. Bennett
                          Corporal Rhinehart Johntz
                          Cook Floyd T. Egelston

PRIVATES   PRIVATES
Andrew Archuletta   Otto Lantinen
Alva C. Brown   Axel C. Lundgren
Frank I. Bruez   Mark D. Sterns
Otis Cutlip   George T. Taylor
Stephen E. Grabowsky.   Paul H. Townsley
Michael Kaunert   Edward J. Week
Leo LaMothe   Leo B. von Gersdorff

1913 Thanksgiving Dinner
Non-commissioned Staff & Band
Second U. S. Infantry
Fort Shafter, Honolulu, H. T.

Menu

Oyster Soup and Crackers

Olives   Mixed Pickles   Celery
Lettuce Salad   Radishes   Green Onions
            Roast Turkey with Oyster Dressing
Brown Gravy   Cranberry Sauce
Creamed Peas   Fried Egg Plant   Mashed Potatoes
           Mince Pie   Apple Pie
Cocoanut Layer Cake   Jelly Roll
Assorted Nuts   Oranges   Bananas   Apples
          Chocolate Ice Cream
                          Bread and Butter
Coffee   Beer and Cigars

Guy Surber, Mess Sergeant.   Floyd Egelston, Cook.

As thousands of young men, along with some women, shipped out to serve in Europe and the Pacific, over a million soldiers and civilian military personnel from the Mainland surged onto Hawai'i's shores like a human tsunami, transforming Island mores and tastes in the process. For one thing, these newcomers craved foods familiar to them, like hot dogs, hamburgers and ice cream. Such items were not so common in Hawai'i at the time—especially not in the small towns that dotted the rural landscape of the Territory.

On the Big Island, for example, the cowtown of Kamuela had a resident population of less than 400 in 1941. From 1942 to 1945, how-ever, some 50,000 Marines occupied a sprawling tent city dubbed Camp Tarawa on the outskirts of the rustic paniolo village.

New-fangled hamburger stands, like Tsugi "Sue" Kaiama's popular Sue's Chuckwagon, quickly became fixtures in town. The *Waimea Gazette* reported that Kaiama used to purchase an entire steer from the nearby Parker Ranch slaughterhouse every day and grind it into hamburger to keep up with the demand. She experimented, adding celery and bread-crumbs to the ground beef to perfect her burgers. Servicemen formed such long lines that locals complained that they never got the chance to taste the legendary burgers. Thanks to the Marines, however, children in Kamuela were treated to ice cream with their school lunches—a rare treat at the time.

It's not hard to understand why war-weary soldiers so far from home would find a juicy, freshly cooked hamburger worth standing in line for. Fresh meat of any kind was a precious commodity everywhere, as the war effort included food shortages and sacrifices on the part of all Americans. Soldiers survived on a diet characterized by C-rations, a variety of dehydrated foods and canned meats that could be stored, shipped and consumed anytime, anywhere. The king of canned meat, of course, was SPAM® Classic, which some soldiers swear they ate several times a day, every day, for weeks on end, as fried SPAM® slabs, baked SPAM® Classic, SPAM® hot dogs, SPAMBURGER® hamburgers and SPAM® sandwiches, to name a few. Durable and versatile, the salty pork product was a natural fit in Hawai'i. The SPAM® brand caught on with the local population and remains an Island favorite today.

If anything, the war and influx of outsiders made local residents more aware of what they held in common with each other. Regardless of their ethnic background, all residents of Hawai'i became occupants of a war zone governed by strict military rule. Everyone abided by curfews and blackout restrictions, carried gas masks wherever they went and stood in line at local schools to receive their ration coupons.

Every resident—regardless of age, ethnicity, economic status or gender—received the same ration coupons. Gasoline, tires, shoes and clothing were rationed during the war as a means of supporting the war effort. Food items such as meat, sugar, butter and coffee were rationed, while bread, milk and beer were not. Spurred on by government directives, many local residents cultivated "Victory Gardens" as one more patriotic means of making up for the shortages in fresh food at home, as American troops overseas needed to be fed and supplied.

Like good Americans, Hawai'i's people adjusted what they ate, following principles promulgated in government pamphlets and food company brochures to stretch their limited sources of protein and substituting ingre-

Opposite page: Period holiday menus provide a record—often the only surviving record—of the men and women who served in Island military units. This page: Among the WWII culinary options for soldiers and sailors in urban Honolulu: The New Eagle Cafe on Fort Street and the Armed Services YMCA on Hotel Street, which today houses the Hawai'i State Art Museum and Downtown restaurant.

dients. Sugarless cookies, eggless cakes and meatless meals may not have been a homemaker's finest creations, but they were what everyone else had to eat, and a high level of national solidarity prevailed.

Not only did the war bring the outside world to Hawai'i; it also

'Eia ke ola...Have a Coke
(HERE'S HEALTH)

...or winning a welcome in Wailuku

Here's health is the happy expression of Hawaiian hospitality. Just as friendly is the *Have a Coke* of the Army flyer. In these three words he says *We're pals.* On a Hawaiian beach, where fishermen toss their nets in the sea...just as in your own home...Coca-Cola brings friendly refreshment to all comers. In Wailuku or Wichita, Coca-Cola stands for *the pause that refreshes,*—has become a symbol of a friendly way of living. Keep Coke on hand in your refrigerator—for your family and your guests.

*   *   *

Our fighting men meet up with Coca-Cola many places overseas, where it's bottled on the spot. Coca-Cola has been a globe-trotter "since way back when".

-the global
high-sign

Coke=Coca-Cola
It's natural for popular names to acquire friendly abbreviations. That's why you hear Coca-Cola called Coke.

COPYRIGHT 1945, THE COCA-COLA COMPANY

In a national Coca-Cola advertisement published in 1945, soldiers share Cokes on a Maui beach.

caused thousands of local residents to experience life overseas. Many soldiers might never have left their small towns and rural lifestyles if not for the military. Instead, thousands of young men suddenly found themselves criss-crossing oceans, undergoing training on the U.S. continent and fighting for their country in Europe, Africa, Australia, Asia and the Pacific. They wore the same uniforms and ate the same food as other American soldiers. More importantly, they fought and they died just like other American heroes.

Those who survived and returned to Hawai'i did so with a radically altered worldview, personal identity and sense of place. Most took advantage of the G.I. Bill of Rights to access housing assistance, small business loans and college scholarships in their pursuit of the American Dream.

Not only had the war confirmed their status as Americans, but it also gave those who lived in the Islands a healthy appreciation for what it meant to be local. On battlefronts around the world, Hawai'i soldiers of all ethnicities tearfully strummed 'ukulele, sang Hawaiian songs and yearned to return home. In Europe, cooks with the 442nd Regimental Combat Team learned to barter with other units for rice, vegetables and bouillon to make pots of beef or chicken hekka. They improvised tsukemono by salting vegetables and reducing the dissolved bouillon down to a dark, salty sauce

that served as an admirable substitute for shoyu. One of the soldiers' favorite hot meals, when they could get it, was hekka served over steamed rice, topped with two eggs.

While the vast majority of soldiers from Hawai'i bravely volunteered for service during the war, a smaller group was forced to leave the Islands against their will. Although most Japanese in Hawai'i were spared the mass incarcerations that took some 120,000 Japanese and Japanese Americans from their homes on the West Coast, approximately 1,444 people from Hawai'i were sent to internment camps on the U.S. Mainland.

They were held there for several years, until the war's end, living in roughly hewn barracks and fed en masse in large mess halls. They were forced to stand in long lines for food doled out on tin plates—whatever the government had by way of surplus, including SPAM™, hot dogs, ketchup and potatoes. It was a far cry from the food and customs to which Japanese families were accustomed.

Like others during the war, they adapted and even acquired a taste for the foods that they were forced to eat. In the years following the war, Japanese Americans routinely ate hot dogs cooked with eggs and shoyu hot dogs with rice. Some also recall being introduced to what was called "SPAM™ sushi," a likely precursor to SPAM™ musubi, in World War II

internment camps.

The war severely tested and then underscored how thoroughly American Hawai'i people were. At the same time, it accentuated what was unique about life in the Islands and how much locals shared in common with one another—not the least of which was their food.

More American Pie: The Food of the Fifties

During the postwar period, Islanders' seemingly innate knack for localizing things American—and Americanizing things local—played a key role in shaping their social iden-tity. At the forefront of this process were those dubbed by journalist Tom Brokaw as "The Greatest Genera-tion"—children of the Great Depres-sion who had come of age during the dark days of World War II.

Although everyone was eager to regain a state of normalcy, this did not mean that they wanted to revert to the lives they had led before the war. Having witnessed their parents' struggles, the goal of this generation was to make life better for themselves and their families. The American economy was surging, and they wanted a piece of the pie.

Besides the G.I. Bill, one of the key factors in shaping Hawai'i's postwar society was organized labor. Building on its success in organizing

⫸⫸ ⫸⫸ ⫸⫸ ⫸⫸ ⫸⫸ ⫸⫸ ⫸⫸

In promoting the modern comforts of their employee housing, Hawai'i's plantations were promoting the realization of the American Dream.

Waikiki LAU YEE CHAI
World's Most Beautiful Chinese Restaurant Honolulu

Waikiki Lau Yee Chai,
Honolulu, Hawaii

》》》 》》》 》》》 》》》 》》》 》》》 》》》

Lau Yee Chai, which opened in the 1930s on Kūhiō Avenue, has been a Waikīkī institution for generations.

West Coast dockworkers, the International Longshore and Warehouse Union (ILWU) enlisted those who worked on Hawai'i's docks and plantations, which at the time comprised the very core of the Islands' economy.

Besides calling for better wages, the ILWU stressed unity and multi-ethnic cooperation, as expressed by its slogan, "Brothers Under the Skin." And, from Labor Day picnics to soup kitchens for its rank-and-file, union leaders literally fed their call for solidarity with pots full of such local classics as rice served with chicken hekka, beef stew and chicken long rice.

In 1999, former plantation worker Joe Hamada described how striking workers at the Oahu Sugar Company pulled together in order to feed everyone even in the leanest of times:

The union organized hunting crew and fishing crews. Everyone had a vegetable garden. They used to cook at the public school in a big wok, and they fed the school students. The guys on strike set up a soup kitchen by the high school. We never went hungry.

Whether one's collar was white or blue, the importance of family lay at the heart of the American Dream. Between 1946 and 1964, the Greatest

Generation bore approximately 76 million babies, a population explosion that inspired the new generation's "baby boomers" moniker.

Hawai'i's extended families became unique multigenerational units comprised of immigrant elders, their Americanized children and an inquisitive brood of baby boomers on the threshold of their formative teen years.

The paradigm for the ideal family was delivered from across the Pacific in the form of television, which made its debut in Hawai'i in 1952, enticing viewers with flickering black-and-white images of American family life and consumerism. And, although most local families did not look or sound anything like those on shows such as *Ozzie and Harriet, The Donna Reed Show, Leave it to Beaver* and *Father Knows Best*, that did not stop them from adapting and adopting what they could. At the very least, local families shared the same dreams as other American families across the country, not the least of which involved owning a house, car, refrigerator, range and, of course, television set.

Popular American foods of the '50s were warmly embraced as well, including hamburgers, hot dogs, ice cream floats, canned soup and dry sweetened cereal. Television advertisements made brand names such as Kellogg's, Coca-Cola, Campbell's Soup and Swanson TV dinners as popular in Hawai'i as they were elsewhere.

People in Hawai'i had actually been primed to buy into the American Dream even before the war, when many Chinese and Japanese worked for companies owned by Caucasians or as domestic servants in Caucasian households. There they learned to prepare Western-style food for their employers. Whites held positions of such wealth and power in the Islands that it was natural to take how they lived and what they ate as reflections of a superior status. Japanese Americans, especially, struggled to overcome the stigma of wartime suspicions regarding their patriotism and

adopted many means of looking and acting like "good Americans." They embraced efforts to stamp out pidgin English and speak standard English; some even changed their religious affiliation from Buddhism to Christianity.

One of the important trends of this period was the fact that people started eating out more often—especially teens, who had access to spending money, cars and other freedoms that their parents and grandparents had never had.

To serve these mobile diners, drive-in restaurants—many featuring carhop service—became a big Island fad in the '50s. KC Drive Inn, on the corner of Ala Wai Boulevard and Kalākaua Avenue, is widely considered to have been the first drive-in in Hawai'i. It originally opened in 1929 and was purchased in 1934 by Jiro Asato, an immigrant from Okinawa who eventually turned the struggling establishment into a hotspot known for its unique waffle dogs and thick "ono ono" shakes.

Nearby, Kau Kau Korner opened on the corner of Kalākaua Avenue and Kapi'olani Boulevard in 1935. Like KC Drive Inn, Kau Kau Korner featured carhop waitresses noted for their short skirts and trademark hats. Other popular drive-ins with carhop service included Alex Drive-In on Kapahulu Avenue and Kalakaua Drive-In at the corner of

Kalākaua Avenue and Ala Moana Boulevard. Kalakaua Drive-In's popularity was boosted by its menu, which went beyond the customary hamburgers, sodas, fries and shakes by offer-

▶▶▶ ▶▶▶ ▶▶▶ ▶▶▶ ▶▶▶ ▶▶▶ ▶▶▶

Felix's Florentine Gardens, rendered here in a 1941 postcard published in Honolululaughs, *offered a Diamond Head view from its location at Kewalo Basin.*

ing local-style plate lunches for less than 50 cents.

Sit-down restaurants also thrived. Interestingly, many of the most popular eateries were owned and operated by people of Okinawan ancestry, though they served American rather than ethnic food. One of the best known was Columbia Inn, founded in 1941 by brothers Fred

"Tosh" Kaneshiro and Frank Gentaro Kaneshiro. Columbia Inn originally opened on Beretania Street before it moved to its better-known location on Kapi'olani Boulevard in 1964.

Steve Nagamine founded the first Flamingo Restaurant in 1950 where the collection of eateries known as Restaurant Row now stands. Flamingo was known for serving

"complete meal" menus, which included soup or salad, main entrée, starch, cooked vegetable, dinner rolls, dessert and drink. This style of dining proved to be very attractive to people who liked receiving maximum value for the price they paid for their meal.

The Wisteria opened in 1952, serving both Japanese and American food. This practice became more and

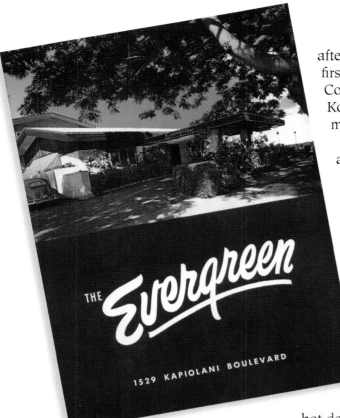

after the national chain opened its first Hawai'i store in 1958. Coco's Coffee Shop replaced Kau Kau Korner in 1960 and made its own mark on Hawai'i's dining scene.

Dozens of burger joints abounded, such as Andy's Drive-In in Kailua. Co-founder Ben Lum reported selling 3,600 hamburgers at 17 cents apiece on opening day in 1957. Other famous burger places included W&M Bar-B-Q in Kaimukī and Kenny's Burger House in Kalihi.

While hamburgers were featured at many locations, the Dog House on Kapahulu turned its spotlight on the other American classic, the hot dog, instead. The drive-in, which was shaped like a doghouse, offered a wide variety of specialty hot dogs from chilidogs to grilled teri hot dogs served with sauerkraut.

Places like Chunky's Drive-In in Mō'ili'ili became known for serving up cheap and tasty plate lunches. Opened in 1959, Chunky's attracted a youthful following—especially when big games and events took place at Honolulu Stadium directly across the street. Souped-up cars were sure to fill its parking lot whenever stock car races were held at the Stadium. Rainbow Drive-In, still serving up great plate lunches in Kapahulu, opened in 1961.

Not only were people dining out more; they could also afford to shop for food in greater quantities and variety. The era of the modern supermarket in Hawai'i started with Foodland in 1947, followed by Times Supermarket in 1949. KTA Super Stores, founded in 1916, opened its first supermarket in 1953, and Star Supermarket joined the group in 1954.

Suburbs and shopping centers soon joined the supermarkets. On Maui, "Dream City," a sprawling subdivision developed in increments by plantation owner Alexander & Baldwin, Inc., gave workers the opportunity to purchase their own homes. The response was overwhelming, with many people waiting through the night for the opportunity to buy. The first residents moved into Dream City in 1950; the Kahului Shopping Center opened nearby in 1951.

Across the Hawaiian Islands, purchasing a new electric range or refrigerator meant that Hawaiian Electric Co. would send one of their trained corps of women known

more common as other dining establishments in Hawai'i noticed that local families loved the flexibility of being able to order from either side of the menu. Like Like Drive Inn opened in 1953, and today the popular Ke'eaumoku Street landmark still serves everything from early-morning breakfasts to late-night bowls of saimin.

Coffee shops also enjoyed great popularity, with local favorites like Kelly's Coffee House opening on Nimitz Highway near the airport in 1951. People also loved eating at the various F.W. Woolworth locations

The Evergreen on Kapi'olani Boulevard was one of three Evergreens in Honolulu in the '50s. Opened in a family home in 1944, The Willows still serves its famous cream pies at the Hausten Street location today.

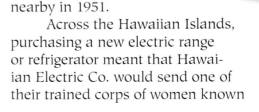

Right: The trained "home economists" of Hawaiian Electric. Below: Boiled peanuts sold at Honolulu Stadium and the sign carried by longtime Stadium vendor Howard Egami. Opposite: Chunky's Drive-In on King Street, just across Isenberg Street from the Stadium.

as "home economists"—properly attired in gloves and silk hose—to the buyer's home to show them how to use the new machines to fullest advantage.

The society in which the next-generation boomers were growing up was indeed a far cry from that of their plantation parents and immigrant grandparents. The brave new world of postwar Hawai'i was starting to look more and more like television America and less and less like rural Hawai'i of the plantation era.

Just as Hawai'i's communities were transitioning from plantations to towns, the Islands' economy was also on the cusp of major, and irreversible, change. Commercial air service to Hawai'i boosted tourism from 15,000 visitors in 1946 to 171,367 in 1958, but that growth would be dwarfed by

the advent of commercial jet service in 1959. Replacing propeller-driven aircraft with jet planes dramatically reduced the time it took to travel to and from Hawai'i. Commercial passenger traffic saw an immediate 33-percent bump in 1960 and didn't slow down for the next 30 years. Tourism, in turn, incited a massive economic boom, including hotel construction and other related infrastructure improvements, supplanting sugar and pineapple as the chief economic engine in the Islands.

With its shores awash with tourists from all corners of the world, Hawai'i had to quickly figure out how and what to feed them in a manner that would meet their expectations and prove worthy of their lengthy journey—maybe something tropical and exotic like coconut flakes or pineapple slices would make anything "Hawaiian"? Welcome to the world of colorful cellophane hula skirts and fruity cocktails adorned with paper umbrellas! Hotel food was destined to establish its own place, both good and bad, in the world of Hawai'i cuisine. It was, after all, what much of the world came to think Hawai'i's kau kau was like.

The Origins of the Plate Lunch

Popular wisdom holds that one of Hawai'i's favorite food traditions— the plate lunch—traces its origins back to the plantation era, when laborers from different ethnic back-

grounds shared their food in the field. It is true that ethnic dishes, many now plate lunch staples, were introduced to the Islands and popularized by plantation immigrants. It is also true that rice, a standard component of the plate lunch, became an Island staple because most of Hawai'i's plantation workers came from such rice-revering countries as China, Japan, Korea and the Philippines.

So is this all one needs to know about the origins of the plate lunch? Not necessarily. To start with, there is still the question of the receptacle for the food, the "plate" itself. Most plantation workers packed their lunches in metal lunch pails called kau kau tins or bento tins—a far cry from the paper plates that gave plate lunches their name. How did we make the leap from these ironclad (mostly aluminum, actually) plantation meals of yesteryear to the plate lunches enjoyed today?

Some historians have theorized that the plate lunch could have

⟫⟫ ⟫⟫ ⟫⟫ ⟫⟫ ⟫⟫ ⟫⟫ ⟫⟫

Complete with carhop service, drive-ins such as Kau Kau Korner were all the rage in 1950s Honolulu. Meanwhile, Island resorts introduced tourists to a sometimes Americanized version of Hawaiian food. Below: An outrigger buffet at the Kona Inn in Kailua-Kona.

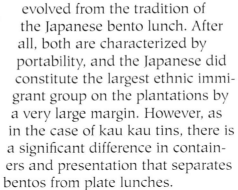

evolved from the tradition of the Japanese bento lunch. After all, both are characterized by portability, and the Japanese did constitute the largest ethnic immigrant group on the plantations by a very large margin. However, as in the case of kau kau tins, there is a significant difference in containers and presentation that separates bentos from plate lunches.

In the days before disposable plastic and Styrofoam containers, Japanese bento bakko (lunch boxes) were rather formal affairs made of lacquered wood with many small compartments to keep different food items from seeping into each other. Bento bakko were often nicely bundled in a furoshiki, or wrapping cloth, for transport. Some bento bakko were multi-tiered affairs, with two or three trays designed to stack on top of each other, all capped with a lid. This might bear some relationship to the dual-level kau kau tins, but not the plate lunch.

Bentos continued to evolve both in Hawai'i and in Japan. Today, they are packed in clear plastic containers or decorative Japanese plastic containers. In Hawai'i, bentos are sold at many supermarkets, drive-in restaurants and even at 7-Eleven convenience stores! Bentos and plate lunches may share similar roots here in Hawai'i,

but the two seem to have evolved as separate branches of the family tree.

It makes sense that while many local food traditions began on the plantations, plate lunches as we know them are more likely to be products of the city rather than the country. There were few, if any, restaurants in the early plantation towns. Aside from worker housing, most towns were comprised of a plantation office, mill, stable (later to become machine shop and garage) and dispensary/ clinic, along with a general store or two. Later, towns would add a barbershop, a tailor, a blacksmith, a post office, churches and a school, and possibly a restaurant. For the most part, however, plantation workers took their lunches with them to the field or mill. They carried no cash in their pockets to buy lunch and, in any event, the lunch break was a very short 30 minutes, taken wherever they happened to be when the luna said it was kau kau time.

On the other hand, in the days before jet travel, the Honolulu waterfront was probably the busiest place in all Hawai'i. There was no shortage of customers who would line up every day for a quick meal or snack. In time, the colorful mix of pushcarts and lunch stands was replaced by lunchwagons and sit-down restaurants, which lined the waterfront from downtown Chinatown through what is now Restaurant Row all the way to

Kewalo Basin. The plate lunch demonstrated back then what it continues to prove today—if you can create a fast, affordable, filling and tasty meal, they will come.

Shave Ice: Shaved not Ground

Cold, sweet and refreshing, shave ice has long been, not surprisingly, one of the most popular year-round treats under the year-round Hawaiian sun.

(An etymological note: In Hilo it is called "ice shave" rather than "shave ice." Nowhere in Hawai'i, however, is it ever referred to as *"shaved* ice.")

Because shave ice in various forms is enjoyed throughout Asia, its presence in the Islands is usually attributed to the influence of Hawai'i's large Asian population. Icy desserts topped with syrups and fruit are found in China. Japanese call their version of shave ice "kakigoori." One interesting story describes how over 1,000 years ago, Japanese people preserved natural ice in winter in "ice rooms" dug deep into the shady sides of mountains. Then, in the summer, they could extract the ice, shave it and eat it with syrup. Japanese also like to add mashed azuki beans sweetened with sugar to shave ice to flavor it. Korean shave ice is called "bingsu"; it often utilizes ice cream or milk at its base, then is topped with sweet beans, canned fruit and soy-

bean powder. Taiwanese shave ice is called "baobing," while halo halo is a popular shave ice dessert in the Philippines.

Rather than the rainbow-colored delights that people order today, anecdotal evidence points to a much more organic beginning in Hawai'i. Old-timers recall that as children they would follow the iceman around as he made deliveries in the neighborhood. The iceman sawed off blocks of ice from the back of his cart to deliver to customers with iceboxes in their homes or businesses, and the kids were allowed to enjoy the ice shavings that fell from the saw.

The next chapter in the shave ice story is related to the advent of ice planers. These were small metal hand planes usually made of aluminum. They fit comfortably in the palm of one hand and featured a covered chamber where the ice shavings collected. Various types of ice planes, almost all of them manufactured in the United States, have been preserved in historical collections. The same is true of the manual shave ice machines that were later used in plantation-era

In downtown Honolulu, Ciro's ("Where Epicureans Meet") hosted business lunches and served an upscale dinner clientele in "air-conditioned luxury" from the 1950s through the '70s.

stores and at picnics and large gatherings. So, although it is tempting to trace shave ice's origins in a direct line to Asia, it appears that it really is a product with roots in different places.

In downtown Honolulu, Kaichi Kaya, founder of K. Kaya Fishing Supply in Chinatown, began shaving

>>> >>> >>> >>> >>> >>> >>>

Brothers Spence and Cliff Weaver's Spencecliff restaurant chain was the state's largest in the 1960s and '70s, including the popular Tops and Coco's coffee shops in Waikīkī.

blocks of ice with a Japanese-style carpenter's plane in the late 1890s. He also brewed his own syrup, and by the early 1900s, he sold shave ice from a pushcart to dockworkers at Honolulu Harbor.

Today's motorized shave ice machines are made in either Japan or the mainland U.S. The key to either is the ability to produce a fine, powdery ice. Sno-cones and other ice desserts are often made of ground ice, which has a coarser texture. One of the distinct differences is that the finer, local-style shave ice holds the syrup better, while in the coarser sno-cone the syrup often runs to the bottom of the cup.

Different flavored syrups are constantly being developed, and different shave ice shops experiment with ingredients and toppings to capture a larger clientele. Shave ice basically comes down to the texture (fineness) of the ice and the quality of the syrup.

Ala Moana Boulevard -- Waikiki

Matsumoto Shave Ice in Haleʻiwa—one of Hawaiʻi's most famous shave ice emporiums— has obviously found the winning formula, serving up to a mind-chilling 1,200 shave-ice cones and cups a day.

Creating the Mixed Plate

Check out the food choices in almost any town in Hawaiʻi or scan the menu at any local hole-in-the-wall restaurant and you'll see how fortunate we are to have such a diversity of food in the Islands. In fact, if you ask anyone who's been away for a while or someone who has moved from Hawaiʻi what he or she missed the most, they're likely to say it's the variety of food we have here rather than any specific food item.

This rich diversity is largely attributed to the number of ethnic groups that have settled in Hawaiʻi. It would be a gross oversimplification, however, to assume that each group simply sailed into the Islands and plopped their favorite dishes down on the local plate lunch counter. The next time you find yourself mulling over which three choices to order for your plate lunch, consider the following issues regarding how each ethnic group has affected Hawaiʻi's mixed plate.

1) Regional Characteristics

Just as "American" food can range from New England chowder to Kansas City barbecue to Louisiana gumbo, each ethnic group that emigrated to Hawaiʻi brought with it the flavors and food preferences unique to their original home—state, province, prefecture, island. Our impression of Chinese, Japanese or Filipino food, in other words, is colored by many geographic and cultural factors and may not necessarily be representative of a universal "national" cuisine.

2) Adaptability

When they arrived in Hawai'i, each ethnic group had to adapt its favorite native foods to what was available in the Islands. Few, if any, ethnic recipes could be replicated exactly as they existed in the old country. Only over time were immigrants able to import seeds and cuttings of plants from their native countries that would grow in Hawaiian soil. Plantations provided small plots of land for workers to grow home gardens, and many of them grew vegetables that were used in their ethnic cuisine. Hard-working immigrants also began to produce foodstuffs that others craved, such as shoyu, tofu, noodles, dairy products and baked goods. Many of these enterprises were started by plantation workers to supplement their meager incomes. The growing availability of these goods allowed people to prepare more and more of their favorite foods and thereby enhance the Islands' diversity.

3) Sharing the Land

For the most part, however, people ate what they could get. This usually meant they used what could

be caught or raised locally, only buying what they had to, when they could afford to. People were extremely resourceful when it came to living off the land. Besides farming, many were skilled at fishing and gathering food from the sea. Hawai'i's coastlines were rich with fish, lobster, eel, tako (octopus), wana (sea urchin), 'opihi (limpets), pipipi (small shellfish), limu and ogo (types of edible seaweed), namako (sea cucumber), crab and mussels. The rivers were filled with

o'opu (goby fish), 'ōpae (shrimp), crayfish and hāhāwai (freshwater shellfish), along with watercress. From the mountains, they hunted and harvested fern shoots, bamboo shoots, wild pig, goat, pheasant and deer. Skilled fishermen and hunters would share their catch with others and usually receive something— fruits, vegetables, prepared food or baked goods—in return. This shared bounty led people of different ethnic backgrounds to adopt many common

➤➤➤ ➤➤➤ ➤➤➤ ➤➤➤ ➤➤➤ ➤➤➤ ➤➤➤

In the 1950s, Spencecliff's first eateries were a diverse lot, from Swanky Burger downtown to the Sky Room at John Rodgers Airport to the legendary Queen's Surf on the beach in Kapi'olani Park.

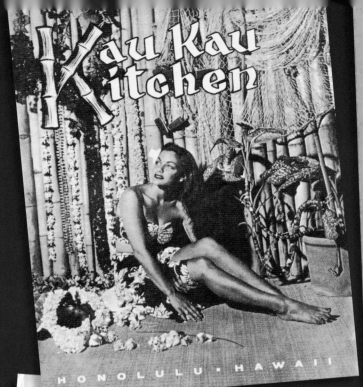

Kau Kau Kitchen

HONOLULU · HAWAII

Aloha Grill

LIQUORS   FINE FOODS

1165 BETHEL STREET

PHONE 5-6363

TAHITIAN LANAI

Appetizers and Soups
E'IA AOTA (Tahitian Marinated Ahi) .... .75
SHRIMP or CRAB MEAT COCKTAIL SUPREME.... 1.00
Cold Vichyssoise 50   Consomme on the Rocks .40
French Onion au Gratin en Casserole .... .60
Fresh Island Fruit Cup .50   Iced Solo Papaya .. .35
Small Mixed Green Salad, Roquefort, French or
1000 Island Dressing .... .50
Chilled Pineapple, Guava, Tomato, Grapefruit Juice .35

POT ROAST OF BEEF
Brown Gravy—Spaetzel
Fresh Vegetable
Banana Muffins or
Rolls and Butter
1.85

Egg Dishes
EGGS BENEDICT 1.85
CRAB MEAT OMELETTE, Parmesan Cheese 1.75
CHICKEN LIVER OMELETTE 1.75
  Served with Hashed Brown Potatoes, Toast and Preserves.
TWO LARGE FRESH ISLAND EGGS any Style ... 1.65
  Served with Ham, Bacon or Sausage, Hashed Brown
  Potatoes, Toast and Preserves.
SCRAMBLED EGGS with Cheese Sauce 1.25

Chilled Salads
FRESH HAWAIIAN FRUIT SALAD 1.50
  Served in one-half fresh Pineapple with Country Style Cottage
  Cheese or Sherbet Topping.
CHEF'S SALAD BOWL 1.65
  Crisp Tossed Island Greens, Garni of Julienne Turkey, Ham
  and Cheese, 1000 Island Dressing.
CAESAR SALAD 1.25
FRESH SHRIMP, Crabmeat or Chicken Salad Bowl 1.85
  All above served with Banana Muffins or Rolls and Butter

Hot Entrees
CRAB MEAT BAKED IN HALF AVOCADO, au Gratin 1.85
FRESH ISLAND MAHIMAHI, Saute, Fine Herbs.... 1.75
  Served with Fresh Vegetable and Shoestring Potatoes.
CHOICE LUNCHEON CLUB STEAK Maitre d'Hotel 2.95
  Served with Fresh Vegetable and Shoestring Potatoes.
CHOPPED TENDERLOIN STEAK, Mushroom Gravy 2.00
  Served with Shoestring Potatoes, Lettuce and Tomato Garni.
COTTAGE CHEESE BLINTZES with Sour Cream ... 1.50
CHICKEN or SHRIMP CURRY, Rice and Condiments 2.25
  All above served with Banana Muffins or Rolls and Butter

Sandwiches
TAHITIAN LANAI'S CHOPPED BEEF TENDERLOIN 1.00
  Served on a Giant Toasted Buttered Bun with Shoestring Potatoes.
TENDERLOIN STEAK SANDWICH on a Toasted Bun 1.85
  Served with Shoestring Potatoes, Lettuce and Tomato Slices.
TOASTED DOUBLE-DECKER CRAB MEAT AND
  BACON SANDWICH, Potato Salad, Garni 1.50
HOT PASTRAMI on Pumpernickel Bread 1.50
  Served with Potato Salad, Garni.
HOT CORNED BEEF ON RYE 1.50
  Served with Potato Salad, Garni.
MONTE CRISTO SANDWICH 1.50
  Served with Tossed Green Salad, Choice of Dressings, Garni
ISLAND TUNA SALAD, Shoestring Potatoes...... 1.00
  Toasted Double-Decker with Lettuce and Tomato.
OUR SPECIAL CLUB SANDWICH 1.50
  A Toasted Double-Decker of Crisp Bacon, Breast of Turkey,
  Lettuce and Tomato served with Potato Salad.
BREAST OF TURKEY on Choice of Breads........ 1.50
  Sliced Tomatoes.
GRILLED AMERICAN AND SWISS CHEESE
  with Bacon or Ham 1.25
  Served with Shoestring Potatoes, Lettuce and Tomato Slices.
ISLAND MAHIMAHI on a Toasted Bun 1.25
  Potatoes, Lettuce and Tomato Slices.

SO. HOTEL ST.
BISHOP STREET

AYH

hob nob

coffee house and cocktail lounge

ALEXANDER YOUNG HOTEL ... IN THE CENTER OF DOWNTOWN HONOLULU

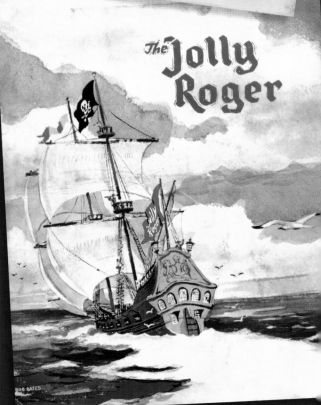

The Jolly Roger

Elliott's

STEWART'S WAIKIKI RESTAURANT (that famous Drugstore Restaurant)

Elliott's * Chuckwagon

1015 Kapiolani Blvd.

Free Transportation to and from
Your Waikiki Hotel. Phone 581161

Today's Special
CREAM OF ASPARAGUS SOUP
CURRIED LAMB
RICE AND CONDIMENTS
2.25

Today's Special
ROAST PORK LOIN
$2.50

Today's Special
SOUP and SALAD
BROILED LOIN LAMB CHOPS
$3.00

Dinner Menu

Choice of:
DAILY SOUP, JELLIED CONSOMME or VICHYSSOISE
TROPICS' TOSSED GREEN SALAD
(With TROPICS' Special Salad Dressing or Parisienne Salad Dressing)

From the Charcoal Broiler

FILET MIGNON with Baked Idaho Russet Potato	5.00
NEW YORK CUT SIRLOIN STEAK with Baked Idaho Russet Potato	5.00
GROUND SIRLOIN OF BEEF	
BROILED SQUAB	2.75
TWO DOUBLE FRENCH LAMB CHOPS with Baked Idaho Russet Potato	3.50
THICK HAM STEAK—Honey Butter Sauce	4.00
PORK CHOPS—Apple Sauce	3.50
BROILED LOBSTER TAIL—Drawn Butter, Shoestring Potatoes	3.50
NEW YORK CUT MINUTE STEAK	3.75
	3.50

Roast

ROAST EASTERN PRIME RIB OF BEEF—au jus	4.50

Entrees

FROG LEGS, Saute, Provencale	
FRESH FRIED CHICKEN, Pan Gravy	3.50
GRILLED FRESH ISLAND MAHIMAHI, Tartar Sauce	3.00
FRESH FRIED LOUISIANA SHRIMP, Hot Sauce	3.00
FRESH FRIED EASTERN SCALLOPS, Tartar Sauce	2.75
GRILLED FRESH JUMBO OYSTERS, Tartar Sauce	2.50
SALMON STEAK MEUNIERE	2.50
GRILLED GENUINE CALF'S LIVER STEAK with Onions or Bacon	2.50
MILK FED VEAL SCALLOPINI SAUTE, Risotto, Marsalla Wine	3.00
BREADED VEAL CUTLETS—Brown Sauce	3.25
ITALIAN SPAGHETTI and Meatballs	3.00
	2.00

Desserts

Assorted Pies or Cakes • Sherbet or Ice Cream • Fresh Sliced Hawaiian Pineapple
Chilled Solo Papaia • Jello

Drinks

LIPTON TEA   or   HILLS BROS. COFFEE

A la Carte Suggestions

FRESH SHRIMP OR CRABMEAT COCKTAIL SUPREME	.85
CAESAR OR CHEF'S SALAD BOWL	1.50
CHICKEN OR TUNA SALAD BOWL	1.75
FRESH SHRIMP OR CRAB SALAD BOWL	2.00
AVOCADO STUFFED WITH CHOICE SEAFOOD	1.75
CRAB MEAT LOUIE	2.00

3½% Hawaii Tax will be added.

THE Tropics

Kapiolani Drive Inn
ALA MOANA AND JOHN ENA ROAD
HONOLULU, HAWAII

We always welcome the opportunity to
serve you and give you the kind of service
that will make you want to come back.

Sky Room

COFFEE SHOP

Honolulu International Airport

---

waikiki pharmacy

"ON THE AVENUE" AT WAIKIKI OPPOSITE ROYAL HAWAIIAN HOTEL

FOUNTAIN SERVICE • BREAKFAST • LUNCHEON • DINNER

Beach Boy

BROILER

HILTON HAWAIIAN VILLAGE ★ WAIKIKI
In the Diamond Head Towers on Dewey Way

>>> >>> >>> >>> >>> >>> >>>

Tuna fishermen work Island waters from the stern of a fishing sampan in the 1950s. Preceding pages: A portfolio of Honolulu restaurants.

food tastes and practices. Food in the plantation era was much more egalitarian than most people think.

4) The Flip Side: A Matter of Style

Some things don't change. Raw 'opihi is what it is. Smoked meat is smoked meat; dried fish is dried fish. Although the same ingredients were available to everyone, different ethnic groups expressed their native cuisine in the different ways they flavored and prepared those ingredients. For example, a simple fish soup, although common to all ethnic groups, would be seasoned in dozens of variations—shoyu, miso, ginger, oyster sauce, patis, lemongrass, chili peppers or tomato sauce, to name just a few—and garnished with kalamungai, green onions, taro, onions, tomatoes, bittermelon, mustard cabbage, pumpkin, squash or other items, depending on the ethnicity of the cook.

Eventually, what flourished were those ethnic foods that held the broadest appeal to the greatest number of people. In some dishes, traditional seasonings or ingredients were adjusted, becoming milder, sweeter, saltier or hotter, to appeal to the prevailing tastes. We'd never have created a mixed plate, after all, if we had not eaten and enjoyed each other's food. In Hawai'i, local people were able to develop an appreciation and an international palate for each other's food that is as broad and as

Perfection in a Can

The SPAM® Family of Products, as it is branded by Hormel Foods, has long been a cause celebre in Hawai'i. We celebrate the ubiquitous canned meat at Waikīkī's annual SPAM JAM® festival, for instance, and in the hundreds of SPAM™ haiku circulating online:

> Can of metal, slick
> soft center, so cool, moistening
> I yearn for your salt

You can find it at every McDonalds, Burger King and 7-Eleven in the archipelago. Why the immense popularity? For starters, it's the perfect illustration of why we eat what we eat in Hawai'i.

The SPAM® brand became an instant hit in the Islands during World War II, just as it did in such war-torn places as Great Britain, Okinawa and Guam. Attribute it to food shortages and war rationing—fresh meat was hard to come by and strict fishing regulations were imposed under martial law. SPAM® Classic was both available and affordable. What's more, many households in Hawai'i were without refrigerators at the time, and canned meat, which requires no refrigeration, quickly became a staple throughout the Islands.

It was also "mo' bettah" for Hawai'i workers, as its saltiness kept it from spoiling long after it was prepared. This was important to plantation laborers and other working-class folks, who packed their lunches in the morning and often had to leave them under the tropical sun for several hours without refrigeration. Less hardy foods could wilt and spoil under such conditions, but not the trusty luncheon meat in the blue can.

The salty flavor of SPAM® Classic made it the perfect accompaniment to rice or bread. A little bit of it was enough to flavor a disproportionately large helping of any starch. So flavorful was SPAM® Classic that more often than not it was cut up and cooked with vegetables such as cabbage or string beans and served with a pot of rice, easily stretching the meager budgets of hungry families.

But perhaps Hawai'i's favorite preparation for SPAM® Classic is the one that has become a symbol of the local culture: the iconic, the one and only, SPAM® musubi.

SPAM® Musubi
Makes 8 musubi

3 c.	uncooked short- or medium-grain rice
4 c.	water
1 can	SPAM® Classic (or other variety)
¼ c.	shoyu
¼ c.	sugar
¼ c.	mirin (rice wine)
5	sheets sushi nori
	Water

Cook rice with water in rice cooker. Cut SPAM® Classic into 8 rectangular slices, approximately ¼" thick. Fry in a large, ungreased frying pan over medium heat until brown and slightly crispy. Remove from heat, drain on paper towels and set aside.

In a small saucepan over high heat, combine shoyu, sugar and mirin; bring just to a boil, then remove from heat. Add fried SPAM® Classic slices, turning them to coat; let sit in marinade until ready to use.

Cut nori in half widthwise so that each strip is as wide as the SPAM® Classic slice is long. In a small bowl, have some water ready to seal the ends of the nori wrapper. Place a sheet of nori on a plate or cutting board.

Position a musubi press lengthwise on the nori so it is centered across the width of the nori. Fill the bottom of the press with approximately ¼ cup cooked rice, on top of the nori; press rice down with the flat part of the press until it is compacted to ¼" thick. Place a SPAM® slice on the rice. Cover with an additional ¼ cup cooked rice and press again.

Remove the musubi from the press by pushing the whole stack down with the flat part of the press while lifting the rest of the press up. Fold one end of nori over the musubi and press lightly onto the rice. Wet the other end slightly, then wrap around the musubi. Repeat the process with the remaining SPAM® slices, making sure to rinse the press after each musubi to keep it from getting too sticky.

IF CAN, CAN!

The Allure of Canned Goods

Canned foods were held in high regard in Hawai'i during the first half of the 20th century. If SPAM™ was king of the cupboard, his court would have been comprised of Vienna sausage, corned beef, tuna, deviled ham and sardines, all of which shared the many virtues of SPAM™. Although less popular than SPAM™ today, canned sardines at five cents a can were immensely popular in the plantation era. Recalled one old-timer: "I never ate anything out of a can until my brother brought back a can of sardines from Hilo. We all shared it."

Can Sardines

This recipe, originally submitted without measurements, was meant to be made to "cook's taste." The suggested measurements can be used as a starting point for your own creativity.

1 clove	garlic, diced
½	Maui onion, sliced
1	bay leaf
1 can	tomato sardines or oil sardines— either variety is okay; whateva you have

Sauté garlic, onion and bay leaf. Remove sardines from can, debone if you like and add to sautéed onions, folding carefully so as to not break sardines. Cover and turn off stove.

Part of the allure of canned foods was the notion that when all you had was homegrown, home-cooked food every day, store-bought food in a can seemed all the more special. Usually the shiny, colorful cans remained tucked

away in the deep recesses of kitchen shelves in households across Hawai'i. There they waited, ready for the next emergency or special occasion. They were there if a guest should happen to stop by unexpectedly, for example. After all, there were no freezers to keep food, much less any late-night convenience stores or supermarkets in the rural camps that dotted the Islands, and our elders would have been ashamed if they had not had anything to offer a guest on such occasions—no matter how humble the fare. This was yet another reason why many local youngsters looked upon canned goods as something special.

The most special canned food of all was not SPAM™, but abalone. One knew a visitor was held in very high regard when that prized can with the pink label was brought out and those tender slices were served like sashimi on a bed of cabbage.

All of this runs contrary to the way in which people in many other parts of the country tend to view canned goods. Perhaps the general

disdain they feel is the result of a lingering association with C-rations, the canned food first doled out to the American military during WWII and later in Korea and Vietnam. Or it could be the perception that canned meat is inferior, "poor man's food." Said an African-American woman from California: "I swore that if I ever made it out of the ghetto and became successful, I would never eat SPAM™ again."

Although considerations such as a lack of refrigeration no longer determine what people in Hawai'i eat, they remain at the root of what we enjoy. Unlike my friend from California, we in Hawai'i tend to look back at our past with nostalgia, and the canned food of that era remains a key part of that past. Corned beef and cabbage in Hawai'i still means *canned* corned beef and cabbage, unless it is specifically labeled fresh. Along with such dishes as SPAM™ with green beans, sardines and onions, SPAM™ and mayonnaise sandwiches and Vienna sausage omelets, it is worthy of a place in the Pantheon of local favorites.

And whatever happened to canned abalone? If it was special then, consider it extinct today. Replaced for a time by cans of more affordable "abalone-like shellfish," today cans of the real and the almost-real abalone are both kept in locked cabinets like expensive jewelry. Sadistic storeowners strategically place these cabinets near the cold beer or by checkout counters in order to keep an eye on them and so that kids of yesteryear, now fully grown, can look up and reminisce about the culinary treasure trapped inside the pink cans. It's a feeling that any canned food was once able to evoke.

sophisticated as you could find anywhere in the world.

On pages 106 and 107 are recipes for suman and mochi, two variations on the basic theme of sweetened glutinous rice that demonstrate the individual ethnic stamp—in this case, Filipino or Japanese—that can be placed on similar dishes.

5) From Plantation to Town

Plantation owners continually recruited workers from different countries in part because of growth in the sugar industry, but also because workers kept leaving the plantations for other occupations. Many former sugar workers found employment in the pineapple, ranching, fishing, farming and dairy industries, while others started up small businesses. In this transition from plantations to towns, entrepreneurs began importing foodstuffs and other goods from their native countries; others manufactured goods that were in demand and opened bakeries, meat markets, produce stands, fish markets and restaurants to meet Hawai'i's rapidly evolving food needs. Eateries such as Chinese restaurants and Japanese okazu-ya and saimin stands helped to define for the public what each ethnic group's food was like.

6) Old and New Immigrants

Hawai'i's ethnic cuisine is usually traced back to the original immigrants who came to work in the sugar fields in the 19th and early 20th centuries. However, more recent immigrants have also heavily influenced ethnic food in Hawai'i. Korean and Filipino immigration, for example, can be viewed in two distinct waves— early and recent. Although Japanese and Chinese cannot claim similarly high numbers of new immigrants, tourists, students and international businesses comprise enough of a critical mass to form essentially a new generation of immigrants to the Islands. Aside from food markets and scores of new restaurants, Hawai'i's foreign-language media (television, radio, newspapers and magazines) and cultural activities (concerts, festivals, fashion and films) have been transformed by the infusion of new immigrants.

While early plantation immigrants generally came from impoverished rural backgrounds, recent immigrants tend to come from more urbanized backgrounds and have made a significant economic and cultural impact on Hawai'i. In the old days, for example, sushi generally referred to inari sushi (vinegared rice in edible aburage cones), oshi sushi (vinegared rice pressed in molds) or maki sushi (vinegared rice with fillings in the middle rolled in a sheet of

CONNECTION

nori). Today, sushi more often refers to nigiri sushi (bite-sized servings of rice with various toppings), temaki sushi (cone-shaped hand rolls) or chirashi sushi (a bowl or box meal with flavored rice on the bottom and fresh seafood arranged on top), prepared by a highly trained sushi chef using the freshest imported ingredients in expensive sushi restaurants. Most sushi toppings (neta)—maguro (tuna), hamachi (yellowfin), ika (squid), tako (octopus), sake (salmon), uni (sea urchin), anago (eel) and other delicacies—for nigiri, temaki and chirashi-style sushi are flown in daily and rushed directly to demanding chefs and their diners.

It's understandable why only the simpler sushi forms like inari, oshi and maki were popular in the Islands in the past, since dried or canned ingredients such as shrimp powder, kampyo (gourd strips) and canned eel or tuna could be used with locally available carrots, cucumbers and eggs.

Yes, Hawai'i's cuisine is greatly influenced by ethnic factors, but what these influences are and how they affect what we eat is in itself a rich and flavorful tale of persistence, adaptability, creativity and sharing that began as human beings from different cultures first started arriving on these shores—and continues to evolve today.

HOW TO ORDER SHAVE ICE

"Rules" for ordering shave ice have long been in place at the iconic Waiola Shave Ice stand in Mō'ili'ili. Partly to alleviate the long lines that frequently form on hot Hawaiian days, efficiency in ordering is critical. If anyone deviates from the requisite procedure, the person taking the order at Waiola wordlessly points to the sign posted above the window:

1. State total number of shave ice and sizes. This allows the server to grab the proper number and sizes of containers, rather than run back-and-forth multiple times just to fill one order.

2. Indicate if you want ice cream, azuki, mochi balls or any toppings. This stuff has to go in on the bottom of the container before the ice. It also determines how the person is going to pack the ice and "finish" it with toppings.

3. Have your money ready. Self-explanatory—don't add precious seconds to everyone's wait by fumbling for your wallet or purse when it comes time to pay. Plus, the faster you pay and put your change in your pocket, the sooner your hands are free to grab your order.

4. Finally, state your flavors. To be more precise, wait until you are asked what flavors you want.

If all this sounds too intimidating, you might be more comfortable simply making your own:

Old-Fashioned Shave Ice Syrup

5 lbs.	sugar
¾ c.	cornstarch
3 qts.	water
	Concentrated flavor extracts
	Food coloring or dye
	Dash of salt

Mix sugar and cornstarch. Add water and stir to dissolve. Bring water to a boil and boil hard, stirring constantly so it will not burn. Remove from heat and add small amount of dye for desired color and enough concentrated extract to flavor according to preference.

THE FIRST PLATE LUNCH?

In 1987, when I was editor of the *Hawaii Herald*, staff writer Wayne Muromoto and I investigated the origins of the plate lunch. We dedicated ourselves to the cause, spending the better part of a year conducting plate lunch "research" all over O'ahu. Besides gaining 20 pounds (each) and compiling a comprehensive directory of plate lunch establishments, we asked dozens of old-timers when and where they remember plate lunches first appearing in Hawai'i.

In keeping with good scholarship, we made our criteria clear: We were looking for actual evidence of the plate lunch, including a paper plate, rice, entrée and macaroni salad. To our surprise, the anecdotal evidence all began to point to the Honolulu waterfront (right, from the old Honolulu Fort, ca. 1900) in the 1920s and '30s. There, Wayne learned, pushcart peddlers served up plate lunches to hungry stevedores, sailors, laborers arriving and passing through the old immigration station, and even cruise ship crews and passengers.

In 1988, we received a letter at the *Herald* from subscriber Leilani Iwanaga, who recalled that her grandmother, Moyo Iwamoto, had sold plate lunches on the Honolulu waterfront in the late 1920s. After her husband died in the Spanish flu epidemic of 1921, Moyo had to raise their six children by herself. She began selling snacks such as candies and oranges at Honolulu Harbor near Pier 7 from a wooden pushcart mounted on two creaky wheelbarrow tires.

Moyo's son, Matsu, helped his mother on a daily basis and was able to provide Wayne with considerable detail about the family business. In the late '20s, Matsu recalled, his mother was able to obtain a larger cart, which she posi-

tioned along Pier 2 (a current cruise ship terminal). There she sold sushi down by the seashore, along with pastries, candies and oranges from a red wooden cart, which sported three-foot-high wooden wheels, a wooden roof and a long push handle. An important feature of the new cart was a compartment designed to hold a large block of ice, which Moyo shaved with a hand plane to make shave ice and milkshakes. She even made her own syrup by mixing sugar, food coloring and various flavorings.

Although he was still a youngster when it was being used, Matsu remembers the pushcart well, as it was his daily assignment to push the bulky contraption from Halekauwila Street across busy Ala Moana Boulevard and along the bustling docks of Honolulu Harbor—about a mile each way.

Later, Moyo was able to lease a small space on Channel Street from the Inter-Island Drydock Co. There, in a hut measuring about 20 by 25 feet, she set up a small cooking area and four long tables. From this simple dockside stand, in the late '20s or early '30s, the Iwamo-

tos began selling honest-to-goodness plate lunches. For 50 cents, hungry dockworkers and other customers could buy an eight-inch paper plate piled high with rice, a vegetable, macaroni salad, kim chee or takuan pickles and a main entrée. Matsu, who did much of the cooking for his mother, remembers that entrées included beef stew, beef tomato, butterfish, chop steak, pig's feet, chicken long rice, pork chops, ham hocks and saimin. Their mixed plate, which included hot dogs, SPAM™, eggs, rice and salad, was one of their biggest sellers.

Business thrived through the war years, as sailors and MPs joined the ranks of stevedores and other regulars. The enterprising Moyo would set up whenever battleships docked at Pier 2, so she could sell snacks, plate lunches and soft drinks to the sailors.

Inter-Island Drydock closed after the war, and the family had to vacate the stand. Undeterred, Moyo bought a truck and started a lunchwagon business selling plate lunches just outside of the Pier 2 gates. She would check the posted schedules and be there to feed the work gangs on both day and night shifts. Moyo Iwamoto worked until illness forced her to retire in 1965 at the age of 81. She passed away a year later. Matsu and his wife, Thelma, continued the business for a few more years before they, too, retired.

Matsu told Wayne that he remembered one other lunch stand, owned and operated by a Kaya family, that was serving plate lunches in the area around this time. The origins of the plate lunch may forever be the subject of debate, for the odds are that variations of the plate lunch were evolving at the same time. Still, the case for Honolulu Harbor as the birthplace of the plate lunch is quite convincing.

HAWAI'I: WHERE MAC SALAD IS KING

Even the most casual survey would confirm that Hawai'i's diverse local cuisine is held together by two elements common to all plate lunches —rice and macaroni salad. It makes sense, as both of these foods are relatively bland and nicely complement just about any form of flavorful entrée, from teriyaki and beef stew to adobo and kim chee, and beyond.

Yet, for its irrefutable importance and enduring popularity, no definitive tale of macaroni salad's origin can be told. Simply based on its main ingredients—pasta (Italian) and mayonnaise (French)—one can infer that macaroni salad's genealogy is rooted in Europe. Potato salad, a likely relative, is also European—specifically German—in origin.

Cookbooks document the popularity of macaroni salad recipes across Mainland America in the early 20th century, and some observers have noted that Mainland chefs were being recruited to run Hawai'i's top hotels and restaurants during the same period, bringing their European-influenced culinary backgrounds—including macaroni salad—with them. Others speculate that sugar and pineapple plantation managers and supervisors, who were mainly of European descent, instructed their domestic help, mainly Asian immigrants, to prepare their beloved potato salad. Both theories are plausible, and it is possible that

macaroni salad had more than one genealogical path to Hawai'i.

Whatever the original dish, the local population eagerly adopted it and set about customizing it to local tastes. If it did originate as potato salad, dried macaroni noodles were cheaper and much easier to obtain and could be stored for longer periods of time than potatoes, so it's no wonder that they eventually replaced potatoes in the local interpretations of the dish.

The local-style macaroni salad also featured mayonnaise—and lots of it. Mayonnaise could be made rather economically at home using vegetable oil and egg yolks, which meant that the entire dish was relatively inexpensive to produce, helped to stretch a family's food budget and tasted good as well.

While the flavor of some foods may vary by ethnic group or by island, macaroni salad tends to vary from cook to cook—even cooks following the same recipe. Many people swear by specific brands of mayonnaise, while others claim that the flavor changes when they prepare the dish anywhere outside of the Islands—even if they have hand-carried the ingredients from Hawai'i! There are literally hundreds of variations on macaroni salad: Do you prefer fat elbow macaroni or thin spaghetti noodles (not exclusive to but very popular on Kaua'i)? Plain macaroni or potato-macaroni? Frozen peas and carrots? Celery? Onions? Canned tuna? Artificial crab? Real crab? Hard-boiled

eggs? How many? Relish? Mustard? What brand of mayo? Can you ever have too much mayo?

The beauty of macaroni salad is that it is quite forgiving and welcomes a wide range of personalization and experimentation. It's a casual dish that easily adapts to any type of food or occasion—it is, in other words, quintessentially local.

Basic Macaroni Salad

To make a basic macaroni salad, you don't need a recipe; just follow these guidelines:

The pasta: Cook 1 pound elbow macaroni (for really local style, cook until soft and fat, but you can go al dente if you prefer).

The flavoring: Stir in ¼ cup very finely grated onion. Not minced, chopped or sliced—grated. It should be liquidy (this is how they do it at Diner's in Kalihi).

The mayo: At least 2½ cups for real local style. But there are no rules, so use less if you like. Or more.

The add-ins: Carrots, watercress, celery, hard-boiled eggs, pickle relish—whatever suits you.

The finale: Salt and pepper, to taste. Stir well; refrigerate.

Macaroni-Potato Salad
Serves 8

½ lb.	macaroni
8	hard-cooked eggs
3	red potatoes, cooked and cubed
1 Tbsp.	salt
1 Tbsp.	vinegar
2 c.	mayonnaise
½ tsp.	ground allspice
½ tsp.	pepper
1 pkg.	frozen peas, thawed and drained (10 oz.)

Cook macaroni according to package directions; drain. Separate egg yolks from egg whites. In a small bowl, mash yolks and chill. Chop egg whites; put into a large bowl with macaroni and potatoes. Stir in salt and vinegar; chill overnight.

Add egg yolks and remaining ingredients; gently mix into macaroni mixture. Chill.

Two Scoop Rice

Two scoops of rice has become the plate lunch standard. But how and why did this come to be? First, at some point in the modern history of Hawai'i, the small arsenal of traditional Asian rice paddles and spoons was replaced with the modern American ice cream scoop. With a quick dip in water to lubricate its shiny metal surface, experienced food servers could quickly scoop and eject the rice onto paper plates and into Styrofoam lunchboxes with a flick of a lever. The result was two perfectly formed round mounds rather than the oddly misshapen glob of grains resulting from a rice paddle. Beyond its aesthetic advantage, the ice cream scoop gave plate lunch providers a means of standardizing their serving portions.

Once the ice cream scoop was established as standard measure, it would appear to be a reasonable matter of one scoop being too little and three scoops being too much, based on the understanding that the amount of rice served should be proportionate to the volume of the non-rice components on the plate, and vice versa.

All Asian cultures have subscribed to this fundamental philosophy of food since time immemorial. Whereas in many Western cultures the starch is secondary to the entrée, or main course, rice is the center of a meal in China, Japan, Korea, the Phil-

CONNECTION

PLATE LUNCH POINTERS

Standing in line to order food at a local drive-in one day, I was reminded of certain nuances in the way one orders a plate lunch. It started when the person at the front of the line cheerfully and politely placed her order—to which the young man behind the counter quickly replied, "Mackotoss?" The customer, suddenly unsure of herself, timidly repeated her order. "Mackotoss?" the counterman repeated.

My mouth was halfway open when the counterperson finally spat out: "You like macaroni or toss …" (now the lights finally flickered on in the eyes of the dazed woman) "… salad?"

"Ohh, tossed sounds good!" the customer said excitedly. Her relief, however, was brief. "Tauzanofrenj?" the counterman asked. Catching himself more quickly this time, he looked the customer in the eyes and said, slowly, "You like Thousand or French" (pause) "dressing wid da toss?"

Replacing the macaroni salad with a tossed green salad used to be a choice only offered by a few select restaurants, but now it has become a widespread practice, I've observed, a trend driven by rising demand for a slightly healthier plate lunch.

Next in line, a young local couple stepped up to the counter and rattled off their order, specifying, "All rice." This is a less exercised option, but an increasingly popular practice among younger generation diners—especially boys. "All rice" is a request to replace the scoop of macaroni salad with a third scoop of rice. According to those who follow this practice, "all rice" is less about eliminating the salt and mayonnaise contained in mac salad than it is to stretch their plate lunch into a more filling meal.

And, as if that were not enough, more and more drive-ins now also offer brown rice as an alternative to white. Now *that* is getting ridiculous.

ippines and other Asian countries. In Japan, the word for cooked rice is "gohan," which also means "meal." It is the same word. That is how critical rice is.

Throughout Asia, rice is consumed in combination with non-rice foods such as seafood, meats and vegetables in order to make a meal. These accompanying foods, sometimes referred to as "side dishes," add

flavors that complement the comforting blandness of the rice as well as provide nutrition. Japanese call these side dishes "okazu." Chinese call them "sung" or "soong." Koreans say "ban chan." In Korea, "baek" means "white" and "ban" means "cooked rice." The word for a meal in Korean is "baek ban," referring to a bowl of cooked white rice served with side dishes.

Like so many other aspects of local culture, Hawaiʻi's modern food traditions are the result of a remarkable coalescence of traditional beliefs, practices and values held by the people who came here from diverse backgrounds. Asian food culture— built on a foundation of rice and accompanying side dishes—found a comfortable home in Hawaiʻi. Traditional Hawaiian culture—along with

Suman

"Kankanen" is the generic Ilocano term used to describe rice cakes made with glutinous rice, coconut milk and sugar. This particular variation is known in the Philippines as "suman."

2 c.   sweet rice
1½ c.   coconut milk
¼ tsp.   salt
              Banana leaf cut in twelve 5"
              strips for wrapping
              Brown sugar, to taste

Wash sweet rice and soak in water overnight. Drain and combine with coconut milk and salt in a large saucepan. Bring to a boil and boil until the liquid evaporates and the rice becomes a glutinous mass.

Taste mixture for sweetness, but do not add sugar yet. Divide mixture into 12 pieces and place each on a banana-leaf strip. If desired, sprinkle 1-2 Tbsp. brown sugar over each piece. Fold the banana leaf closed. Tie the wrapped pieces together in pairs so that the folded ends are facing each other. These double bundles are the suman.

Boil a pot of water and put the 6 suman in, making sure they are completely covered by water. After 1 hour, check the consistency of the rice inside the packets. If it is soft, they are done.

Serve suman still wrapped in the banana leaves, which should be unfolded and discarded before eating. The rice filling may be dipped in extra sugar while eating if desired.

other Polynesian societies—also categorized food into two main types. The only difference was that, instead of rice, the bland staple at the heart of the Hawaiian diet was called "'ai." 'Ai refers to a vegetable food, usually poi, but it can also mean taro, sweet potato, breadfruit or yam. This starch was paired with i'a, the term for any tasty accompaniment that enhanced the enjoyment of consuming the 'ai. I'a was almost always fish or other edible delicacies from the sea—including salt—but other sources of meat such as pig, dog and chicken were also i'a.

The heart of local dining, then, was to balance 'ai and i'a—rice and okazu—to create a meal. This remains largely true today—one without the other would not be considered a complete meal.

Meals primarily composed of a starch seasoned with small amounts of savory, more nutritious foods also grew out of the culture of scarcity in which many in Hawai'i were raised. When flour or rice were more easily obtained and stored than meat or vegetables, eating a lot of okazu and not enough starch might be considered selfish or impolite. Even after these conditions of scarcity no longer existed, the habits of diet remain. Two scoops of rice were determined to be a comfortable amount with which to balance a certain quantity of food that could be consumed to satisfy a diner's hunger. A mini-plate gears down the proportions to exactly half the amount of meat and only one scoop of rice. Conversely, many local restaurants will accommodate their customers' request for "all rice," adding a third scoop of rice in place of macaroni salad.

Part of the appeal of foods such as SPAM™ musubi is that they take the guesswork out of serving the right amount of meat and rice. Here, the rice is shaped to precisely conform to the dimensions of a slice of SPAM™. Thicknesses may vary, but the coverage is the same, so there is no mistake—every bite ensures a mouthful of meat and rice. The same could be said about nigiri sushi, where raw fish or seafood is cut and laid out on a small block of rice. In the case of maki, or rolled, sushi, the filling runs the entire length of the rice roll covered in nori (a sheet of dried seaweed).

The Rest Is Gravy

Another important element in local plate lunch culture is the popularity of sauces and condiments. Sprinkling shoyu or furikake (seasoned seaweed or dried bonito flakes) on rice is an increasingly popular practice. These condiments function as flavorful buffers between the 'ai and i'a. Ume (pickled plum) in the middle of a musubi (rice ball), lomi-lomi salmon on poi, or kim chee on the side are other classic examples of this practice.

Basic Mochi

2 c.	water
¾ c.	sugar
1 pkg.	mochiko (10 oz.)
1 can	tsubushi-an (sweetened red bean paste)
	Katakuriko (potato starch)

Boil water and sugar. Remove from heat and add mochiko. Mix until well blended. Cook 5 to 10 minutes at medium heat, stirring constantly. While mixture is cooking, coat cutting board with potato starch. Pour hot mixture on cutting board.

Cut a piece of mochi; coat hands in potato starch and place mochi in your hand. Put a spoonful of an on mochi and bring edges of mochi together by pinching the edges to make them stick.

Place mochi, pinched side down, on tray pre-coated with potato starch. Cool well before packing.

Sandwiches and milk from glass bottles fill the bill for school lunches in the 1940s.

One of the ultimate means of flavoring any bland starch is gravy, as in mashed potatoes and gravy. Locally, not only can diners slather their meatloaf, roast beef, roast pork, hamburger steak, chicken cutlet or loco moco with gravy, they can also order any one of these dishes with "gravy on the rice." Some may consider this overkill, while others believe one really can't get too much of a good thing. There was a time when gravy on rice—just gravy and rice—constituted a filling (if not so nutritious) meal for cash-strapped college students at places like the now-legendary Maruzen restaurant in Mōʻiliʻili, or for carbo-craving surfers at Rainbow Drive-In in Kapahulu.

It is also one more reason why saucy foods like beef stew, tripe stew or beef curry are so popular. These dishes provide solid meat and vegetable components along with rich, tasty sauces that seep down through the rice. Chili is considered to be a traditional "local" food in part because it has the right viscosity to be mixed with rice, like a thick and well-seasoned gravy (e.g., Zippy's chili and frank or chili and chicken mixed plate).

Soups—like miso soup, oxtail soup and Portuguese bean soup—are also very popular, because they can easily be combined with rice (or poi or bread) to make a hearty meal. Other foods include some sauce that is not gravy or soup but still adds flavor to rice, like pork tofu, pork and squash, salt meat and watercress, chicken hekka or sukiyaki. ◙

CONNECTION

PLATE LUNCH MIXOLOGY

A final note on the subject of soups, sauces and gravy dishes on rice: Be careful how you combine these foods. You might call Hawai'i a one-bowl or one-plate culture. You could be at a family potluck, a banquet buffet or a lunch-wagon at the beach when you're presented with an option of several entrées to go with your two scoops of rice.

Most locals have either the experience or the innate intelligence to choose items that will not completely run into each other. I was made painfully aware of this issue by my friend Bob from L.A. Bob loves coming to Hawai'i and eating local food—all kinds of local food—so I always take him to as many different places as I can while he is here. Like a kid in a candy shop, he stands in front of the drive-in menu, agonizing over his choices for the two- or even three-choice mix plate.

You must understand that Bob has waited many long months and lost many sleepless nights waiting for this moment. Finally realizing that he is taking too long and beginning to upset the hungry blue-collar folks in line behind him, he whispers to me: "I am thinking that the tripe stew, beef curry and chicken hekka sound good. What do you think, Master?"

My heart sinks. I have neither the heart to scold him nor the time to explain the do's and don'ts of plate lunch mixology. All I can offer is, "Why don't you have what I'm having?"

Later, I am able to take him aside and explain what any third grader in Hawai'i already knows: Do not mix several gravy-based, saucy or soupy dishes together on one plate. They will run together to form an indistinguishable and unappetizing puddle. Get one gravy-rich dish, like tripe

stew or chicken curry, to anchor your meal and flavor your rice, then add one or more non-gravy dishes, like teriyaki beef or mahimahi or Korean chicken or pork adobo. These are your classic combos, like katsu-curry or chili-frank.

"Wet and dry, soft and crunchy, sweet and sour, bland and salty. Balance. It's all about balance, Grasshopper," I tell him softly.

CHAPTER FIVE

The Hawaiian Renaissance

A Revolution in the Kitchen

The 1950s culminated in a big way in Hawai'i. Besides marking the start of jet service to the Islands, 1959 was also the year that the sprawling Ala Moana Center opened. The largest shopping mall in the entire United States at the time, Ala Moana stood as a dramatic symbol signaling the dawn of a sophisticated consumer age never even dreamed of by many older residents. But most of all, Hawai'i's long-time campaign for statehood finally came to fruition in 1959, leading Islanders to proclaim that they were no longer "second-class" American citizens.

In many respects, the powerful influences of Americanization that impacted the Islands in the '40s and '50s extended their grip in the '60s and '70s—including what people ate and where they ate it. The first McDonald's restaurant in Hawai'i opened on O'ahu in 1968, and the franchise quickly spread throughout the state. Other major national fast food chains and franchises, such as Dairy Queen, Kentucky Fried Chicken, Burger King, Jack in the Box, Wendy's, Pizza Hut and Taco Bell also became familiar sights throughout Hawai'i.

>>> >>> >>> >>> >>> >>> >>>

Established in 1904, the Oahu Market has long been a gathering place for Chinatown's immigrant population—Chinese, Japanese, Koreans, Okinawans, Filipinos and, more recently, Vietnamese and other ethnic groups from Southeast Asia and the South Pacific. Opposite: Executive Chef Yves Menoret of the Hilton Hawaiian Village's Bali by the Sea typified the culinary blend of East and West gaining popularity in the 1980s: (left to right) Abalone Napped in Basil Sauce, Grilled Veal Chop with Essence of Macadamia Nuts and 'Opakapaka in Ti Leaf Wrap, and Fruit Sorbets with Haupia and Rasberry Coulis.

>>> >>> >>> >>> >>> >>> >>>

Stylized menu renderings like this Windward O'ahu hukilau incorporated Hawaiiana into the local dining experience— especially in the resort restaurants.

The advent of jet service to the Islands helped morph tourism into the state's primary economic engine, far outstripping both sugarcane and pineapple. Owners and managers of Hawai'i's booming hotel industry began to rely heavily on Mainland- and European-trained chefs to run their all-important food and beverage operations. As a result, much of the high-end food served in hotel dining rooms and in the numerous restaurants that popped up to accommodate the tourist trade was strongly influenced by French and European cuisine, and many of the ingredients that went into its preparation were imported from other parts of the world.

One rather unwelcome outcome of these external influences on Hawai'i's culinary reputation was that visitors came to assume that what was being served to them in these hotels and restaurants was really "Hawaiian" food.

Visitors had their choice of dining in pricey restaurants on frozen, shipped-in, picked-before-it's-ripe food, or in tourist establishments that distorted traditional Hawaiian cooking for Western tastes. Small wonder that Hawaii had long been regarded as a paradise for beaches but a wasteland for food.
—Janice Wald Henderson,
The New Cuisine of Hawaii

How bad was it? One has only to look through any number of "Hawaiian" cookbooks aimed at national audiences to get a sense of what was being foisted upon unsuspecting diners as "Hawaiian cuisine." A 1974 recipe for Tuna Delight Salad Mold, for instance, calls for the combination of such unlikely ingredients as canned pineapple in syrup, canned tuna, lime gelatin, mayonnaise, monosodium glutamate and evaporated milk. The good news: This kind of misguided combination would ultimately lead to a flowering of culinary excellence.

Redefining the Meaning of Local

Local food, not the hotel-Hawaiian variety, still held its place among local eaters in the diners, coffee shops and drive-ins that flourished in the '50s. In 1966, for example, brothers Charles and Francis Higa opened the first Zippy's restaurant on South King Street in midtown Honolulu.

Other legendary eateries that helped popularize local-style kau kau included the original L&L Drive-In on Liliha Street, which opened in 1959, and Masu's Massive Plate Lunch on Makaloa Street, which made its debut in 1974. L&L was purchased the following year by entrepreneur Eddie Flores, who then partnered with his friend Johnson Kam in 1976 to grow the business into one of Hawai'i's largest and most successful food

franchises and, later on, to expand nationwide under the L&L Hawaiian Barbecue brand.

In the early 1970s, Grace's Lunchwagon became a fixture near the corner of University and Metcalf Streets by the University of Hawai'i at Mānoa, offering hungry students cheap and tasty alternatives to the institutional offerings served up by the on-campus food service provider, SAGA Foods. Students lined up for filling plate lunches like Grace's hot dog/chow fun plate, with two scoops of rice, macaroni salad and kim chee, for about $1.65.

The lunchwagon, in fact, may well be ultimate symbol of Hawai'i's casual food and lifestyle; these mobile diners flourished through the '60s and '70s and remain popular today. The converted step vans, outfitted with cook tops, counters, coolers and a cut-out side window with counter, generally stake out favored locations near beach parks, playgrounds and well-trafficked worksites. Over time, they become part of the scenery, fixtures in the neighborhood. At lunchtime, these mobile chow wagons attract a very democratic clientele, with buttoned-down office workers and executives standing in line along with students, construction workers, hungry surfers and tourists.

In spite of rising fuel and food costs, lunchwagons remain a relatively affordable alternative for hard-

Honolulu restaurateur George "Cass" Castagnola built a loyal following at his Castagnola's restaurants in Mānoa and Waikīkī by featuring imported ingredients— San Marzano tomatoes, extra virgin olive oil and Parma ham from Italy, for example—and spawned a number of competing Italian restaurants opened by former employees. Here, he shows off his imported products in a 1992 promotional photo.

working entrepreneurs—and their customers—when compared to the capital and operating costs of traditional brick-and-mortar restaurants. And while old-timers sometimes lament that their old favorites are fast disappearing, according to the State Department of Health there are still more than 600 lunchwagons with permits to operate in Hawai'i—almost all of them on O'ahu.

The Renaissance Takes Shape

The optimism and prosperity of the decades following statehood were tempered by political tensions

>>> >>> >>> >>> >>> >>> >>>

Launched in 1944 in an old University-district flower shop, Kuhio Grill was a watering hole of renown in the 1960s and '70s.

and social upheaval wrought by the anti-war, civil rights, environmental and women's rights movements, all of which stoked the fires of the turbulent '60s. After spreading across the Mainland, these issues soon found expression in the Islands. The radios and television sets that brought Hawai'i *I Love Lucy* and *American Bandstand* also began flooding local living rooms with images of Selma and Saigon, Woodstock and Wounded Knee.

By the 1970s, the nation's profound reassessment of its most basic beliefs and institutions had led to important corollary developments in Hawai'i. The Protect Kaho'olawe 'Ohana, for example, sought to end U.S. military bombing of the island of Kaho'olawe, while an assortment of grassroots organizations protested the eviction of pig farmers from Kalama Valley, taro farmers from Waiahole Valley, and longtime residents from communities in downtown Chinatown, Ota Camp in Waipahu, and Nukoli'i on Kaua'i, to name a few. Local environmental groups Save Our Surf and Life of the Land organized campaigns to curb development that they viewed as detrimental to the Islands' ecology.

One of the most compelling cultural milestones of this era was the successful launching of *Hōkūle'a* in 1975 by the Polynesian Voyaging Society. The traditional double-hulled canoe was widely embraced

as a powerful symbol of pride in the abilities of ancient Polynesians to navigate long ocean voyages. Meanwhile, events such as the Merrie Monarch Festival (1963), King Kamehameha Hula and Chant Competition (1973) and Prince Lot Hula Festival (1977) celebrated the revival of traditional hula.

In Hawai'i, this social and cultural revolution inspired a burning curiosity about and appreciation for one's roots and culture, regardless of a person's race or ethnicity. Students at the University of Hawai'i at Mānoa succeeded in establishing an Ethnic Studies Program in 1970. The program encouraged the practice of recording oral histories of working-class people, in keeping with its slogan, "Our History, Our Way."

Alex Haley's *Roots*, which aired as a television miniseries in 1977, further fanned the firestorm of interest in ethnic history and family genealogies. Ethnic diversity was celebrated by such arts organizations as Temari: Center for Asian and Pacific Arts

(1979), which focused on teaching traditional arts and crafts; Cane Haul Road (1977), which designed and printed T-shirts with clever local images and phrases; Talk Story, Inc. (1977) and Bamboo Ridge Press (1978), which encouraged the development of local literature; and Kumu Kahua Theatre (1971), which

THE LEGEND OF KUHIO GRILL

There are many dining establishments across Hawai'i, now gone, that are fondly remembered by kama'āina. Only a few, however, will ever assume the legendary status attributed to the Kuhio Grill in Mō'ili'ili. A modest family restaurant by day, at night Kuhio Grill was transformed into a bustling pub or izakaya—in Japan, a bar serving food to accompany drinks—revered by legions of students who attended the University of Hawai'i at Mānoa between the late 1940s and 1979.

There were neighborhood regulars who frequented the joint, but it was mainly UH dormitory residents, most from the Neighbor Islands and rural O'ahu, and student-athletes who found sustenance and intellectual stimulation in the endless bottles of cold beer and plates full of tasty pūpū that packed "KGs" nearly every night.

In a rite of passage, students made the pilgrimage down either of two decrepit wooden stairwells that hugged the cliff separating Upper Campus from "the Quarry." Now known as Lower Campus, the Quarry wasn't hard to navigate, being just an unpaved, often flooded, parking lot, grass playing fields, a track and a smattering of portable buildings. The intrepid students ventured past the makai campus gate and athletic dormitory, down a darkened Kalo Lane and finally through the creaky back door and bustling kitchen of the restaurant. For many, it felt like coming home.

Kuhio Grill was the creation of Mark Kamemori Miyashiro, a hardworking immigrant from Okinawa who had come to Hawai'i in 1917. Miyashiro got into the restaurant business, operating the Aloha Coffee Shop in downtown Honolulu, then the Olympic Grill on Ala Moana Boulevard. In 1944, he purchased a building in Mōili'ili and converted a market and flower shop into Kuhio Grill. The restaurant was expanded in 1949 to seat approximately 100 customers and employed up to nine waitresses in its heyday. Murakami's nephews, Kinji and Charlie Miyashiro, took over the operation in 1967. Murakami himself visited the restaurant regularly until his passing in 1973 at the age of 72.

Kuhio Grill served mainly American food, starting with breakfast at 6 a.m. Its lunch and dinner menus included such dishes as hamburger steak, veal cutlet, beef stew, shrimp tempura, liver and onions, beef tomato, and occasional Hawaiian specialties.

But the magic of KGs was that it stayed open until 1 or 2 a.m., operating on a concept that appeared deceptively simple on its surface: Patrons bought their drinks and the waitresses provided complimentary pūpū. That was it in a nutshell. What a waitress served was left entirely to her discretion and could range from less-costly "house" pūpū all the way to such delicacies as fried chicken, steak, shrimp tempura and sashimi. Musubi (rice balls) instantly turned the plates of pūpū into a full-blown meal.

This system of service relied on the premise that customers would account for the food that was served to them and leave an appropriate tip at the end of the evening. Even after paying a proper tip, the meal and drinks were still a great bargain. Of course, the more generous the tip, the better the impression the customers left on their waitress. So, intending to return time and again, treating waitresses as friends rather than servants and tipping them well as a way of saying "thank you" assured customers of good service and lots of good, high-grade pūpū. For the students who understood the importance of relationships, it all added up to their best—and in some cases, only—meal of the day.

Over time, however, the Kuhio Grill crowd changed. Word got around that you could get a "free" meal at KGs by simply ordering a beer or wine cooler, eat all of the great pūpū and leave without tipping for the food. Waitresses grew more guarded as to what they served and to whom. Nevertheless, Kuhio Grill maintained its free pūpū policy until it closed in 1979.

More than the food it served, the real reason that Kuhio Grill lingers in our collective memory is what it represented in the way of local culture and values. These days, dozens of popular drinking places serve food—good food—which customers order from pūpū menus with prices clearly listed. It's a whole new world. Patrons never ordered what they wanted to eat at KGs. That would have been considered rude, because technically there was no pūpū menu to order from. It's as if one stopped by a friend's house for a few beers and started ordering food. Customers might hope to have certain dishes served to them, but that was up to the waitress to decide. The pūpū were like a gift, a friendly gesture on the waitresses' part that also signaled a leap of faith that patrons were akamai (knowledgeable) enough about local ways not to stiff them for the cost of the food they ordered in the kitchen on their behalf. It was all about reciprocity and trust, a system more in keeping with yesterday's Hawai'i.

ZIPPY'S: A MIXED PLATE OF TRADITION AND INNOVATION

In an informal email poll, college students from Hawai'i attending schools on the Mainland were asked, "Where is the last place you go to eat when you're leaving Hawai'i?" and "Where is the first place you go to eat when you return?" The poll resulted in a list of diverse places, but the clear winner—not surprisingly—was Zippy's. While many longtime local establishments struggle to survive, Zippy's has evolved from its origins as a single McCully area eatery in 1966 to a chain of 24 restaurants in 2009. Founded by brothers Charles and Francis Higa, Zippy's has thrived on a simple-yet-effective formula melding tradition and innovation.

Charles (right), who continued to lead the company after Francis' death in 1999, reflects on his family's humble roots with great appreciation. His father, Yeiko Higa, worked at a Chinese market, while his mother, Kameko, stayed home to raise the couple's four boys. They ate what they could get back then, Charles explained. His father brought home less-than-premium items like pork fat, beef tongue, pig's feet or chicken feet from his job at the market. There was enough room behind their Nu'uanu house for the boys to raise goats, rabbits and chickens. "All parts of the animal were used," Charles said. And, always, a little meat was mixed with lots of vegetables to stretch what they had. "All kinds of soup," Charles recalled. "Chicken soup … goat soup …" Rather than shame or regret, Charles said, "I feel glad that I had such a background. I think we were fortunate, really, because today's kids didn't go through that. I think it makes you strive to do better."

In 1946, his father purchased the market he

worked for and started Higa Market, a wholesale meat and pork distributor still in operation today. Working with their father and brothers, however, it was apparent to Charles and Francis that the family business could not support all of them and their growing families. After briefly considering a carwash, they decided to open a drive-in restaurant with a saimin stand in back—naming it Zippy's after the still-new U.S. ZIP code system.

According to Charles, their business plan was simple: Serve good, straightforward local food, such as beef stew, saimin, hamburger curry, chili, fried chicken and teriyaki beef at reasonable prices. Charles credits his wife, Helen (above), for her work on the menu items, and chef Shiro Matsuo for helping them during the all-important start-up period. Keeping the restaurant open 24 hours a day since they started, Charles and Francis took turns running

the operation around the clock, getting little sleep and limited time with their families.

In addition to hard work and good food, Zippy's success over the years has also hinged on its ability to adapt to changing times—freely adding and removing menu items as customers' tastes dictated. "Older folks concerned about high blood pressure and diabetes wanted healthier, low-sodium menu items," Charles explained, "and more fish, like salmon. Young folks' tastes change—and they can eat whatever they like."

Still, Zippy's success is fueled by the enduring popularity of its core menu items, led by its chili and fried chicken. Charles—who recently handed over the reins of the company to his nephew, Jason Higa—believes in trying new things. He tweaked and updated as basic an item as the restaurants' teriyaki sauce, because he had never been completely satisfied with it over the years. Even Zippy's famous chili—all 220,000 pounds of it served each month—can now be enjoyed with or without beans, with turkey and even vegetarian-style. A significant portion of Zippy's chili is sold online and shipped off to displaced Islanders overseas.

Charles "craves the foods that he grew up with," said Helen, who admits that it took her a little while early in their marriage to learn how to cook her husband's favorite foods. Perhaps that is one thing that has helped Zippy's to keep the old—oxtail soup, local-style beef stew (with soupy gravy) and Zip Pac bentos—along with the new throughout the years. "It's perfect for families," Helen said of Zippy's menu. "There really is something for everyone."

▶▶▶ ▶▶▶ ▶▶▶ ▶▶▶ ▶▶▶ ▶▶▶ ▶▶▶

At the Polynesian Palace ca. 1980, Jonathan Winters, James Brolin, Clint Eastwood, Lee Majors and Farrah Fawcett are wined and dined at the Don Ho Show, Waikīkī's biggest draw for decades.

provided a venue for local playwrights and actors.

Chinese Hot Pot

My dream of America
Is like dá bìn lòuh
With people of all persuasions
and tastes
sitting down around a common pot
chopsticks and basket scoops
here and there
some cooking squid and others beef
some tofu or watercress
all in one broth

like a stew that really isn't
as each one chooses
what he wishes to eat
only that the pot and fire are shared
along with the good company
and the sweet soup
spooned out at the end of the meal.
—Wing Tek Lum

Music and entertainment blossomed, with major live events as diverse as the Diamond Head Crater Festival (1970) and Kanikapila (1970), to such '70s hotbeds of live local music as the Territorial Tavern,

Rainbow Villa, The Sty, Chuck's Cellar, Black Angus, Oceania Floating Restaurant, Toppe Ada Shop, Kojak's and the Gold Coin.

Local humor—much of it delivered in pidgin English—exploded in popularity during this period, thanks to the creative efforts of Booga Booga, Mel Cabang, Rap Reiplinger, Frank DeLima and Andy Bumatai. To the delight of audiences, the humor often made it a point to target Mainland-influenced "American" culture as the butt of its jokes, while proudly championing a local Hawai'i lifestyle as

▶▶▶ ▶▶▶ ▶▶▶ ▶▶▶ ▶▶▶ ▶▶▶ ▶▶▶

In 1948, Irish immigrant Maurice Sullivan opened Foodland at Market City in Kaimuki, the first in a chain of more than 114 stores in Hawai'i and on the Mainland, including Foodland, Sack N Save, Food Pantry and Kalama Beach Corp. Sullivan also opened Hawai'i's first McDonald's franchise in 1967.

being "mo' bettah," superior.

In time, people began calling this outpouring of political, cultural and artistic energy the Hawaiian Renaissance. It is fair to say that the Renaissance did not affect everyone in the same way. Instead of consensus, the times invited debate, offered variety and encouraged choice. While some donned denim jeans and tie-dyed tank tops, others gravitated to wearing slick polyester Angel Flights and making the scene at popular '70s discos like the Point After, Hula Hut, Sting, Infinity, Spats, C'est Si Bon, Bobby McGee's, Oasis, Tiki's, La Mancha and Foxy Lady Too.

This much is certain, however. The Renaissance did touch everyone, regardless of their political persuasion or taste in music, whether or not they were consciously engaged in it. The times promulgated an attitude and a mindset that affected how even the most commonplace things were viewed—what people wore, or what they ate. T-shirts, tank tops, rubber slippers and palaka shirts and shorts best expressed the casual, unpretentious local style. Palaka, a sturdy plaid fabric that was widely used in the plantation era, came to represent one's local roots and was popular with politicians and entertainers of

the time.

In a similar fashion, local foods—from shave ice, malasadas, SPAM™ musubi, li hing-flavored snacks and loco moco to Okinawan andagi doughnuts—were viewed as more than just food; they were symbols of what made Hawai'i unique. Local foodways were so important that people even sang tributes to them, as in the Ka'au Crater Boys' rendition of "He 'Ono" ("Delicious"), composed by Bina Mossman:

Shooa me ka beef stew,
heavy on the extra salad
Two scoops rice on a hamburger bun
Hot dog, kim chee, chili peppa water
Akule, aku, mahimahi sandwich
Top it all off with the Kikkoman shoyu
He 'ono toumi ta ho'i tau
i to pu'u te momoni aku
Manapua, manapua, pepeiao, okole.
A he 'ono no

Whether one had spent the evening doing the Hustle at a flashy dance hall or listening to political speeches, most everyone later adjourned to one of many popular late-night eateries such as Like Like Drive In, McCully Chop Suey or Tin Tin Chop Suey, to slurp down a bowl of saimin, won ton min or sam see mein.

During the Hawaiian Renaissance, of course, Hawai'i people did more than just celebrate long-popular

CLASSIC HOME COOKING

Beef Tomato
Serves 4-6

Marinade
2 tsp.	shoyu
2 tsp.	sugar
1 tsp.	wine
1 tsp.	cornstarch
2 Tbsp.	oil
1"	piece ginger, crushed
1 clove	garlic, crushed

1 lb.	beef (sirloin, round, etc.), thinly sliced

Gravy
1 tsp.	cornstarch
1 tsp.	shoyu
1 Tbsp.	ketchup
2 tsp.	sugar
½ tsp.	Worcestershire sauce

2 Tbsp.	oil, divided
2	stalks celery, sliced diagonally
3-4	green peppers, cut in wedges
½	onion, cut in wedges
3-4	tomatoes, cut in wedges
1	green onion, cut in 2" lengths

Mix marinade ingredients together in a large bowl. Add beef and marinate for 30 minutes. Mix gravy ingredients in a separate bowl and set aside.

Heat 1 Tbsp. oil in wok or deep frying pan. Stir-fry onion, celery and green pepper until almost cooked. Add tomatoes and cook 1 minute. Remove vegetables to a bowl. Using the same pan, heat 1 Tbsp. oil and cook beef, with marinade, until medium rare. Remove garlic and ginger. Add vegetables, green onions and gravy and bring to a quick boil, then remove from heat.

Chop Steak & Vegetables
Serves 4-6

¼ c.	shoyu
3 Tbsp.	sugar
1 Tbsp.	sherry or other wine
1 clove	garlic, crushed
1"	piece ginger, crushed
3½ Tbsp.	oil, divided

2	stalks celery, sliced diagonally
2	bell peppers, sliced
1	large sweet round onion, sliced
1 lb.	beef (flap meat, sirloin, flank, etc.), thinly sliced
	Black pepper, to taste

In a small bowl, combine shoyu, sugar and sherry. In a wok or frying pan, brown garlic and ginger in ½ Tbsp. oil and add to shoyu mixture. In same pan, heat 1 Tbsp. of oil in and stir-fry celery, green peppers and onion.

Pour approximately half the sauce over the vegetables and cook until half done. Remove from pan. Heat remaining oil and brown beef in it; add remaining sauce and cook until medium rare. Add the vegetables and stir-fry until cooked. Season with black pepper, if desired.

➤➤➤ ➤➤➤ ➤➤➤ ➤➤➤ ➤➤➤ ➤➤➤ ➤➤➤

Local food to go is always the daily special at Hawai'i lunchwagons like Haili's in Honolulu, run by sisters Donna Pang, Lorraine Haili-Alo and Rachel Haili, and Hanalei Taro and Juice Co. on Kaua'i, owned by Lyndsey Haraguchi-Nakayama and Brad Nakayama.

ethnic foods; the local palate also continued to expand. The Immigration Act of 1965 particularly paved the way for new Asian immigrants, which in turn increased the number and type of ethnic foods and ethnic restaurants in Hawai'i. New arrivals from Taiwan and northern China, for example, led to a boost in popularity of Mandarin, Szechuan and other regional cuisine. Winter Garden, considered the first northern Chinese restaurant in Honolulu, opened at Kahala Mall in 1969. By the late '70s, waves of other Asian immigrants had boosted the popularity of foods from the Philippines, Vietnam, Korea and Thailand. In 1977, restaurateur Keo Sananikone opened the Mekong, followed by the immensely popular Keo's restaurant in Kapahulu in 1981.

In Hawai'i as well as on the Mainland, the growing popularity of health foods—now more than just "hippie" fare—also continued to grow and spread its appeal across a wider demographic spectrum. Maintaining that Americans needed to get back in touch with nature, devotees of the so-called health food movement espoused eliminating preservatives and replacing the processed foods in their diet with foods eaten in their more natural state—granola, soybeans, bean sprouts, yogurt, vegetarian chili, guacamole and whole grain bread. To meet the demand for healthy goods, food cooperatives such as Kokua Country Foods, founded in Hawai'i in 1970, grew in popularity and mainstream appeal.

In fact, the boom in natural and

vegetarian dishes continued through the '70s, these foods eventually finding their way onto the menus of many popular restaurants and food columns in major magazines and newspapers. Some of the country's biggest food manufacturers began putting out their own "natural" and organic products, such as granola and "home-style" breads, to capitalize on the bandwagon. In this way, the food of the 1970s, while perhaps not extremely glamorous or memorable in itself, did help plant the seeds of the budding regional cuisine movement, with its emphasis on fresh, natural, locally produced ingredients.

In contrast to the earnest, well-meaning food of the '70s, gourmet cooking became immensely popular across the country in the follow-

KAU KAU
CONNECTION

LOCO MOCO:
ODE TO A SUPERSTAR

It's indeed a rare honor when you can claim to have a personal relationship with a legend—sort of like saying you grew up with Elvis. That's one reason why I consider myself so lucky to have grown up in Hilo, home of the internationally acclaimed loco moco. Today my childhood friends and I can look back and reflect proudly on how we were able to enjoy, in person, the now-iconic bowl of plate lunch perfection—rice, hamburger, egg and gravy—well before the rest of the world was even aware of it.

It is an even greater source of pride that our loco mocos were the real deal, in the sense that they came from what is widely considered the home of the loco moco—the Graceland of loco mocos, to continue the Elvis analogy—Cafe 100.

Like all legends, a trace of intrigue surrounds the origins of the loco moco. The mystery was first raised in an article written in 2006 by the late *Honolulu Advertiser* columnist Bob Krauss, who retold a story about hamburger, rice and gravy being served "more than 50 years ago" at the now long-defunct Lincoln Grill in Hilo. According to Krauss' source, the restaurant owners, Nancy and Richard Inouye, dubbed their dish "loco moco."

Mystery? Perhaps. Controversy? No. Current Cafe 100 owner Gail Miyashiro (right, with mother Evelyn) does not dispute the tale. "My father never claimed to have invented the loco moco," she said. "It was probably created at a neighborhood diner (e.g., Lincoln Grill)

by teenaged boys and working men looking for a cheap and filling meal they could eat on the go." What Miyashiro does know for a fact is that her father, Richard, founded Cafe 100 in 1946 shortly after he returned from fighting in World War II with the 100th Infantry Battalion in Europe—naming his restaurant after his proud fighting unit. He then began serving his signature loco moco—with an egg—around 1949.

You have to have an egg. There is a huge, Kīlauea Crater-sized gap between a plain bowl of hamburger, rice and gravy and a true loco moco with an egg. Saying that the egg came later is akin to saying that you invented baseball—but without bases or foul lines.

It is the egg, after all, that sets the loco moco apart from the simply mundane and catapults it into the realm of Kau Kau Hall of Fame genius. You start with a generous bed

of steaming-hot white rice. Add a homemade hamburger patty, fried so that the juices are still dribbling out of it. Gently slide an egg onto the burger so its yolk (sunny-side-up or over-easy) does not break until you're ready to eat it. Cover the whole concoction with brown gravy. Break the yolk so that it oozes down into the hamburger juices and brown gravy. Together, the yolk and juices and gravy cascade down into the starchy depths of the rice, filling every nook and cranny and completing the exquisite symphony of flavors that is the joy of loco moco. Of course, many aficionados like to punch up their loco mocos with ketchup, shoyu, Worcestershire or a dash of Tabasco—all conveniently laid out at the Cafe 100 counter.

Some of us have mixed emotions as we watch the loco moco rise to greater heights around the Islands, across the West Coast and even further. It is no longer uncommon to see Japanese tourists clutching their guidebooks as they make their way up to local drive-ins and coffee shops. My daughter has even sent me pictures of loco moco drive-ins in Japan.

I am swept by nostalgia as I remember the days of our youth when plate lunches were $1.50—which was just a tad above the hourly wage of the time, by the way. A loco moco was 75 cents. It was perfect as a "second serving" for growing boys for whom a regular plate lunch was not quite enough. It was also the perfect after-school snack to settle our rumbling stomachs and tide us over until dinner without filling us up. More substantial than a hamburger, lighter than a full plate lunch and completely 'ono, there's little wonder why the loco moco has catapulted to superstar status.

ing decade, and Hawai'i wasn't far behind. Extra virgin olive oil, balsamic vinegars and food processors became kitchen necessities. Williams-Sonoma became a national favorite, while local foodies rejoiced when Richard Field launched an upscale market in Kaimukī in 1977. Field later opened R. Field Wine Co. in the Ward Centre in the early '80s. Strawberry Connection made its debut in 1984 in Kalihi. In spite of an inconvenient location off Nimitz Highway, Strawberry quickly lured home-gourmets and notable professional chefs alike.

As people began using more esoteric imported ingredients, regional chefs and interest in local food remained part of the larger redefinition of things local, including a rekindled interest in and respect for tradition and a deeper appreciation of diversity and Hawai'i's multiethnic society. Change occurred and movements grew as much in reaction against unabated Americanization and the amalgamation of food as in favor of more localized regional cuisine.

Local people rejected the idea that Hawai'i's best hope lay in following the standards set by Mainland models. In the food industry, this translated into redefining what others thought Hawaiian food should look and taste like and what "fine dining" truly meant. One of the key byproducts of this movement was an

expression of pride in Hawai'i's ability to produce high-quality ingredients, rather than relying on frozen foods and other ingredients shipped or flown in from overseas. Just as it did in politics and the arts, the Renaissance inspired Hawai'i's cooks to take what they knew and elevate it to the highest levels of cuisine. It was time for Hawai'i's people to reclaim their special heritage—one with much to contribute to the rest of the world.

All of these seemingly disparate forces: the postwar influence of American-style foods and food establishments; a dominant European bias in Hawai'i's giant restaurant and resort industry; the trend toward using fresh, locally grown ingredients; and the deeply felt, emotional reassessment of Hawai'i's history and local culture known as the Hawaiian Renaissance were all brought together by a budding young generation of chefs who were learning their craft in the '70s.

Hawai'i Regional Cuisine

As celebrity chefs like Wolfgang Puck took the stars by storm in Hollywood and Paul Prudhomme made Cajun food the rage in New Orleans, a rising group of talented new chefs prepared to put themselves and Hawai'i on the culinary map. Hawai'i Regional Cuisine was a phrase that would gain substance and momentum in the '90s, but its roots are firmly

set in the changing beliefs and attitudes of the '60s and '70s, during the Hawaiian Renaissance.

An outstanding culinary arts program developed by Kapi'olani Community College (KCC) influenced many of these dynamic chefs. O'ahu North Shore product Sam Choy graduated from the KCC program in 1972; future James Beard Foundation Award winner Alan Wong graduated in 1979. Other distinguished KCC alumni include Russell Siu, Kelvin Ro and Glenn Chu. Still other influential chefs took different paths to perfect their trade. Colin Nishida, for example, broke into the restaurant business in 1972 as a dishwasher and cook at C's Diner in Kalihi. He then became a partner in a plate-lunch operation called Take's before opening his popular Side Street Inn bar and restaurant in 1992. In 1979, D.K. Kodama decided to take a break from his engineering studies at the University of Hawai'i by moving to Seattle, where he worked as a bartender before getting into cooking.

These and other homegrown chefs forged a powerful culinary alliance with more recent arrivals like Roy Yamaguchi, who graduated from the Culinary Institute of America in New York in 1976. Yamaguchi moved to Los Angeles in 1984 and opened Roy's in Hawai'i in 1988. Peter Merriman came to Hawai'i in 1983, Amy Ferguson Ota in 1985 and George

CHEF ROY YAMAGUCHI

After graduating from New York's Culinary Institute of America and opening the popular Los Angeles restaurant 385 North, Japan-born Roy Yamaguchi moved to Hawai'i and launched the chain of restaurants with which he would spread the Hawai'i Regional Cuisine message farther afield than any of the other HRC founding chefs—nearly 40 restaurants from Tampa to Tokyo. In 1988 he opened the very first Roy's in Hawai'i Kai, where his Seared Spicy Scallops (right) drew raves from the many devotees of his new fusion cuisine.

Seared Spicy Scallops with Marinated Japanese Vegetables
Serves 4

4 oz.	red kelp
4 oz.	green kelp
	Pinch of black sesame seeds
	Pinch of white sesame seeds
2 tsp.	rice wine vinegar
1 tsp.	sesame oil
1 Tbsp.	bamboo shoots, julienned
½	carrot, julienned
2" piece	gobo, julienned
2-3	stems watercress, cut in 1" pieces
½" piece	ginger root, minced
1 clove	garlic, minced
1 tsp.	shoyu
12	scallops
¼ tsp.	shichimi (Japanese 7-spice seasoning)
1 Tbsp.	peanut oil
2 oz.	golden caviar

Place red and green kelp in separate bowls. Add black and white sesame seeds and 1 tsp. vinegar to each bowl and mix; marinate 1 hour.

In a frying pan heat sesame oil and sauté bamboo shoots, carrots, gobo, watercress, ginger and garlic. Stir in shoyu. Remove from heat. Dust scallops on one side with shichimi and coat with peanut oil. In another frying pan, sauté scallops to desired doneness. To serve, arrange three scallops on each plate, alternating with mounds of green kelp, red kelp and Japanese vegetables. Place golden caviar in center of plate.

"Chef Mavro" Mavrothalassitis in 1988.

In her 1994 book, *The New Cuisine of Hawaii*, author Janice Wald Henderson forever immortalized chefs Sam Choy, Roger Dikon, Mark Ellman, Amy Ferguson Ota, Beverly Gannon, Jean-Marie Josselin, George Mavrothalassitis, Peter Merriman, Philippe Padovani, Gary Strehl, Alan Wong and Roy Yamaguchi as the pioneering co-founders of Hawai'i Regional Cuisine. These chefs first gathered in 1991 to address the still-lingering perception of the Islands as a food wasteland. The following year, the same dozen chefs founded a non-profit organization called Hawaii Regional Cuisine, Inc., "to promote and develop Hawaii Regional Cuisine to benefit everyone in Hawaii who works with local products." Although now defunct, the organization's namesake lives on—forever seared into the lexicon of local culinary history.

What exactly is Hawai'i Regional Cuisine, and how did it affect what we eat in Hawai'i? The main impetus behind its founding was to respond to the negative perceptions outsiders had of Island food. In her book, Janice Henderson noted that while all food in Hawai'i was not lousy, visitors were being subjected to lousy food. It was a perspective that was echoed by the HRC chefs who felt compelled to defend the integrity of their trade—as well as the honor of their home turf.

Up through the 1980s, … the joke was that the best food you'll get in Hawai'i is on the plane ride coming over here.
—Alan Wong

Consider the mission accomplished. Today, most visitors to Hawai'i are quickly made aware of Hawai'i Regional Cuisine and the high standards of the culinary arts throughout the Islands. In fact, negative perceptions of food in Hawai'i seem to have been effectively extinguished, with dining out now ranked on equal terms with shopping, surfing and sightseeing as visitor "musts."

Eating well is easy to do, really, for some form of very good food can be found in nearly every nook and cranny of every island these days—from small, intimate restaurants to big, exclusive resorts. Much of it bears the distinctive attributes of Hawai'i Regional Cuisine. Most notably, one of Hawai'i Regional Cuisine's first precepts was to showcase the high quality of locally produced ingredients. Many chefs now work closely with local farmers, fishermen and ranchers in order to obtain specialized ingredients, from sweet corn, hybrid tomatoes, fresh herbs and exotic specialty greens, to lamb, grass-finished beef, farm-raised fish and lobster, and specialties like goat cheese and lavender.

A key component to regional cuisine is its strong element of cre-ativity and the desire to experiment with exciting ways of utilizing both new and traditional ingredients.

My style is evolving. I like to experiment with flavors.
—Roy Yamaguchi

Hawai'i Regional Cuisine embraces an extremely personalized cooking philosophy and methodology. Each chef brings his or her family, education, travel and work experiences to the table. Some base their creations on an Asian foundation; others are more European. While terms such as Pacific Rim and fusion cuisine are sometimes used to describe the new blend of the 50th State's Polynesian, Asian, American and European food traditions, today's chefs resist being categorized by trendy labels.

"Dirty Mouths"

Chef Sam Choy once cautioned that it is not enough to simply take an Asian ingredient and give it a European sauce, or vice versa. That may be "fusion," but it is not Hawai'i Regional Cuisine, he insisted. In Choy's opinion, Hawai'i Regional Cuisine must maintain a more fundamental connection to the flavors and traditions of local food.

Even as Hawai'i Regional Cuisine snowballed in popularity in the '80s and '90s, however, its influ-

CHEF SAM CHOY

Born and raised on O'ahu's North Shore, Sam Choy cut his culinary teeth at the family restaurant in Lā'ie—Sam's Place, named for his father, Hung Sam Choy. After stints at the Hyatt Kuilima Resort and the Waldorf Astoria in New York, he went on to become one of the 12 founding chefs of Hawai'i Regional Cuisine, a celebrity with restaurants in Hawai'i, Guam and Japan. In the late 1980s, when he created this Shrimp Curry (right), he was executive chef of the Big Island's Kona Hilton Beach & Tennis Resort.

Shrimp Curry
Serves 4

1 lb.	shrimp (16-20 count)
6 Tbsp.	butter, divided
1	small onion, finely chopped
1 Tbsp.	curry powder
1 tsp.	sugar
½ tsp.	salt
¼ c.	flour
2 c.	heavy cream
1 c.	chicken stock
2 c.	tender-crisp cooked vegetables (a combination of celery, carrots and peas is good)
¼ tsp.	turmeric
	Salt and pepper, to taste

Peel, devein and rinse shrimp; set aside. In a heavy skillet, melt 2 Tbsp. butter and sauté onion and curry powder until onion is translucent. Add shrimp, sugar and salt; sauté 2 to 3 minutes. Remove shrimp from pan and set aside.

Melt remaining 4 Tbsp. butter in same pan; stir in flour and cook 5 minutes. Slowly add heavy cream and chicken stock, stirring constantly, until mixture is smooth and thick. Stir in shrimp, vegetables and turmeric. Season to taste with salt and pepper.

ence didn't always trickle down to the average diner's daily menu. The gap between Hawai'i Regional Cuisine and everyday local food could be attributed in part to cost. To use only the finest, freshest—and sometimes hard to get—ingredients pushed the cost of regional cuisine higher than what folks spent on their "local food." Elegantly designed and decorated restaurants situated in prime commercial locations added to the cost, as did the phalanx of well-trained employees needed to provide top-notch service. Fine-dining quality, of course, didn't come at plate lunch prices. Many local people couldn't afford to dine on the new regional cuisine, while others didn't feel comfortable in such fancy environments. Food writer Betty Fullard-Leo described the dichotomy between local food and Hawai'i Regional Cuisine this way:

Mention local food in Hawaii and people think of fish and poi, plate lunches with macaroni salad and rice, squid luau made with taro leaves, or poke made of raw fish and seaweed. Mention regional cuisine in the Islands and people picture exquisite plates of beautifully prepared food, incorporating the freshest of fish and produce, often with aromatic flavors of ginger, soy and garlic, or ingredients unique to Hawaii, perhaps fern shoots gathered in Waipio Valley, or goat cheese from the Puna District.

The impact of Hawai'i Regional Cuisine would grow over time, however, to inspire the general population to appreciate local foods and the deep traditions behind them, raise awareness to the creative possibilities of celebrating and utilizing fresh local ingredients, and emphasize the fact that local food is as good as any regional cuisine to be found anywhere in the world. Fullard-Leo continued:

As recently as 20 years ago, international gourmands would never have believed that pig and poi, shoyu and somen, dim sum and daikon could blend in Hawaii's melting pot to produce a regional cuisine as distinctive and delicious as the Creole or Southwestern styles found on the Mainland.

Although there are differences between Hawai'i Regional Cuisine and traditional local food, the two are connected in some very fundamental ways. Sam Choy maintains that when he worked and studied in New York, he felt he had a distinct advantage over his peers because his palate was so acclimatized to the entire range of flavors—Eastern, Western and everything in between—because people in Hawai'i grew up that way.

Lifelong exposure to that kind of variety is what has made people from Hawai'i so competitive in the food

business. By virtue of our cultural heritage, I believe our taste buds are naturally educated, extremely sensitized. I often say that Hawai'i people have "dirty mouths." What I mean by that is we have very sophisticated senses when it comes to taste; we really know the difference between what is good and what isn't.
—Sam Choy

David Cruz, a chef of Hawaiian, Japanese, German and Guamanian extraction, agrees with Choy that Island-born chefs—many, like Cruz and Choy, with multiethnic family backgrounds—have an advantage in integrating local flavors and cooking styles. In her article "Getting to the Roots of Hawaii Regional Cuisine," Betty Fullard-Leo quotes Cruz as saying, "When I was growing up, my mom experimented with every ethnic culture. There was no food that she didn't cook; so I grew up tasting all of these different kinds of foods and applying them to new things."

The relationship between everyday local food and Hawai'i Regional Cuisine is a complex one. They remain connected in some very fundamental ways, including their freedom and willingness to combine flavors and ingredients from different traditions, and a palate for taste that is as broad and as diverse as the people of Hawai'i.

Plain old local food, in other

CHEF PETER MERRIMAN

Pittsburgh-born Peter Merriman trained in Europe and the U.S., including the Four Seasons Hotel in Washington, D.C., before hiring on at the Mauna Lani Resort on the Big Island's Kōhala Coast, where he began developing close ties with producers of fresh local ingredients—Puna goat cheese, Lalamilo strawberries, salmon from the aquaculture farms of Keahole-Kona and many others. Since then he has carried this eat-local approach to the restaurants he operates throughout the Islands. The first of these was Merriman's in Waimea, opened in 1988, where he built a faithful clientele with specialties like Pizza Soup (right), made with tomatoes, onions and herbs supplied by neighboring farmers.

Pizza Soup
Serves 4

	Pizza dough *or*
1	loaf French or Italian bread
	Olive oil and anchovy paste for pizza rounds (optional)
1	onion, chopped
1	bell pepper, chopped
1 Tbsp.	olive oil
2 cloves	garlic, chopped
2 tsp.	basil
1 tsp.	oregano
1 tsp.	marjoram
½ tsp.	fennel seed
¼ tsp.	crushed red pepper
2	tomatoes, peeled, seeded and diced
¼ c.	tomato juice
1 qt.	chicken stock
	Salt and pepper, to taste
2 c.	grated cheese (combining provolone, Parmesan and Mozzarella is good)

Preheat oven to 350°F. If making pizza rounds, cut pizza dough to fit soup bowls. If making toast rounds, cut bread into slices. Brush with olive oil and anchovy paste, if desired. Bake rounds until golden brown. Bread may be toasted in a toaster oven instead.

In a frying pan sauté onion and bell pepper in oil. Add garlic, basil, oregano, marjoram, fennel seed and red pepper. Sauté briefly. Stir in tomatoes, tomato juice and chicken stock. Bring to a boil; reduce heat and simmer for 15 minutes. Adjust seasoning with salt and pepper.

Place rounds in bowls. Pour soup into bowls and sprinkle with grated cheese mixture.

words—no matter how humble its origins—can inspire the finest cuisine. Stuff that people in the Islands have enjoyed for generations is indeed worthy of such attention. Major supermarkets and localized farmers markets now offer a wide range of island-fresh goods. And family dinners, office potluck parties and football tailgate gatherings frequently include offerings as elegant as nori-wrapped macadamia nut-encrusted ahi. This is the true and lasting legacy of Hawai'i Regional Cuisine, the bold and imaginative flavors which now infuse and inspire the food of the masses.

The Power to Comfort

Enterprising young chefs like Elmer Guzman, another KCC graduate, herald a bright future for Hawai'i's evolving food scene. After receiving his culinary training at Kapi'olani Community College, Guzman began working for, and was mentored by, Alan Wong. Like Wong, he went on to complete an apprenticeship at the prestigious Greenbrier resort in West Virginia, and he later worked for Emeril Lagasse in New Orleans before returning to Hawai'i. Guzman became the executive chef at Sam Choy's Diamond Head restaurant before opening his own eatery in Waipahu—The Poke Stop.

As impressive as Guzman's resume may be, he honors his local

roots in the laid-back nature of his restaurant, his moderate prices and the esteem in which he holds his mother's traditional fish sabao soup. The sabao, in which whole fried fish are added to a broth flavored with ginger, garlic, onions and tomatoes, served with a bowl of rice, "brings back memories of my childhood, when my mom used this preparation to make a simple but soothing Filipino soup dish," Guzman explained.

"Simple but soothing"—one could not find a more precise definition of comfort food.

To be sure, food is inherently comforting in that it wards off hunger, but comfort foods are special in that they are imbued with unique—apparently paranormal—characteristics. They have the ability to whisk us home from far, far away; they can pick us up in a warm, healing embrace when we're feeling down; they can turn back the hands of time when life seems to be moving too swiftly, and they remind us of life's simple pleasures in a world grown too complex.

Soup, like Guzman's mother's fish sabao, is one of the most universal comfort foods in the world. All around the globe some kind of chicken soup, miso soup, bean soup, oxtail soup, jook (rice soup), tomato soup, noodle soup, vegetable soup, pig's feet soup or chowder heads the lists of comfort foods. Soup just seems naturally disposed to the role:

It is flavor; it is aroma; it is texture; it is instant warmth that fills the body and stimulates the brain.

Soups are also simple and economical to prepare, allowing families to stretch limited food budgets in order to feed a tablefull of hungry children. For many local families, fish soup could be created for next to nothing by anyone with a fishing pole, spear gun or fishing net and a vegetable garden. Stews and noodles also rank very high on the list of comfort foods. Almost anything associated with one's childhood—including cookies, milk and ice cream—certainly qualifies.

As in Guzman's example, even Hawai'i's most celebrated chefs often crave their favorite comfort foods over the fancy dishes they prepare for others. Side Street Inn—an unassuming restaurant-bar in Kaka'ako—is a favorite place for chefs like Alan Wong, Roy Yamaguchi, Russell Siu, Hiroshi Fukui and others to eat, drink and relax after work. Colin Nishida, Side Street's owner and chef, is famed for his local dishes such as poke, pork chops, chicken gizzards, smoked pork and fried rice. "It's comfort food," Fukui said. The food is "very local—it hits home," Wong observed. "People think chefs like to eat only fancy, very complex food; in reality, chefs look for very simple stuff." Siu agrees. "I don't eat at work," he says. "I usually pick up a plate of beef stew or something on my way home."

CHEF JEAN-MARIE JOSSELIN

It's a long way from Neuilly, France—where Jean-Marie Josselin was born—to Kapa'a, Kaua'i, where he opened his first Hawai'i restaurant, A Pacific Café, in the late 1980s, following a stint at the Hotel Hana-Maui. After opening restaurants of the same name on O'ahu and Maui, he exported his Hawai'i Regional Cuisine to Las Vegas, where he launched his luxe 808 restaurant at Caesar's Palace. Among his popular appetizers at A Pacific Café: Pan-Fried Oysters with Scallion Sauce (right).

Pan-Fried Pacific Oysters with Scallion Sauce
Serves 4

20	Pacific oysters
1 c.	cornmeal
1 Tbsp.	curry powder
1 c.	white wine
2	shallots, chopped
4	mushrooms, sliced
1 c.	heavy cream
1 c.	unsalted butter
	Salt and pepper, to taste
½ c.	diced green onions
3 Tbsp.	vegetable oil
	Tobiko, for garnish

Remove oysters from shells. Rinse and reserve shells. Combine cornmeal and curry powder and dredge oysters.

In a saucepan combine white wine, shallots and mushrooms; bring to a boil and reduce by two thirds. Stir in heavy cream and reduce by two thirds again. Cut butter in small pieces and add gradually, whisking continuously. Season to taste with salt and pepper. Strain liquid into food processor or blender and add green onions; blend until smooth.

Fry oysters in vegetable oil for a few seconds, until lightly browned. Replace oysters in shells and top with sauce. Garnish with tobiko.

COMFORT FOOD, PLANTATION-STYLE

Sometimes, simpler is better. When they lived and worked at Waipahu Sugar Company, the Tokujo family could seldom afford to eat meat. When the family's second-eldest son, Roy, returned from college on the Mainland, he bought steak and asked his mother to cook it. His mother prepared the steak the way she knew best, which was to stretch the meat in order to feed the entire family.

Roy, who later established himself as one of Hawai'i's most successful entertainment and hospitality industry entrepreneurs, was initially dismayed when she took that nice, juicy steak and prepared what the family called "Japanese Hamburger." Since then, however, it has become a family favorite. Originally, cheaper cuts of meat were used, but as the family grew more affluent, more expensive cuts were included.

Hamburgers Tokujo Style demonstrates another way to stretch meat. Today, when these dishes and other family favorites are prepared, it is occasion for the entire extended Tokujo clan to get together and enjoy this plantation-inspired comfort food.

In the following recipes, the amount of meat is not specified. The original assumption was that one would buy as much meat as one could afford; nowadays, individual taste can determine the protein-to-starch ratio.

Japanese Hamburger

	Steak, cut in small pieces
2	potatoes, cut in matchstick strips
1	onion, cut in matchstick strips
2	eggs, beaten
6 Tbsp.	flour, or as needed for consistency
	Salt and pepper
	Vegetable oil for deep-frying

Mix all ingredients in a large bowl. The consistency will be sticky. Form mixture into gobs approximately the size of an egg, making sure at least one piece of steak is in each gob. Deep-fry until golden brown.

Hamburgers Tokujo Style

	Hamburger
1-2	potatoes, grated
1	onion, diced
	Leftover bread, as much as necessary for consistency, soaked in milk or water and crumbled smooth

Mix all ingredients well. Form into patties and pan-fry.

Tofu Umbusa

Tofu, cut in cubes
Green onions, chopped
Hondashi, to taste
Salt and pepper, to taste

Mix all ingredients together in a pot and heat.

Fried Somen

1 pkg.	somen
1 Tbsp.	vegetable oil
	Salt and pepper, to taste
	Green onions, thinly sliced

Cook somen according to package directions. Drain and lightly fry, seasoning with salt and pepper as needed. Serve sprinkled with green onions.

When asked what his idea of comfort food was, the Japan-born Yamaguchi replied, "A dish called ochazuke. It's a seared filet of salmon, served in a broth over rice flavored with green tea and nori. In Japan, we think of it as a hangover cure."

The salmon ochazuke that Yamaguchi serves at his Roy's restaurants is a popular—albeit somewhat formalized—take on this dish. For most Hawai'i folks of Japanese descent, ochazuke is simply made by pouring hot tea over a bowl of leftover rice. The beauty of the dish lies in its simplicity, which seemingly allows it to balance or absorb overly rich food—or even alcohol—in one's system. For this reason, in Japan, ochazuke is often served as the final course after an elaborate meal, as a late-night snack or, as Yamaguchi points out, as a hangover cure.

Ochazuke follows the enduring food formula of complementing the blandness of the rice and tea with flavorful, often salty, side dishes. There are ready-made ochazuke seasonings—individually sealed packets of dried nori (seaweed), ume (pickled plum) or katsuoboshi (dried bonito)—to simply sprinkle over the rice. Or, in the absence of a filet of salmon, other local side dishes might include any sort of leftovers; hot dogs, Vienna sausage, canned corned beef or SPAM™ cooked with shoyu and sugar; fried, dried or smoked fish; or

SAIMIN: THE ULTIMATE COMFORT FOOD?

Saimin Broth
Makes 8 servings.

1 c.	dried shrimp
5	dried shiitake mushrooms
1	thumb-sized piece fresh ginger
1	small sheet dashi konbu (dried kelp)
2 qts.	water
1 tsp.	Hawaiian salt, or more to taste
1 tsp.	monosodium glutamate (MSG or ajinomoto)

Bring all ingredients except Hawaiian salt and MSG to a boil. Lower heat and simmer, covered, about 2 hours. Add Hawaiian salt and MSG. To serve, add cooked saimin noodles and desired condiments, such as strips of scrambled egg or slices of roast pork or luncheon meat.

Fried Saimin

1 bag	saimin noodles
	Char siu, sliced, to taste
	Green onions, minced, to taste
	Kamaboko, sliced, to taste
	Dashi no moto or powdered saimin soup base, to taste
1 Tbsp.	vegetable oil, or more to taste

Boil noodles, drain and rinse in cold water. Heat oil in a frying pan, then add char siu, green onions, kamaboko and noodles. Stir fry for about a minute. Add dashi no moto or soup base, mix well and fry for another minute. Since saimin can be such a personal thing, all quantities are approximate.

"Saimin" is a contraction of the Chinese words "sai" (thin) and "mein" (noodle). Saimin noodles are unique in that they contain eggs and are curly and slightly chewy when cooked. The popular staple (see photo page ii) dates back to the plantation era, when it cost 10 cents for a large bowl, 5 cents for a small one, at Waipahu's Shiroma Saimin stand in the 1930s. Saimin is served alongside hot dogs and burgers throughout the Islands—only in Hawai'i is it found on the menu at Jack in the Box and McDonald's. Hamura's Saimin Stand on Kaua'i was even recognized by the prestigious James Beard Foundation as one of America's Classics in 2006.

a variety of pickles ranging from Japanese takuan to Korean kim chee.

The true power of comfort food, however, has more to do with context than it does with content. It has more to do, in other words, with the love that permeated one's family's kitchen than the freshly baked cookies and cold glass of milk enjoyed there, or the comfort of being nursed back to health rather than the curative properties of soup itself, or the company of old childhood friends rather than the

drive-ins frequented with them.

We need to eat to survive—it is a basic human instinct. But, beyond that, food unites people in intimate ways. Comfort food, especially, and the memories it triggers in us, provides an emotional—even spiritual—power to connect people from different geographic, economic and ethnic backgrounds into families, communities, cultures. It has the power to bind us as human beings in its universal embrace. ◙

CHAPTER SIX

A Boundless Buffet

What Price Progress?

The pace of change in the Islands only accelerates with time. These days, the final roll call of those who comprised the Greatest Generation is recorded in the obituary pages of the daily newspapers. Even baby boomers, who stormed the '60s and '70s with an indomitable spirit of rebellion and innovation, now teeter on the threshold of retirement. And, besides bidding aloha to the departed loved ones in our lives, longtime Hawai'i residents also lament the closure of many longtime local businesses— mom-and-pop general stores, hole-in-the-wall restaurants, shave ice stands, neighborhood bakeries and okazu-ya—which occur with alarming regularity.

Most closures are attributable to financial reasons, such as a drop in business, increase in operating costs, expiration of leases or redevelopment, while other owners simply want to retire and have no heirs to take over. With the loss of people and places that link the past with the present, memories of the war and plantation life in Hawai'i grow slightly dimmer with each passing day.

Longtime local favorites like Tasty Broiler, which served fresh seafood across Nimitz Highway from Honolulu Harbor, are now preserved only in memory or in nostalgic artwork like this painting by Honolulu artist Doug Young. Below: Plate lunch fare at the Kapi'olani Community College Farmers Market

>>> >>> >>> >>> >>> >>> >>>

Chef Elmer Guzman (right, with parrotfish), Kapi'olani Community College graduate and owner of The Poke Stop, developed a culinary niche market in preparing fresh Island fish. Among them:

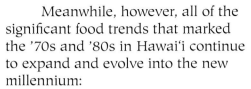

1. *Mū (big-eye emperor)*
2. *'A'awa (Hawaiian hogfish)*
3. *Ōmilu (bluefin trevally)*
4. *White ulua (giant trevally)*
5. *Toau (blacktail snapper)*
6. *Uhu uliuli (speckled parrotfish)*

1.

2.

3.

4.

5.

6.

Meanwhile, however, all of the significant food trends that marked the '70s and '80s in Hawai'i continue to expand and evolve into the new millennium:

- "American" influences from the Mainland cast an ever-more-dominant shadow over local foodways.
- Pride in Hawaiian culture and local identity finds expression across the Pacific Ocean.
- Eating healthy is more than a fad; it is a way of life.
- Hawai'i Regional Cuisine—and its emphasis on locally grown ingredients—gains greater traction and interest with each passing year.

Parts of Hawai'i are starting to look a lot like the Mainland, with a commercial landscape dominated by well-capitalized corporate giants such as Walmart, Costco, Sam's Club, K Mart, Safeway, Walgreens, Home Depot, Lowe's, Sears, Target, Sports Authority, Office Depot, Office Max and Best Buy. In addition to meeting the growing demands of local consumers, these and other nationally known companies enjoy a high brand-recognition factor among Hawai'i's visitors and large military population.

The same holds true of major Mainland food franchises, which continue to expand their presence in Hawai'i's major malls, resort properties and entertainment centers. The ranks of longtime businesses such as Dairy Queen, McDonalds, Burger King, Jack in the Box, Wendy's, Sizzler's, Taco Bell, Kentucky Fried Chicken and Pizza Hut have been joined by Arby's, Carl's Jr., Subway, Quizno's, Ruby Tuesdays, TCBY, Cold Stone Creamery, Chili's, Denny's, IHOP, Starbucks, California Pizza Kitchen, Coffee Bean & Tea Leaf, Seattle's Best and Jamba Juice. This growth has been so extensive that it would appear entirely possible for an individual or family in Hawai'i to dine out for weeks without ever stepping into a locally owned dining establishment and not even be aware of it.

Saturating the media with sophisticated national marketing campaigns, these large Mainland enterprises hold an especially strong

Pan-Fried Toau (Blacktail Snapper) with Fried Garlic-Edamame Sauce and Pea Shoot Salad
Serves 4-6

8   toau fillets (10 oz. each)
            Salt and pepper, to taste
            Seasoned flour (see recipe),
            as needed
1 c.   vegetable oil

Season toau with salt and pepper and lightly dredge in seasoned flour. Heat oil in a large frying pan over high heat. Sear fillets for 3 minutes on each side. Place fillets on individual plates and drizzle with garlic-edamame sauce (see recipe). Top with pea shoot salad (see recipe).

Seasoned Flour
2 c.   flour
1 c.   cornstarch
½ Tbsp.   salt
1 Tbsp.   Chef E Spice (see recipe below.
            Also available at The Poke Stop in
            Waipahu.)

Combine all ingredients. This will make more than you need, but it can be stored in a tightly closed container in the freezer.

Chef E Spice
½ c. minus 4 tsp. iodized salt
Scant ¼ c. paprika
1½ tsp.   cayenne
2½ Tbsp. ground black pepper
2½ Tbsp. granulated garlic
1½ Tbsp. onion powder

¼ c.   dried oregano
¼ c.   dried thyme
2 tsp.   togarashi (Japanese seasoning)

Combine all ingredients. This will make more than you need, but it can be saved in a tightly closed container and is very useful.

Fried Garlic-Edamame Sauce
1 Tbsp.   chopped garlic
1 Tbsp.   oil
5 Tbsp.   shoyu
1 Tbsp.   oyster sauce
1 lb.   unsalted butter, cut in chunks
            Shelled, boiled edamame, to taste

In a small frying pan, fry garlic in oil until crisp and golden brown. Combine shoyu and oyster sauce in a saucepan. Simmer until reduced by a third. Slowly whisk in butter until incorporated. Sprinkle with fried garlic and edamame.

Pea Shoot Salad
¼ lb.   fresh pea shoots
            (available at farmers markets)
            Red onion, thinly sliced, to taste
6-8   grape tomatoes, halved
1 pkg.   enoki mushrooms
            Balsamic vinaigrette, to taste (whisk
            3-4 parts vegetable oil with 1 part
            balsamic vinegar)
2 Tbsp.   grated Parmesan cheese

Combine vegetables in a bowl and toss with vinaigrette to coat slightly. Sprinkle with Parmesan cheese.

Eggplant and Zucchini Soufflé with Tomato Sauce
Serves 4-6

1	round eggplant
	Olive oil
2 lbs.	zucchini
	Table salt
½ c.	mascarpone cheese
¼ c.	shredded Parmesan cheese
2	eggs, beaten
2 tsp.	onion powder
2 tsp.	granulated garlic
	Kosher salt, to taste
	Pinch of white pepper
4	long Japanese eggplants
1 c.	tomato sauce (see recipe)
1 Tbsp.	butter
	Large pinch of fresh herbs
	Fresh rosemary stalks, for garnish

Preheat oven to 350°F. Cut round eggplant in half and score the flesh. Lightly oil and place cut side down on a baking sheet; bake about 30 minutes, or until soft. Remove from oven and let cool. Scrape the meat from the skin with a spoon and purée in a blender. Run purée through a strainer to remove the seeds and set aside. Do not turn oven off.

While eggplant is baking, cut zucchini into quarters lengthwise and remove seeds. Shred zucchini, place in a strainer and sprinkle with salt. Squeeze out excess water and set aside.

In a large mixing bowl, combine eggplant purée, shredded zucchini, mascarpone, Parmesan, eggs, onion powder, granulated garlic, kosher salt and white pepper; mix well. Chill in refrigerator until ready to use.

With a mandolin or slicer, thinly slice long egg-plant. Lay slices on a baking sheet, lightly oil and place in oven for a few minutes, until soft enough to shape in molds. When eggplant is cool, lightly oil the insides of six 8-oz. ramekins and arrange sliced eggplant inside with both ends draped evenly over the edge, until the ramekins are covered with one layer. Fill ramekins with souf-flé mixture, leaving an ⅛" lip. Fold the hanging eggplant slices over the top to cover the mixture.

Place the soufflés in a 4"-deep pan and care-fully pour warm water into pan until it reaches halfway up ramekins' sides. Cover pan with foil and bake in oven for 1 hour or until the soufflé is set.

Measure out 1 cup of tomato sauce, reserv-ing the rest for another recipe. Stir in butter and herbs. Make a lake of sauce on each plate and set a soufflé in the middle of it. Garnish with a stem of fresh rosemary.

Tomato Sauce
This recipe makes more sauce than is needed for the soufflés, but it freezes well and is useful to have on hand.

1	small round onion, chopped
5 cloves	garlic, peeled and chopped
1 Tbsp.	olive oil
½ c.	white wine
1 tsp.	whole peppercorns
2	bay leaves
4 c.	whole peeled tomatoes (canned is fine), seeds squeezed out
1 Tbsp.	brown sugar
10	basil leaves
	Salt and pepper, to taste

In a saucepan over medium heat, sauté onion and garlic in vegetable oil until onion is trans-lucent, about 1 minute. Deglaze pan with white wine.

Tie peppercorns and bay leaves in a piece of cheesecloth and add to pot, along with toma-toes. Bring to a boil, add brown sugar and lower heat. Simmer for 30 minutes. Add basil and simmer 5 minutes more. Add salt and pepper and remove from heat.

Remove the sachet of peppercorns and bay leaves and discard; blend sauce in a blender until smooth.

appeal for young consumers, who will ultimately determine the future of food in Hawai'i.

Although there are no definitive lines explaining exactly who or what these younger generations are, they are most commonly referred to as Gen (Generation) X and Gen Y. For discussion purposes, Gen X-ers are generally described as being born between 1965 and the early '80s, which means they now range in age from their late 20s to middle 40s. Gen Y, meanwhile, is comprised of those born between the early '80s and early '00s, which means they range in age from under 10 to their late 20s today.

These two generations share much in common, differing largely in terms of degree. Both are technologically savvy, for example, with Gen X-ers growing up in front of the television watching *Sesame Street*, eating microwave meals and being introduced to computers at a young age. The '80s and MTV were heavy influences on X-ers during their formative teen years. It's no surprise that many from this generation ended up working with computers and now occupy positions as managers and entrepreneurs—as well as parents.

Gen Y, by comparison, not only grew up with television; its members were plugged into cable TV boxes with hundreds of channels to choose from. They not only had computers; they had cell phones, MP3 players and instantaneous access to information via the Internet as well.

What kind of foods the younger generations prefer is closely tied to who they are. Diversity is changing not only what Americans look like but what they like to eat. Nationally, an estimated 36 percent of Gen Y comes from minority backgrounds. The U.S. Census Bureau also reveals that Hawai'i leads the nation in diversity, with 42 percent of its population being Asian, 8.5 percent Native Hawaiian or Pacific Islander and 21 percent of mixed ancestry. This high degree of cultural diversity is reflected in the popularity of an ever-widening range of foods and flavors. Spicy and exotic Thai, Vietnamese, Indian and Mexican foods, for example, are popular additions that stretch the boundaries of the Islands' mixed plate.

Young people are generally more knowledgeable, adventurous and sophisticated eaters than their parents were when they were the same age. Placing a high value on speed, flexibility and convenience, both Gen X-ers and Gen Y-ers like to eat out and are quick to judge what they eat based on taste, quality, ambiance and service, easily rejecting what they don't like.

Keeping pace with the evolving tastes and increasing demands of diners, the Hawai'i Regional Cuisine movement has likewise grown. Established chefs such as Alan Wong, Sam Choy, Roy Yamaguchi, Chef Mavro, Russell Siu and others are now being

joined by younger chefs—some of whom they mentored—who are creating new and creative ways to combine fresh local ingredients with Eastern and Western culinary traditions. These chefs, like Elmer Guzman of The Poke Stop, are blazing their own trails while celebrating Hawai'i's local roots through their cooking.

Almost everyone these days has some interest in eating healthy—it's particularly important to the young and the very old, who base their food preferences in part on their desire to reduce or eliminate fat, sugar, salt or any sort of artificial additives in their diets. Hoping to drop pounds, lower cholesterol and improve their health in general, customers eagerly buy food products touted as low- or

Chef Chai Chaowasaree (above left with Hawai'i Farm Bureau Federation president Dean Okimoto at Okimoto's Nalo Farms in Waimānalo) seasons Hawai'i Regional Cuisine with the flavors of his native Thailand. Opposite: Chaowasaree's Eggplant and Zucchini Soufflé.

reduced-fat alternatives, as well as anything tagged "organic."

In many cases, these concerns tend to converge, overlap and influence each other. For example, the Moloka'i (or Wai'anae) Diet advocates a return to the basics of the traditionally high-carb/high-fiber/low-fat diet that Hawaiians adhered to before Westernization. Its popularity is fueled by cultural as well as health-related reasons.

The desire to eat healthy has even influenced popular plate lunch choices, with brown rice and tossed greens offered as alternatives to white rice and macaroni salad. Smaller portions, called mini-plates, are almost universally available at most drive-in restaurants as a means of allowing patrons to enjoy rich, tasty local food while still cutting back on their daily intake of calories, salt and fat by simply eating less.

At Kapi'olani Community College (KCC), which boasts the state's most progressive culinary arts program, classes and community outreach efforts stress eating local—and healthy. KCC's influence extends well beyond the 300 students enrolled in its food service program at any given time. In fact, you can find evidence of the school's influence on Hawai'i's food scene nearly everywhere you look. Its graduates include many of Hawai'i's top chefs—including a young generation of rising stars—and scores of the professionals who lead

CONNECTION

THE JOY OF SOY

It's official. In 2008, Merriam-Webster added "edamame," along with more than 100 other new words, to its revised Collegiate Dictionary. Lots of folks in Hawai'i have taken to using this now-popularized Japanese term, although for generations the dish has been known either by its other Japanese name, daizu, or simply as "soybeans."

Soybeans, a.k.a. edamame, were first cultivated in China, then spread to Japan in ancient times. Missionaries are believed to have spread soybeans from China to Europe in the 1700s.

One result of the current edamame phenomenon is that the beans can now be purchased frozen, shelled or unshelled, very economically at almost any supermarket or health food store. In the old days, daizu were grown in home gardens throughout Hawai'i and simply boiled with salt as a basic local snack. Try it yourself.

Boiled Soybean Snack

Boil soybeans in the shell in salted water. Add whole star anise for extra flavor. Drain and enjoy as pūpū.

Chili-Garlic Edamame

These days, a variety of flavored edamame pūpū (right) has become popular at bars and restaurants around Hawai'i. You can replicate it by quickly steaming edamame in the microwave or boiling them, then stir-frying them in a mixture of shoyu, minced garlic, ginger, oyster sauce, sesame oil, chili-garlic sauce or any other sort of seasoning for 1 or 2 minutes, or until most of the liquid has evaporated.

Cucumber Bisque with Grape Tomato Garnish
Serves 4

Soup

4	Japanese cucumbers, peeled and chopped in large chunks, about 8 c.
½ c.	chopped cilantro
¼ c.	chopped green onions
2 c.	low-fat plain yogurt
1 Tbsp.	olive oil
2 Tbsp.	fresh-squeezed lime juice
½ tsp.	salt
¼ tsp.	black pepper
1 c.	grape or cherry tomatoes, halved or quartered
4 tsp.	olive oil
4 tsp.	chopped cilantro
4 tsp.	chopped green onions
1 tsp.	cracked or fresh-ground black pepper (optional)

Combine soup ingredients in a blender and blend until smooth. Adjust flavors to taste. Pour into individual serving bowls and garnish with cherry tomatoes, a drizzle of olive oil and a sprinkle of cilantro and green onions. Season with pepper, if desired.

Hawai'i's restaurant, hotel and hospitality industries. Chefs such as Alan Wong, Sam Choy, Wayne Hirabayashi, Russell Siu, Elmer Guzman, Shane Masutani and Keith Ogata are but a few of the KCC graduates who have made their mark in Hawai'i.

Student awards and celebrity chefs aren't the only measure of KCC's impact on the community. Frank Gonzales, director of the school's non-credit program, is proud of the dozens of classes designed to connect directly with the general public. "Many local people—young and old—aren't used to trying different things," he said. Classes in Southern cooking, Mexican food and Mediterranean cuisine encourage students to step outside of their comfort zone and expand their culinary horizons. Other

non-credit classes, which nearly always sell out, combine tours of local farms, or Honolulu's Chinatown, with cooking and tastings. Equally popular is KCC's "Cooking Local" series, led by Chef Grant Sato and other noted KCC instructors. Students are taught to prepare a variety of local favorites, such as kalbi, shoyu chicken, shoyu pork and oxtail stew. Still other programs, such as the Dietary Approach to Stop Hypertension (DASH), focus on educating students and the public about healthy eating and presenting them with healthier ways to prepare local favorites.

As a significant segment of the local food scene morphs into healthier, higher-end alternatives, many diners have come to view unadulterated local classics as com-

KAUAʻI'S FLYING SAUCERS

Even in the age of globalization, there are still some foods that can only be found in certain places. There are others that can only be found at certain times of year. The ultimate specialty food may very well be one that can only be found in a certain place at a certain time of year.

The flying saucer, which appears only on the island of Kauaʻi during Obon (the Japanese festival for the dead), is just such a specialty item. It is named not for its elusiveness but for its shape: This rare treat is round and flat and looks a UFO.

Each flying saucer is comprised of two slices of bread filled with what resembles a Sloppy Joe mix, topped with a slice of American cheese. The genius of this Kauaʻi specialty lies in its preparation, which requires special round "pie irons" that are used to toast the circular sandwiches over a charcoal grill. The pie iron is heated, lightly toasting and sealing the edges of the two pieces of bread together—ideally, day-old bread. The corners and crust of the bread are then cut away to form a neatly sealed, perfectly round flying saucer.

In a 1998 newspaper interview, longtime flying saucer cook Flora Fujii recalled that Lihue Hongwanji once tried switching to square irons

when they had trouble replacing old ones. But square was no good, she confided, and they were scrapped in favor of the round ones again. "There was always dry bread in the corners of the square ones," Fujii explained.

Not even Fujii, however, could account for the origin of the flying saucer, which remains a mystery to this day. Fujii did remember its introduction as a new item sometime in the early '60s. "We weren't the first," she said. "We heard about it from Kapaa Hongwanji, I believe, where it was a good seller." Fujii contacted Kapaa Hongwanji and someone agreed to teach the members at Līhuʻe how to make the specialty item. Lihue Hongwanji was then able to purchase its own set of irons from a store in Līhuʻe.

Today, each Buddhist temple on the island

has developed its own recipe, which generally involves a tweaking of the basic ingredients of ground beef, ketchup, Tabasco and Worcestershire sauce, along with some herbs. Circular-shaped pie irons can still be found in mail-order catalogs or online sites specializing in camping and outdoor gear.

Ted Inouye of Lihue Hongwanji said that in 2006 his organization prepared 2,000 flying saucers each night of its two-night Obon festival—exactly twice what Fujii reported in 1998—and sold out both nights. One thing has remained the same for more than 40 years however: When the last taiko drumbeat echoes, bringing the Obon festival to a close, the venerable cooking irons will be cleaned and carefully put away for yet another year.

fort foods—dishes savored to remind them of where they've come from and of simpler times past. To some degree, local grinds are in today's parlance a "brand"—one that is proudly flaunted not just in Hawai'i but across the country and in foreign lands by expatriates who have left the Islands for jobs, housing or other reasons, or college-bound students who are venturing forth and resettling elsewhere in greater numbers than ever before.

It used to be that those who had a hankering for a taste of home while living away could obtain their fix via "CARE packages" sent by loved ones in the Islands. To some degree, this tradition continues, with cardboard boxes most commonly filled with goodies like instant ramen (packages or cup style), cans of SPAM™, macadamia nuts, mac nut candies or cookies, arare (Japanese rice crackers), furikake (rice seasoning), guava jelly, Kona coffee, Chinese preserved seeds or li hing powder, or dried ika (cuttlefish).

In certain parts of the Mainland, however, people can now just hop into their cars and drive to get a loco moco or some reasonable semblance of a Hawaiian plate lunch at any number of diners and drive-ins. This is especially true of cities up and down the West Coast from Seattle to San Diego, at dozens of Las Vegas eateries, and even in restaurants as far away as New York and Tokyo—attesting to the booming popularity of local Island foods.

Due to the estimated 500,000 Island tourists who fly to and from Las Vegas each year, plus some 50,000 former Hawai'i residents who now call the Nevada city and its environs home, Las Vegas has been dubbed the "Ninth Hawaiian Island." Hawai'i folks need look no further than the shelves of Las Vegas' Long's Drugs or ABC Stores to find an assortment of local snacks—or visit any downtown Boyd Gaming casino eatery to enjoy saimin, oxtail soup, loco moco and other Island favorites.

Northern California is also home to a booming population of Hawaiian expatriates, as are Southland cities such as Long Beach and Garden Grove. According to the *San Francisco Chronicle*, more than 44,000 people moved from Hawai'i to California between 1995 and 2000 alone. L&L Hawaiian Barbecue has almost 40 outlets in Northern California, while Ohana Hawaiian BBQ is also expanding, along with restaurants such as Hukilau and Hawaiian Drive Inn. Large social gatherings of people from Hawai'i, including annual ho'olaule'a (festivals), take place at various cities on the West Coast and in Las Vegas, featuring Hawaiian music, crafts and food. According to ex-pat columnists Kyle Tatsumoto and Keith Kamisugi (the "Two Japanee Bruddahs"), it's become easier to find a loco moco in the Bay Area than a Double-Double from In-N-Out Burger.

If a person happens to live in a place where local-style meals are not readily available, he or she can still acquire almost anything from Hawai'i via the Internet, with coffee, macadamia nuts, candies, Portuguese sausage or sweet bread, shortbread cookies, or Zippy's chili and rice delivered to the door—sort of a self-help CARE package. As the "Hawaiian Diaspora" continues to fan out across the globe, food becomes the flag that Island expatriates proudly fly. Another indication of how far local food has evolved is the expanded role that it plays in the plans of visitors to Hawai'i. More and more people now schedule their trips around events such as the Waikīkī

The Hawai'i Farm Bureau Federation has expanded its network of farmers markets to include weekly events throughout the state.

>>> >>> >>> >>> >>> >>> >>>

Among the offerings at the Farm Bureau's farmers markets: Organic produce from Ma'o Farms and Hawaiian-style chili from North Shore Farm.

Ho'olaule'a, SPAM JAM®, Matsuri in Hawai'i, Okinawan Festival, Kona Coffee Festival or other events in which food plays a big part. Other savvy travelers carefully scour the Internet and seek advice from dozens of online food blogs prior to their trips in order to incorporate dining more consciously into their Hawai'i vacations, scheduling tours and activities to include meals and snacks at key venues around the Islands.

A number of creative enterprises encourage this growing fascination with food as a pastime, including candy factories; wineries; and coffee, macadamia nut, goat cheese and lavender farms that are designed to accommodate visitors, offer tours, serve food and, of course, provide a well-stocked gift shop.

There are other positive initiatives, such as the effort to revive Hawai'i's cattle industry through the development and marketing of grass-fed beef; a growing cadre of farmers who sell their homegrown produce directly to consumers at public markets; and high-tech aquaculture operations that raise ogo (an edible seaweed), fish (moi, kampachi, tila-pia), lobsters and abalone—to be sold both locally and to markets in Asia.

Omiyage: Then and Now

The tradition of omiyage has also fueled the development of new and innovative local food products, just as it has helped preserve many of the traditional favorites. In Hawai'i, people of all ethnic backgrounds often refer to the tradition of gift giving by this Japanese term. Perhaps this is because people of Japanese descent once comprised such a large percentage of the local population. Or perhaps it's due to the degree to which gift-giving is emphasized in Japanese culture, where omiyage are gifts or souvenirs that a person brings home from a trip for friends, family or co-workers.

Gift-giving, of course, is a universal practice common in all cultures, including the Hawaiian host culture. In her seminal work *'Ōlelo No'eau: Hawaiian Proverbs and Poetical Sayings*, revered cultural expert Mary Kawena Pukui translated the phrase "I hele i kauhale, paua pū'olo i ka lima" to "In going to the houses of others, carry a package in the hand." In plain terms, Pukui said, it means, "Take a gift."

Also nestled deep within the pages of Pukui's text is another key phrase: "Ko koā uka, ko koā kai": "Those of the upland, those of the shore. Poi, taro for fish, seafood. Visits were never made empty-handed."

Together, these two phrases reflect the underlying spirit of omiyage, which usually means not only bringing a gift, but selecting something that is special to one's place.

In days past, before souvenir shops and gift shops were conveniently situated in hotel and airport lobbies, gifts were usually things one grew or caught or made and shared with neighbors. Vegetables from one's garden and fruit from backyard trees were commonly given with profuse apologies for their inferior quality and value. Fishermen gave fresh or dried fish, hunters gave fresh or smoked meat, and bakers gave cookies stored in clean glass mayonnaise jars with waxed paper lining the lids or coffee cans with plastic covers.

Along the line, our world got larger. Neighborly visits became weekly commutes from country to town, then from island to island, to frequent trips to the Mainland and even beyond. As the vast Pacific became more of a pond, inter-island specialties gained fame, like manju from Maui, manapua from O'ahu, cookies from Kaua'i and Punalu'u Bake Shop sweetbread from the Big Island. Visitors from afar took fresh pineapple, Kona coffee and macadamia nuts home with them as mementos of Hawai'i. Today, the variety of omiyage items is far more diverse and growing by the day.

Few food items are as synonymous with Hawai'i as macadamia nuts, which may very well be the king of Hawai'i omiyage. Mac nuts actually originated in Australia and were introduced to Hawai'i in 1881. Commercial cultivation and processing of the so-called "world's perfect nut" began in the early 1930s. Ellen Dye Candies—a small candy shop in Honolulu—is credited as the first company to dip macadamia nuts into chocolate. Mamoru Takitani purchased Ellen Dye Candies in 1960 and renamed the company Hawaiian Host, which is the largest purveyor of chocolate-covered macadamia nuts in Hawai'i today. Besides being sold salted and roasted whole and dipped in chocolate, macadamia nuts are crushed and used in cookies and desserts, and as a signature ingredient in a number of regional dishes, such as macadamia-crusted fresh fish.

One of the best examples of the bridge from old to new is Big Island Candies, founded in 1979 by Hilo-born Allan Ikawa. Following his entrepreneurial instinct, Ikawa entered the confectionary business by producing chocolate-covered macadamia nuts for a major corporate grower. When that client decided to make its own candies, he was forced to regroup and retool his business. Taking a big risk, especially given his location in Hilo on the Big Island, Ikawa refocused his efforts to tap the potential of the omiyage market, focusing first on visitors from Japan and the U.S. Mainland, steadily

building his local clientele, and then harnessing the power of the exploding mail order and Internet sales frontiers.

"The important thing about omiyage-type sales is that people want to give the best," Ikawa said. "Even if it costs a little more, they want to express their feelings by giving something that will make the recipient feel special." It is a mantra that is internalized by all of his employees. Premium-quality macadamia nuts, 100-percent Kona coffee, Hawaiian cane sugar and even fresh island eggs keep Big Island Candies products as tied to the Islands as possible, a fact

Fresh Puna papaya for sale at an open market in Honolulu's Chinatown.

CONNECTION

BOILED PEANUTS

Whether for a perfect pūpū or a nostalgic stadium snack, people in Hawai'i have long preferred boiled peanuts to roasted peanuts by a large margin.

Boiled peanuts very likely found their way onto Hawai'i's potluck menu via Chinese immigrants. Peanuts were spread to Asia from South America by Portuguese sailors in the 16th century.

Because boiled peanuts are also very popular in such Southern states as Georgia, Alabama and South Carolina, some have speculated that American soldiers might have brought the treat to the Islands during World War II, but in fact boiled peanuts were already popular in Hawai'i before the war.

In fact, peanuts were grown in Hawai'i from the 1830s, though not on a large commercial scale. The rich soil and warm climate in the Islands are quite conducive to growing peanuts. Besides being made at home, boiled peanuts were produced and sold by many small family-run stores, street vendors and specialty peanut and snack shop operators. Boiled peanuts now sold at Aloha Stadium and other Hawai'i sports venues

remind fans of the tradition established by sidewalk vendors at the old Honolulu Stadium a generation ago.

Local-Style Boiled Peanuts

2 lbs.	raw peanuts, in the shell
	Water, sufficient to cover peanuts
2 Tbsp.	Hawaiian rock salt
1	whole star anise

Rinse peanuts, place in a large pot and cover with water. To keep peanuts submerged, cover with a plate that fits into the pot and hold it down with a weight, like a heavy can. Soak overnight.

Rinse peanuts several times until water runs clear. Return peanuts to pot and cover with fresh water. Add salt and star anise. Cover and bring to a boil. Simmer 30 minutes.

Taste for doneness—peanuts should be medium-soft but not mushy. Let them soak in cooking water for 1 hour, then drain.

that is underscored by the practice of carefully limiting sales of his products outside of the Hilo factory, by mail order or online. As a result, Big Island Candies' distinctive hand-carried airline boxes are a familiar sight at the Hilo airport.

Persimmons to Pineapple Wine

Brand-new or "value added" omiyage items are constantly being created and growing in popularity. On the island of Maui alone, there are cleverly packaged raw cane sugar from Hawai'i's last surviving sugar plantation; jams and scone mix from Hashimoto Persimmon Farm; gourmet cheeses from Surfing Goat Dairy, lavender lotions and salad dressings from Ali'i Kula Lavender and even a unique pineapple-passion fruit wine from the slopes of Haleakalā.

And the list of Island-made products goes on statewide: Nalo Greens, North Shore Farms, Big Island Abalone, Kahuku Corn, Ma'o Farm organic produce, locally produced beef, honey, coffee, eggs, duck eggs and so much more. One of the positive results of this proliferation of locally grown food is the opportunity for people to interact with farmers and other producers, noted veteran O'ahu chef Alan Wong, proprietor of Alan Wong's and the Pineapple Room in Honolulu: "At farmers markets, the public can buy all sorts of premium, fresh ingredients that were once available only to restaurants."

Savvy farmers, he observed, now sell prepared foods using their own locally grown ingredients—like Jeanne Vana of North Shore Farms, who makes pizzas with her farm-grown tomatoes. This practice further encourages customers to purchase the fresh ingredients, take them home and try new culinary ideas on their own. "People try to recreate what they see and taste at the markets or at a restaurant," Wong said. "This helps fuel demand, which in turn is good for the farmers."

The great interest in food these days is fed in part by a smorgasbord of cooking shows on television and a crowded calendar of foodie fundraisers. "I think if we participated in every fundraiser we're invited to, we'd be doing one every week," he observed. This interest has affected what local people like to eat. Traditional Island potlucks, for example, still feature an array of familiar local dishes, such as teriyaki beef and macaroni salad. But now it's not unusual to find at least one or two new dishes inspired by some cooking show, cookbook or restaurant experience, Wong observed. "Local people travel more, eat out more often and have developed a more sophisticated palate than in the past," Wong said. "It's our job (as chefs and restaurateurs) to meet that challenge."

Yet not everyone fits this consumer profile: "Money is a big factor—there are many people who cannot

afford to buy high-end ingredients or dine out." Wong also sees a significant number of young people who don't know how to cook. "Lots of parents these days are so busy that they tend to eat out a lot," Wong said. "It means that many kids have no clue how to cook traditional ethnic foods—Filipino pinakbet, Japanese nishime—that their parents or grandparents used to make for the family. They might know where to go get certain foods, but not how to prepare them at home. Because of that, their kids won't know how to cook. That's sad."

When Alan Wong was growing up, his entire family always sat down together for dinner: "My father started, and then everyone else would eat. No TV—you had to talk to each

⫸ ⫸ ⫸ ⫸ ⫸ ⫸ ⫸

The Hilo Farmers Market is an institution in downtown Hilo.

COFFEE, TEA OR…'ŌKOLEHAO: HOME BREWS AND OTHER BEVERAGES

It's hard to believe, in today's highly commercial consumer society, but there was a time when Hawai'i residents grew and made not just what they ate, but most of what they drank as well. If we were forced to do without Starbucks or soda machines today, how would we fare?

Hawaiians drank herbal teas from ancient times, mainly for health reasons. The mamaki and ko'oko'olau are two prominent examples. Tea had also migrated from China to Europe and England in the 16th and 17th centuries. With this as background, and with so many Asian immigrants in Hawai'i, it's no surprise that tea was a very popular beverage throughout the Islands.

Tea plants were grown in Hawai'i as early as 1887, and the Hawaiian Coffee and Tea Co. established a five-acre tea plantation in Kona in 1892. Tea, however, did not meet with the commercial success that coffee did.

Many immigrants grew, dried and brewed their own tea from a variety of plants, such as lemongrass, kalamungai and even fungus. Japanese dried and roasted the seeds of the habucha (black tea) plant for daily consumption at home.

In the 1970s, beer can hats were worn as a sign of local pride. Right: The S.I. Shaw Saloon, a 19th-century "drink enterprise" in downtown Honolulu.

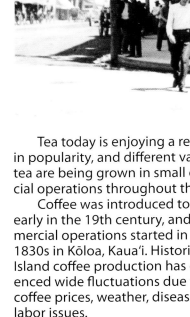

Tea today is enjoying a resurgence in popularity, and different varieties of tea are being grown in small commercial operations throughout the Islands.

Coffee was introduced to Hawai'i early in the 19th century, and commercial operations started in the 1830s in Kōloa, Kaua'i. Historically, Island coffee production has experienced wide fluctuations due to global coffee prices, weather, diseases and labor issues.

Shortly after 1900, large coffee plantations in Kona were broken up into smaller parcels, typically five to 15 acres in size, and leased to tenant farmers, mainly Japanese immigrants eager to escape the hardships of sugar plantation life. By 1910, these small Japanese family farms comprised 80 percent of Kona's coffee industry. Throughout its commercial ups and downs, coffee has always been a popular beverage locally. People also grew their own coffee for home use.

In the 1980s, as sugar production moved to more cost-effective growing centers overseas, many of the canefields were planted with coffee, rejuvenating the industry in

No longer just a Kona specialty brand, Island coffee is now grown from Ka'ū to Moloka'i to 'Ele'ele.

the Islands. Today, coffee is a major agricultural crop in Hawai'i, grown on more than 8,200 acres statewide, and Kona coffee is prized worldwide as a premium product. And while it was the Kona variety that put the Island bean and brew on the map, premium roasts are now produced throughout the archipelago from Ka'ū to 'Ele'ele—Maui Mountain, Moloka'i Muleskinner and dozens of others.

Generations ago, every ethnic group had its own version of a preferred alcoholic beverage, which were produced at home and shared with friends and neighbors. 'Ōkolehao, for example, is an 80-proof Hawaiian liquor made from the roots of the ti plant. ('Awa was used more for ceremonial purposes than for daily consumption.) Japanese brewed sake, Portuguese made wine and others brewed homemade beer and "swipe." Swipe was a crude drink made by placing fruit such as pineapple or pānini from cactus trees in containers with a little sugar and leaving the mixture out in the sun to ferment. Some extracted the juice from fruits with a homemade press and put it into plastic buckets covered with cheesecloth. Yet another method was to ferment molasses with water and yeast for a week. It was all consid-

ered "swipe," as was the pineapple workers' practice of cutting off the top of a growing pineapple out in the field and letting it ferment in the sun.

The cost of importing sake from Japan led immigrant Tajiro Sumida to establish the Honolulu Sake Brewery in Honolulu in 1908. It was not only the first sake brewery in Hawai'i; it was the first outside of Japan. The resilient and innovative Sumida pioneered a refrigerated brewing method in order

to overcome Hawai'i's tropical climate. During Prohibition (1920-1934) the company operated as an ice plant. Later, when the rice it fermented was needed for food during World War II, the factory produced shoyu.

Hawai'i's first commercial beer producer, Honolulu Brewery, was launched in 1854, and dozens of beer brands have come and gone since—including the iconic Primo, first brewed in 1901 in a red brick building that still stands on Queen Street in downtown Honolulu. Today, there are craft breweries and home brewers through the Islands.

Hawai'i-produced wine has also seen a surge in popularity in recent years. Wine grapes are raised with success on the cool flanks of the great volcanoes—most notably, at the Big Island's Volcano Winery and Maui's Tedeschi Vineyards, both of which have also diversified into the likes of macadamia nut wine, pineapple-passion fruit wine and raspberry wine.

≫≫≫ ≫≫≫ ≫≫≫ ≫≫≫ ≫≫≫ ≫≫≫ ≫≫≫

Aliʻi Kula Lavender co-owner Aliʻi Chang hosts a group of visitors at the Upcountry Maui farm.

other." These days, going out to dinner together may be one way for people to connect not only with food but with each other.

Celebrated in Hawaiʻi and abroad for the elegance and innovation of his cuisine—he is a past James Beard Award winner—Wong is nevertheless partial to comfort food. "When you work with food every day, you crave something simple," he explained. "For me, that means any kind of noodle soup—it's filling and warms your stomach." Wong also fondly recalls the foods his mother prepared for him as a youngster growing up on a Wahiawā pineapple plantation, like kimpira gobo and miso soup.

In Wong's opinion, tradition and change go hand in hand. "Just look at Zippy's," he said. "They have the standard stuff, but they also adjust to the times." With celebrity chefs and television programs serving up inspiration, local farmers and ranchers are providing flavorful foods and fresh new ingredients that continue to satisfy and expand the local palate. "Things like asparagus, artichokes, mushrooms and hearts of palm used to only come to us in cans," Wong recalled. "Now, we grow all that stuff here." Now these and other locally produced foods have found their way from Hawaiʻi's high-end restaurants, fancy fundraisers and cooking shows to local kitchens, backyards, potlucks and dinner tables.

What Price Progress?

While the successes of the niche-market and "value-added" products are encouraging, they can hardly make up for the fact that Hawaiʻi now imports nearly all of its food—between 80 and 95 percent of it—from outside sources. While the decline and near-total demise of the sugar and pineapple industries in the Islands have been well documented, less concern has been raised by the closure of the last poultry farm in Hawaiʻi, and the fact that the dairy, pork and egg industries in Hawaiʻi are now reduced to but a few farm operations statewide.

These changes are driven by economics, of course, and so the future of the farm industry in Hawaiʻi really depends on the ability to make these critical food-producing enterprises economically viable again, just as Hawaiʻi's regional chefs have boosted the viability of other locally grown products. More important, perhaps, is the idea that the inhabitants of the Hawaiian Islands have always felt that the need to produce their own food is one of the most fundamental of life's instincts. Abdicating food production to outside sources would appear to completely contradict the Island identity of Hawaiʻi's people.

Meanwhile, people of Hawaiʻi are now faced with more choices than they have ever had before. The key to this rich scenario is that local people tend not to view their food choices as being separate or exclusive of each other. Just as they instinctively switch from standard to pidgin English depending on the context in which they find themselves, local people are able to do the same with food. There is a place for local comfort foods, high-end cuisine, traditional ethnic food, mainstream American food, fast food and health food—often all at the same table. Hawai'i people love food, period, and most of all they enjoy the variety and seamless integration of food trends and traditions that make Hawai'i such a unique—and flavorful—food haven.

Thus, while one can find plate lunches in California and order oxtail soup in Las Vegas or loco moco in Japan, every Hawai'i resident knows how good it feels to return home after being away for any length of time. Upon closer examination, it is not so much that local residents couldn't find some of their favorite food choices elsewhere, but that what they miss over the long haul is the luxury of accessing the endless spectrum of food in Hawai'i. The taste of home could be a teriburger and saimin combo; or Portuguese sausage, eggs and rice available at McDonald's; or the opportunity to mix chili and chicken with rice and mac salad at Zippy's.

In this brave new world of limitless food choices, one is left to ponder what remains to distinguish local food from what the rest of the world

eats. To determine what defines local food, one might go back to traditional Hawaiian foods and the collective local cuisine—kau kau—that was developed by those immigrants who followed. Practitioners of Hawai'i Regional Cuisine, for example, are highly cognizant of maintaining a connection to this food heritage no matter how innovative their food creations might become. If certain foods lack any ties to this legacy, there's a very high likelihood that that they are merely mimicking something from somewhere else.

Perhaps that is one reason why locals agonize so deeply over every shuttering of a longtime restaurant or old-fashioned country store, for these closings serve to dramatize just how fragile the ties to the past really are. After serving generations of Hawai'i residents for decades, many of these places endeared themselves to their customers and represented a way of life and a set of values that people shared during simpler times.

In time, there may be no more such places left, which is what makes their replacements all the more important. Rather than Zippy's—if that is all that is left standing someday—or what the next level of regional cuisine might serve up, the most crucial factor in determining Hawai'i's food future might very well be how well Island families manage to pass their food traditions on to younger generations, so that they may continue

Big Island Candies owner Allan Ikawa inspects a batch of shortbread cookies. Left: The Hilo company's signature hand-dipped cookies.

⫸⫸⫸ ⫸⫸⫸ ⫸⫸⫸ ⫸⫸⫸ ⫸⫸⫸ ⫸⫸⫸ ⫸⫸⫸

The venerable Punalu'u Bake Shop welcomes visitors to the Big Island town of Nā'ālehu. Right: Loaves of Punalu'u Bake Shop sweet bread. The soft Hawaiian version of Portuguese sweet bread was introduced in 1958 by King's Hawaiian Bakery owner Robert Taira, who later exported his product to the Mainland.

to practice them. A case in point: the edamame and boiled peanuts recipes on pages 138 and 144, which demonstrate that such foods can still be recreated while at the same time innovating with modern seasonings.

It is also important that younger generations don't go so far in their fascination with food that they forget the premises and standards of the past in dealing with the present. This issue becomes self-evident when perusing some of the online Hawai'i food blogs that thrive on critiquing local food and food establishments based on some sort of sophisticated epicurean standard. Online foodies eagerly fill blogsites with opinions about local food that can be devoid of any social or cultural context. They view food for food's sake, judging

dishes solely on the basis of taste, texture, presentation and cost. Some of these critics mercilessly revile and ridicule certain dishes, chefs and restaurants for not meeting their high expectations.

Certainly such opinions are fair game in this day and age. People pay money—often a lot of money—and have a reasonable expectation receiving something of like value in return. This approach to food, however, also serves to point out how far today's high-tech, highly commercialized world has drifted from a time and place in Hawai'i when food and drink had everything to do with satisfying one's hunger and quenching one's thirst—and little to do with gastronomical posturing—where the act of sharing food was in itself greater than anyone's right to judge or to reject what was offered. Is it even possible in this day and age to expect young people to relate to the simple pleasure of drinking a glass of ice water after a day of hard labor? Or the satisfaction of eating a simple ball of rice or bowl of poi flavored only with a little salt?

In fact, it is not the food itself that is important in this discussion; rather, it is the act of producing, preparing and sharing food that has played such an important role in binding people together. To forget this truth at this juncture of Hawai'i's social evolution could spell

the demise not only of local food but of the very heart of local itself.

A Case Study:
Tradition and Change in Big Island Beef

There is an aura of timelessness that infuses the hundreds of thousands of acres of rolling pastureland that stretch across the island of Hawai'i. Perhaps it is the mist that so often enshrouds the distant herds of grazing cattle, or the stands of gnarled trees that bow respectfully to ka makani, the omnipresent wind, that make time seem to stand still. And while the past and the present, the old and the new, commingle elsewhere throughout the Hawaiian Islands, nowhere are they more integrally linked than in parts of the Big Island where the cattle industry's proud past—and its

THE DOLLAR DILEMMA

Regardless of nationality or economic status, every cook since time immemorial has tried to make food taste good, as author and chef Anthony Bourdain intones on his weekly television food show. With this simple truth ringing in my head, I ventured out to a dinner party at a high-end Honolulu restaurant one night. Our host had preordered the dinner for 10 at a cost of $150 or more per person, not counting the wine. Everything was delicious. The meal and service were shining examples of how enjoyable a first-class dining experience in Hawai'i can be. And although I don't get out very much, I do understand the value of always striving to be better; to take local cuisine to the proverbial next level; to be what is referred to as "world-class." From the unmitigated success of Hawai'i Regional Cuisine chefs around the world, one could argue that Hawai'i's food has indeed succeeded in achieving such premiere status.

My only concern about this progress, however, was also underscored at the same dinner party. As I practically licked my plate clean after each course, I noticed that half our table of 10 barely picked at some of the dishes that were served. Out of earshot of the host, I overheard a few of the guests whisper some negative comments about certain dishes.

You can't just raise the bar without being somewhat critical, it seems. It would be like good athletes receiving only praise from their coaches, rather than the criticism they need to push them to get better. This is very apparent on food blogs. I'm what bloggers call a "lurker," in that I read others' opinions but never post my own. It's hard not to be impressed by the passion and sophistication that many of these food aficionados bring to their discussion of food in Hawai'i.

Sometimes, however, I wonder if we are becoming too discerning and sophisticated as connoisseurs of food and wine. Similar to those comments made by some of the dinner guests that evening, following are online critiques of three of Hawai'i's most popular restaurants—all owned and operated by high-profile Hawai'i Regional Cuisine chefs.

- "The salad was unmemorable, thai lobster soup was way over-spiced, yet was flat … and a sesame crusted mahi-mahi was charred within an inch of its life, and some excellent quality tuna was also charred on the outside. We sent back the charred outside pieces, and ate the sushi-grade center."

- "I am not a fan of this haphazard way of slapping unmatching ingre-dients together left and right and calling it fusion cuisine."

- "We were sorely disappointed by the service, which barely gave you a chance to catch your breathe between courses, and the lackluster food that we were served!"

One can also argue that patrons have a right to express their opinions and to expect the best. But is this where we want to go as a food culture? It's impossible to go backwards or even stay the same, and you can't just stay home and eat comfort food all the time, yet I can't help wondering if the price of excellent food is worth it if it negatively impacts our perceptions and personalities as people.

⫸⫸⫸ ⫸⫸⫸ ⫸⫸⫸ ⫸⫸⫸ ⫸⫸⫸ ⫸⫸⫸ ⫸⫸⫸

Ernest and Stephan De Luz: A hardscrabble tale and the importance of family.

future—reside.

It was here on Hawai'i Island, at Kealakekua Bay in Kona, that Captain George Vancouver introduced cattle to the Islands in 1793 as a gift to King Kamehameha the Great. Additional gifts of cattle arrived on subsequent voyages, delivered up the coast at Kawaihae.

Protected by the King's royal kapu, these animals proliferated. Herds roamed unrestricted through the countryside, damaging crops and threatening the populace. In 1816, a young seaman from Massachusetts named John Palmer Parker arrived in Hawai'i. After marrying into Hawaiian royalty, he started a ranch and was given special permission to hunt the feral cattle. Parker did so with

great success, selling the meat, hides and tallow to visiting ships.

A much broader effort would be needed to control the feral cattle population, however, so around 1832 King Kamehameha III engaged the services of Spanish vaqueros (cowboys) from Mexican-held California. The vaqueros taught Hawaiians how to break and ride the wild horses that had been introduced to Hawai'i in 1804 and gave them the skills to finally control the feral cattle. The local cowboys called themselves "paniolo," from the Spanish word "Espanol"—a tribute to their spirited teachers.

More than a century and a half after it began, the cattle industry still dominates much of the Big Island's landscape. Most of the state's 850,000 acres of pastureland are here, parceled amongst the island's 400-plus cattle ranches, which range from small family operations all the way up to the seemingly boundless reaches of Parker Ranch.

Founded in 1847, at its pinnacle Parker Ranch alone spanned a staggering half-million acres. Today, at approximately 200,000 acres and some 30,000 to 35,000 head of cattle, it remains one of the oldest and largest cattle ranches in the country.

A few miles south of Waimea, along the Hāmākua Coast, three generations of the Ernest and Marian De Luz family pull together to manage an operation of some 1,450 breeding

cows. The hardscrabble tale of patriarch Ernest De Luz's life is etched on his face—a life built on hard work and determination following the death of his father when Ernest was only five and his mother when he was just 16. Driven by his love for horses and cattle, he broke into ranching in 1952 and has pursued it full-time since 1987. Today, Ernest works alongside his son, Stephan, who manages the ranch, and his grandson Shane.

The importance of family is a powerful theme that runs throughout the island's cattle industry. Nowhere is this more evident than at Kahuā Ranch, perched some 3,000 feet above sea level on the slopes of the Kōhala Mountains. Herbert M. "Monty" Richards, Jr., chairman of Kahuā Ranch, is the nephew of Atherton Richards, who co-founded the ranch in 1928 with Ronald von Holt. Richards lives on the ranch with his wife, Phyllis, his four children and their families. Son Tim serves as president and general manager of Kahuā Ranch, while also working as the veterinarian for Parker Ranch. Monty's son John oversees the ranch's diversified enterprises, including a Kawasaki dealership and an extensive visitor program.

Kahuā Ranch's family-first values include the ranch's employees, Tim Richards points out. This is demonstrated in the continued practice of one of the ranch's longest-running traditions, "house meat." House meat is the practice of periodically slaughtering a cow and dividing the meat amongst the ranch's employees, a tradition that goes back to the earliest days of the ranch's existence.

Far from relying on their rustic charm, however, Hawai'i's ranches are driven by the need to change—or face extinction. Kahuā Ranch, for one, has garnered a well-deserved reputation for its willingness to experiment, to innovate. Back in the mid-'60s, Kahuā became the first ranch in Hawai'i to implement the practice of artificial insemination to genetically improve its livestock; in the '80s, it incorporated motorbikes—called "Japanese quarter horses"—to greatly improve the ranch's efficiency. Ranch managers have cultivated flowers, tomatoes and lettuce utilizing hydroponics and built windmills to capture electricity from the wind.

Today, Kahuā Ranch's inventive spirit can be seen in its inclusion of sheep (the wool is sold to Mainland manufacturers; the meat is sold locally) and Wagyu beef, the buttery-tender meat popularly known as "Kobe" beef, to diversify its livestock operations. The ranch now generates much of its own electricity via photovoltaic solar panels and runs a Kawasaki ATV retail outlet and service center. It offers an extensive list of visitor activities, including horseback riding, wagon rides and ATV ranch tours; it operates a well-stocked retail store and offers a dinner and entertainment package, Evening at Kahuā Ranch.

Parker Ranch also offers a wide variety of visitor activities, including ATV rides, tours, horseback riding and hunting. It is run like a modern corporation and includes commercial leasing, real estate and retail ventures.

More importantly, Kahuā and other ranches in Hawai'i are implementing the latest scientific tools in managing their pastureland. The new "rapid rotational" method is helping the industry to evolve at a most critical point in its proud history. Basically, the practice involves subdividing large grazing areas into an intelocking series of smaller paddocks. Instead of leaving the cattle to graze randomly over a large area for a long period of time, they are systematically herded from one grid to the next.

It sounds simple, but this method is yielding important benefits. For one, it allows the cattle to eat only the more nutritious leaves and tops of the grasses rather than the tougher, lower-quality stems close to the ground, which in turn results in significantly faster growth rates and higher-quality meat without the addition of any artificial supplements to their diet. It also allows the grazed area to recover faster and helps prevent erosion, which means that ranches are able to maximize the carrying capacity of their acreage.

The De Luz family is not about to add visitor activities to its ranch

operations, but it has implemented rotational grazing practices with good results. There was a time in the early '80s to early '90s when nearly all Hawai'i-raised cattle had to be sent to feedlots to be grain-finished, Marian De Luz recalled. After the last O'ahu feedlot closed, most of the ranches sold their calves to buyers on the U.S. Mainland. Rising fuel prices and correspondingly higher shipping rates make it harder and harder to turn a profit. Now, thanks to improved practices, Stephan De Luz says that their cattle can be ready for market in 24 to 36 months, and their all-natural beef is turning up in supermarkets and on the menus of some of Hawai'i's finest restaurants, such as those at the Four Seasons Resort Manele Bay and The

CTAHR's Glen Fukumoto and Milton Yamasaki: Forage-finished or grain-finished beef?

»»» »»» »»» »»» »»» »»» »»»

Kulana Foods' Brady Yagi: In the footsteps of his grandfather. Right: KTA Super Stores' Derek Kurisu displays a few of the offerings in the chain's Mountain Apple brand, which includes scores of food items from local growers and producers. Far right: Kurisu's recipe for the classic plantation dish chicken hekka.

Lodge at Koele on the island of Lana'i.

Many of these innovative—indeed revolutionary—livestock management practices are the result of a partnership between the ranchers and the Mealani Research Center in Waimea, a facility run by the College of Tropical Agriculture and Human Resources (CTAHR) of the University of Hawai'i. Glen Fukumoto, a county extension agent for CTAHR's Cooperative Extension Service, and Milton Yamasaki, Mealani Research Station's manager, have been leading the effort to improve livestock production. Mealani's studies include rotational grazing and testing different types of forage plants for cattle. Its research shows that Hawai'i's grass-fed, or "forage-finished," beef is an all-natural product with many nutritional benefits that grain-finished beef lacks.

One of the remaining challenges confronting the cattle ranchers is the lingering public perception that grass-finished beef is not as good as grain-finished beef, even if recent consumer studies have shown that improved forage plants and rotational grazing have dramatically improved the quality of local grass-fed beef.

To demonstrate that forage-finished beef was as tender and as tasty as grain-finished, Fukumoto and Yamasaki in 1996 created A Taste of the Hawaiian Range, a food and agricultural festival. Today, the event has grown into one of Hawai'i's largest and most anticipated annual food events. Held at the Hilton Waikoloa Village Resort, it draws more than 2,000 people each year to sample the offerings of some 50 of Hawai'i's top chefs.

One of the unique aspects of A Taste of the Hawaiian Range—and

Uncle Derek's Chicken Hekka

2-lb.	chicken, cut in pieces
3"	piece ginger, peeled and sliced
	Vegetable oil for frying
½ c.	shoyu
½ c.	sugar
2 cans	sukiyaki no tomo,* drained (8.75 oz. each)
1 can	chicken broth (14 oz.)
2 Tbsp.	butter
	Dash of sake (rice wine)
6	shiitake mushrooms, sliced
1	carrot, thinly sliced
2	round onions, sliced
	Salt, to taste
	Watercress (optional)
1-2	bundles long rice, soaked in water until soft (optional)
	Aburage (optional)
1 bunch	green onions, chopped

Fry chicken and ginger in a large pot with a little vegetable oil. Heat shoyu and sugar in a small saucepan over medium heat until sugar dissolves. When chicken is almost cooked, add shoyu-sugar mixture and sukiyaki no tomo. Add chicken broth and remaining ingredients, except green onions. Cook to desired doneness and taste for seasoning. Sprinkle green onions before serving. (See photo page 1.)

*This includes bamboo shoots, mung bean thread and mushrooms.

KAU KAU

C O N N E C T I O N

PIPIKAULA AND SMOKE MEAT

To connect with the traditional heritage and changing manifestations of Hawaii's paniolo past, try preparing these two iconic products:

Pipikaula

Pipikaula, literally "rope beef," is a Hawaiian-style beef jerky that played a big part in the diets and lifestyle of Hawaiʻi's paniolo. At its most basic, pipikaula was prepared by simply rubbing strips of beef with paʻakai (Hawaiian salt) and drying them outdoors in screen boxes to protect the meat from flies. After a day or two, the meat would reach the desired texture (dry outside, still a little moist inside). Drying the meat allowed cowboys to stretch and preserve meat after a cow was killed and dressed, and it provided them with an excellent source of food that did not need refrigeration when they traveled far from home for days or weeks at a time out on the open range.

Pipikaula also lends itself to many flavor variations reflecting the taste and creativity of the cook. Some of the most popular versions involve rubbing or marinating the meat with crushed garlic, shoyu, brown sugar and spices.

1 lb.	boneless chuck roast
½ c.	shoyu
½ c.	water
2 cloves	garlic, minced
1	red chili pepper, minced (optional)

Cut meat, with the grain, into ½"-thick strips. Place in a shallow container or plastic bag.

Combine shoyu, water, garlic and red peppers, if desired, and pour over meat. Marinate in refrigerator for at least 2 hours.

Traditionally the meat was then placed in a dry box for a day or two, but nowadays most people use an electric dehydrator or oven. If using a dehydrator, follow manufacturer's instructions. If using an oven, lay the meat on baking sheets or position the oven rack at the highest level and hang the strips of meat from the rack, using bent paper clips. A drip pan or layer of foil should be placed on the bottom of the oven to catch the drippings.

Set oven at 150°F to 200°F and cook meat for 5 to 7 hours, with the oven door slightly ajar, checking occasionally to see whether desired texture has been achieved.

To serve, fry in oil with sliced onions or watercress and slice across the grain.

Smoke Meat

With exception of cowboys and ranchers, most folks in Hawaiʻi did not have access to fresh meat—certainly not in the sort of quantity needed to be making pipikaula. What were accessible, however, were the wild pigs that populated the forests on every island. These pigs were descendents of the domesticated Polynesian pigs that arrived with the first settlers of the Islands, interbred with the European boars introduced by Western sailors. Plantation workers hunted pigs for meat as well as sport, smoking the meat in their backyards in simply constructed smoke houses made of corrugated metal roofing panels. Smoke (not "smoked") meat was the jerked meat for the masses.

Smoke meat approximates pipikaula in that it can be prepared simply with Hawaiian salt and a little paprika or marinated with all sorts of other ingredients such as ginger, garlic, sugar and chili pepper. Some people like to use commercially bottled shoyu-style barbecue sauce to marinate the meat before smoking.

Rather than jerry-rigging a smokehouse, most people today use a store-bought smoker or large (Weber-style) kettle grill. The key to the latter is to position the hot coals off to one side of the grill while placing the meat away from the hot coals and over a drip pan containing water. Kiawe (mesquite) chips soaked in water are sprinkled on the coals to generate and flavor the smoke.

Cover the grill and smoke the meat for about 4 hours. Keep the grill covered, with the lower grill vents and cover vents open. Monitor the smoke rising from the cover, and open the cover only when it's necessary to add more coal or wood chips and check the meat. The smoke meat is done when the outside is a light medium brown (or to taste).

To serve, cut the meat strips into bite-size pieces and fry with a little oil.

WE FEED EACH OTHER AT FUNERALS

In addition to all of the major holidays, Hawaiʻi people seem to mark major life milestones with food—baby lūʻau, graduations, weddings, housewarmings, grand openings, retirements, golden anniversaries and yakudoshi.

Of course the dress code is nearly the same for every affair—comfortable. It ranges from "casual" (aloha shirt, shorts, sandals or slippers) to "business" (aloha shirt, pressed, tucked in, with slacks and shoes) to "formal" (*nice* aloha shirt with sports coat or jacket). No matter how casual the dress may be, however, food-wise these are not simple chip-and-dip affairs; there is no need to fill up on cheese-and-crackers and vegetable sticks at these parties.

We feed each other at funerals, which are often scheduled around either lunch or dinner times so that the bereaved family can feed the scores of relatives, friends, neighbors, coworkers and community representatives who turn out. Immediately following the funeral services, everyone is invited to partake in a buffet that usually includes fried chicken, shoyu pork, nishime, chow mein noodles, sushi and macaroni salad. In fact, it's not unlike what you'd find at a picnic.

Stories are exchanged over platefuls of food. Deep sighs are expelled. Eyes swollen with grief slowly soften, lightening for the first time in weeks or even months. Friends seek out those they haven't seen in a long time, and conversation shifts to the present—trying to identify the kids and grandkids racing about, since they grow up so fast. There is time for cake, mochi and andagi doughnuts for dessert, with fruit punch, coffee or hot tea. Finally, people smile; and after a few chuckles, lots of hugs and gentle pats on the back, mourners head home. They would no doubt have left feeling empty if not for the kau kau, which in turn offered the time to heal and the chance to reinforce the bonds that hold us together. There is so much food at funerals, in fact, that you must take a plate with you when you go.

one of its greatest lures—is that it showcases all parts of the animal, including heart, liver, tongue, tripe and, yes, "mountain oysters." Beyond adding an air of exoticism, this policy creates an important connection between today's sophisticated Hawaiʻi Regional Cuisine and the traditional food practices of the past, in which nothing was wasted.

Besides the food tasting, a Forage Field Day—designed to educate members of the food industry about the latest improvements being made to local beef—is an important part of the event. Thanks to the efforts of researchers, ranchers, meat processors and retailers, Hawaiʻi's beef cattle industry anticipates continued growth of natural grass-finished beef sales.

Another key player in this unfolding success story is Kulana Foods, one of two slaughterhouses and meat-processing facilities on Hawaiʻi Island and one of the main supporters of A Taste of the Hawaiian Range. Founded by James S. Yagi in 1939 as Standard Meat Market, the company is now run by his grandson, Brady Yagi. In many ways, Kulana Foods is a throwback to the old days, still servicing customers who might want a single cow or pig killed, trimmed and packed for home use. It also works with many of the island's major ranches, however, including the De Luz, Kahuā and Parker spreads. Kulana purchases cattle, pigs and sheep and sells the packaged products

to supermarkets, hotels and restaurants. It has been instrumental in promoting grass-finished beef to high-end clients throughout the state and even on the Mainland.

Occasionally, Yagi even gets requests for salt beef, the venerable staple of the high seas that first made its way to Hawaiʻi's shores more than 200 years ago. It is a testament to the young Yagi's knowledge gained from his father and grandfather that he is able to fill what is now such an unusual order.

Such is the story of the cattle industry in Hawaiʻi, where niche marketing the latest in grass-finished beef to Hawaiʻi's most exclusive restaurants segues seamlessly with a request for an archaic product like salt beef. The moral of the tale may be that the future of ranchers and farmers in Hawaiʻi is equally dependent on their ability to make the old new again as well as on the ability of local consumers to see the value of locally produced foods—from salt beef to gourmet grass-fed steaks—or risk becoming nothing more than an ocean-bound outpost of the U.S. Mainland.

Life on a Modern Island

There is something about life on an island that is difficult to explain. Most Islanders are used to it, of course, this notion of being surrounded in all directions by water. But as normal and natural as it might seem to them, there are others who have difficulty becoming reconciled to it. For example, there's the simple notion that directions such as North-South and East-West are not nearly as useful in Hawai'i as mauka (toward the mountains) and makai (toward the sea). Or the realization that if one drives in the same direction long enough, one will end up back at the beginning—enough to give some people a full-blown case of "rock fever."

As experienced *Hōkūle'a* crewmembers point out, there is a direct similarity between life on an island and life on a canoe. While food and water are more abundant on an island, they remain finite resources, and their use must still be carefully protected, managed and shared.

Despite the fact that we still inhabit the most isolated landmass in the world, we have drifted far from the self-sufficiency of the original settlers. Due to modern communication and transportation, our economy today depends heavily on outside sources to meet most of our basic needs, including the importation of more than 80 percent of our food and the vast majority of other consumer goods.

All that is necessary in order to appreciate the deep, psychological grip that this near-total dependency has on our psyche is to experience a shipping strike—or the mere threat of a shipping strike. When, in 2009, Big Islanders heard word of a labor dispute affecting West Coast dock-

workers, there was an immediate groundswell of shoppers at local supermarkets. There was no frenzied panic at this point, just cautious residents stocking up in case the situation worsened. Within minutes, one store manager began posting handmade signs limiting purchases of certain items to two per customer. All sorts of products were filling the shopping carts, with bags of rice, dry dog food, various canned goods and toilet paper among the most coveted items. Had it been a full-blown strike, the situation would have changed and escalated considerably. One need not be stricken by rock fever to be reminded that we live on an island.

Learning to live well on islands is a microcosm of learning to live well everywhere. Here in Hawai'i we are surrounded by the world's largest ocean, but, as master navigator Nainoa Thompson of the Polynesian Voyaging Society reminds us, Earth itself is also a kind of island, surrounded by an ocean of space. He adds:

In the end, every single one of us—no matter what our ethnic background or nationality—is native to this planet. As the native community of Earth we should all aspire to live in pono—in balance—between all people, all living things and the resources of the Earth—our island home in an immense sea of space.

Troubled in Taipei

A number of years ago I accompanied a contingent of Hawai'i high school athletes who were invited to play a series of goodwill games in Asia. These involved both boys' and girls' all-star teams in different sports.

Near the end our stay in Taiwan, the hosts held an elaborate dinner party at a restaurant near our hotel in downtown Taipei. It was Chinese fare, of course, served in a familiar manner. Just as in Hawai'i, the food arrived in courses, each dish rotated on a lazy Susan to be enjoyed family-style by the dozen or so guests seated at each table.

It was obvious to everyone at our table—mainly parents and chaperones—that the dishes being served were special. Each dish was greeted

The Huli-Huli Chicken brand was trademarked by Island poultry pioneer Ernest Morgado in 1954, and the tasty rotisserie chicken, a popular fundraiser item, is often marketed today as moa moa chicken.

CONNECTION

THE LI HING MUI FAMILY

A good example of locals' ability to mix cultural palates—and to combine old and new—is the relatively recent craze for li hing-flavored everything. Li hing mui is remarkable stuff, dating back over 2,000 years to ancient China. The characters for li hing mui translate to "traveling plum," which indicates that these preserved fruits seasoned with licorice, sugar and salt were the ideal pack-and-go food for travelers to nibble while on the move.

Chinese preserved seeds and fruits, which come in many types and flavor variations, all come under the general heading of "crack seed" in Hawai'i. They were first imported from China, but entrepreneurs in Hawai'i soon began producing them locally, at least by the early 1900's. Crack seed was a hit with the general population, and these affordable snacks were soon made available at crack seed shops and general stores all over Hawai'i.

Li hing mui may still be the most popular of all crack seed varieties. It is an addictive sweet and salty combination of flavors: sugar, licorice, salt and star anise, among others. Today, li hing mui is also sold as a powder or syrup that can be used to flavor just about anything edible, including gummy bear candies, popcorn, dried fruits, shave ice syrup, salad dressings and even martinis.

Li Hing Mui Snack

This "recipe" is easy enough: Just get some li hing mui powder and then assemble any of the following:

• Dried fruits—mangoes, cranberries or apricots are good

• Microwave popcorn

• Gummy bears

Sprinkle li hing mui powder on any of these or whatever you feel like eating—it tastes good on anything!

Japanese Ume

The Japanese equivalent of li hing mui may very well be umeboshi—ume for short—a salty Japanese pickled plum. It is used as a seasoning but is most famous for occupying the middle of a musubi (rice ball). Ume inside of a musubi added flavor and helped to keep the rice from spoiling.

The fruit, actually an apricot rather than a plum, is picked green, dried and pickled in salt and shiso or chiso (beefsteak plant) leaves. Weights are placed on top, and the ume is left to pickle for anywhere from two months to several years.

The liquid that the umeboshi creates as it pickles, ume-su, is used to season okai (rice gruel) or a cup of hot tea, and is believed to have health-giving properties. Today, ume-flavored furikake is popular, as are ume-flavored dressings and sauces.

Fun with Fruit

Finally, for a true local take on the salt/fruit combination, there is the "sour lemon," known to citrus-gathering kids all over the Islands for decades, though less popular today. It'll take some time, but try to make some: It's the taste of childhood.

Start by washing 15 or 20 lemons (or limes) well before starting—local kine mo' bettah—enough to fill a gallon jar. Some people prefer their fruit a little on the green side.

Put the lemons in a gallon jar and cover with boiling water for at least 10 minutes. This will help the salt to penetrate the skin later. Some folks also advocate rubbing with Hawaiian salt. It's especially important to clean store-bought lemons that have had their skins waxed.

Drain the water. The lemons can go straight to the jar from here, or they can dry in the sun for a few days.

Sprinkle the limes with about a pound (1 to 1½ cups) of Hawaiian salt.

Cover the top of the jar with heavy-duty plastic wrap, wax paper or plastic from a sandwich bag and seal the cover. Shake the jar daily for one week, then once a week for two months, then let sit outside in the sun for one year, shaking occasionally. Check the level of the liquid in the jar to make sure the lemons are in contact with it.

After a year, dry the lemons in the sun. A cardboard box works well and will not rust. Just cover with netting to keep the bugs out. Lemons will wrinkle and salt crystals form on the surface. Store them in jars—they will keep for years.

with oohs and ahs and savored with appreciative nods. At the end of the evening, the empty platters on our table indicated just how much we had enjoyed the food. As we exited the banquet hall, however, we had a shock. There on the tables where the Hawai'i kids had been seated sat platters full of food left virtually untouched.

As we approached the buses, I could hear parents asking their kids what was wrong and the students complaining about the food—saying it was "junk" or "tasted weird." Anger and shame began to boil inside of me. If my child had been part of the group, I would not have minced any words in letting my feelings be known. I managed to restrain myself—though I felt I was going to explode.

After expressing what I considered only mild disapproval, the parents shrugged and boarded the buses. On the way back to the hotel, the bright lights of a McDonald's restaurant suddenly appeared—a beacon of familiarity in a sea of strangeness. The students pleaded for the driver to stop, and the parents, apparently concerned that their kids would go to bed hungry, agreed. The caravan of buses ground to halt and the kids spilled out onto the curb, whooping and hollering as they dashed toward the glowing arches.

I've experienced many more important, life-changing events since that trip, but years later I'm surprised at how vividly I still recall this incident in Taipei. Watching that line of kids slowly snake into McDonald's gave me lots of time to sit and stew over the situation. *How far have we drifted from the cultural values of our forbears?* I wondered. *What happened to such principles as not wasting food and never insulting the generosity and hospitality of others?* These precepts—pounded into us as youngsters—were fundamental to the dynamics of local culture. In the process we were taught not only to eat just about anything, but to actually enjoy eating a wider variety of food.

That night I remember feeling for the first time the full brunt of the term "ugly American." In my travels, I had encountered others whose ethnocentric and arrogant attitudes were deserving of the moniker, but this was the first time I was made to feel like one myself. I could only imagine what the event's hosts and restaurant staff were thinking back at the restaurant as they cleared tables piled with uneaten food. *Where are we headed, I fumed, when these youngsters, so privileged to represent Hawai'i abroad, could sully the image of the Aloha State by behaving like spoiled brats?*

I've mellowed since then, and today I try to think of this incident

Hawai'i Regional Cuisine chef Alan Wong: With Island foods, tradition and change go hand in hand.

as an isolated one—a case of road-weary kids who missed home and the comforting flavors of pizzas, burgers and fries. Nevertheless, I think the reason this experience still haunts me is that it is a stark reminder of how fragile our local culture really is. As our choices broaden from generation to generation, we must be vigilant in passing on our lessons learned to future generations—lest my troubled memory of Taipei become our daily reality. ◙

IN A LAND WITHOUT SEASONS

To people living elsewhere in the world, Hawai'i is a land without seasons. Actually, locals and longtime residents are accustomed to the rhythm of having two seasons a year: a hotter, more humid "summer" that runs roughly from May to October, and a colder, rainier "winter" that stretches from about November to April. The difference is rather subtle, however, as the average daytime temperature varies by about seven degrees, from 85 degrees in summer to 78 in winter.

While most newcomers appreciate Hawai'i's year-round temperate climate, others miss the experience of having four distinct seasons each year—leaves changing color in autumn, snow falling in winter, flowers blooming in spring and the heat rising in summer. They claim that the subtler seasons in Hawai'i make it more difficult to measure the passage of time.

But Islanders can rely on traditional seasonal holidays to help maintain their bearings as the year passes. What's more, a smorgasbord of ethnic festivals and cultural observances further helps mark the passage of time. You might say that—in a land without seasons—it is necessary to party one's way through the year, using food as a guidepost to help chart the course of memory through time.

New Year's

New Year's celebrations in Hawai'i literally start the year off with a bang, with celebratory fireworks and enough food to last the rest of the year. New Year's resolutions, champagne toasts and singing "Auld Lang Syne" are merely backdrops to the many deeply rooted and

New Year's Eve

richly layered Asian traditions—usually involving food—practiced to ensure good luck and prosperity. One of the most important times of the year, New Year's in Hawai'i lasts far longer than just one night.

Food assumes great symbolic value in Asian cultures—especially at New Year's. Japanese, for example, associate mochi (pounded rice cakes) with New Year's. The ritual of making mochi is still practiced today by extended families, churches and community groups who get together about a week before New Year's Eve to steam and pound the mochi rice with wooden mallets (kine) in a traditional stone mortar (usu). These days, many more gather in kitchens around automated mochi-making appliances or purchase their mochi in supermarkets and department stores. On New Year's morning, it is important for families to eat ozoni, a soup made with mochi dumplings, along with various side dishes.

Food names play an important role in why certain foods are eaten at New Year's. The word for red snapper, for example, "tai," is part of the word "medetai," which evokes happy or celebratory events. Toshikoshi soba (buckwheat noodles), or "year-crossing soba," suggest a life that is long and unbroken like a soba noodle. "Konbu" or "kombu" (a type of seaweed) sounds like the second part of "yorokobu," the Japanese word for happiness. "Kuromame," the word for black beans, can also mean "hardworking or healthy," while eating kazunoko (herring roe) means one will have lots of children and therefore prosper.

Chinese New Year

Chinese New Year arrives on the first day of the first new moon. It is actually celebrated for 15 days from the New Moon to the Full Moon—usually late January through early February.

During the Chinese New Year celebration, special foods are prepared, such as jai and gau. Jai is a vegetarian dish also known as "monk's food." It is traditionally eaten for breakfast on the first day of the New Year as a sign of respect to the Buddha. Although jai is made in many different ways, some of its common ingredients include mung bean thread or vermicelli, ginkgo nuts, black mushrooms and fungus, soybean sticks, deep-fried tofu, won bok, Chinese dates and fermented red bean sauce. Each ingredient holds special meaning, such as good luck, wealth, long life and prosperity. Gau is a sweet, sticky dish made of rice flour sweetened with coconut milk and brown sugar. Like Japanese mochi, it symbolizes cohesiveness in the family.

Chinese New Year is an especially big and colorful event in the Chinatown district of downtown Honolulu. Thousands of people of all ethnic backgrounds enjoy the bazaars, live entertainment, lion dances, fireworks and food booths at the Chinese Cultural Plaza and along Beretania and Maunakea streets. The Narcissus Festival, which crowns the Narcissus Queen and Court, is also part of the Chinese New Year celebrations on Oʻahu.

Lion dance, Chinese New Year

Tet

Hawaiʻi's growing Vietnamese population also celebrates its traditional Tet lunar new year in late January to early February. Food booths, lion dances, cultural displays and traditional games are celebrated at Kapiʻolani Park.

Punahou Carnival

The Punahou Carnival, held in February, is acknowledged to be the best-known and most-anticipated school carnival in Hawaiʻi. Along with entertainment, rides, games and plant and white elephant sales, the Punahou Carnival is also famed for its food offerings, such as malasadas, Hawaiian plates and Portuguese bean soup.

Shrove (or "Fat") Tuesday

The day before Lent was historically a time when households feasted before fasting. In England they eat pancakes, in Germany they eat doughnuts and in Hawaiʻi we eat malasadas.

Malasadas are round, sweet and delicious Portuguese yeast doughnuts (no holes) that are deep-fried in hot oil and liberally coated with sugar. Enjoyed year-round, they are specially honored on Fat Tuesday, which is known as Malasadas Day in Hawaiʻi. Portuguese immigrants would use up all of their lard, butter and sugar prior to Lent by making large batches of malasadas, but though the doughnuts are still a tradition in Hawaiʻi, nowadays most people buy them. Long lines outside Leonard's Bakery and Champions Bakery attest to the satisfaction local people take from perpetuating traditional foodways. Recently malasadas filled with cream or fruit custard have appeared in bakeries, but the originals remain the most popular.

Boys' and Girls' Day

In Japan, Girls' Day (March 3) and Boys' Day (May 5) have been combined into a joint Children's Day celebration observed on May 5. In Hawaiʻi, however, old customs die hard. Families display colorful ningyo (dolls) on Girls' Day and koi (carp) banners on Boys' Day. Special foods, especially mochi, are often eaten on these occasions.

Ching Ming

Ching Ming is a Chinese custom that is observed in April. It involves the cleaning and repairing of family gravesites. Participants pray and burn incense along with symbolic pieces of paper. Ching Ming is known for special foods such as fruit, rice, chicken, pork, cakes and tea, which are ceremonially presented at the gravesite. A meal may be eaten at the grave as a gesture of sharing with one's ancestors and deceased relatives. It is not necessarily a sad occasion, but a time to remember and honor past generations.

This is a classic Chinese-inspired sweetmeat to make in honor of the dead—or the living.

Chinese Almond Cookies

3 c.	flour
1 c.	sugar
1 tsp.	baking powder
¼ tsp.	salt
1 c.	shortening
1	egg, beaten
1 tsp.	almond extract
	Almonds for garnish, if desired
	Red food coloring, if desired

Preheat oven to 350°F. In a large bowl, combine flour, sugar, baking powder and salt. Cut shortening into dry ingredients until mixture is crumbly. Add egg and almond extract. Mix, then knead until soft. Form into small balls on ungreased baking sheet and flatten slightly. Make a dent in the center of each cookie. Garnish dent with an almond or a dab of red food coloring. Bake 10 to 15 minutes.

Easter

Easter is widely celebrated by nearly everyone in Hawai'i, regardless of their religious faith. It is a time when people gather for potluck or go out to enjoy a nice brunch, lunch or dinner at their favorite restaurants. Traditional Easter dishes such as lamb, ham, turkey and potatoes are augmented by a range of local favorites, from sashimi and poke to kalbi and kim chee. Egg sales soar.

Khmer

Although not great in number here, Cambodians celebrate New Year in April, at the end of the harvest season. During this three-day celebration, people clean their homes thoroughly to rid them of any unclean spirits, buy or make new clothes to represent new beginnings, and bring food and other offerings to place before the monks and share with others.

Cinco de Mayo

Cinco de Mayo, which marks the Mexican army's victory over the French in 1862, is celebrated with great enthusiasm and plenty of Mexican food and beer in downtown Honolulu at Murphy's Bar & Grill and on Merchant Street near Murphy's, as well as at the Aloha Tower Marketplace.

Memorial Day

On the last Monday in May, Hawai'i joins the rest of the nation in honoring its servicemen and -women who died in service to their country. Due to the Islands' proud military history and strong contemporary military presence, services are held at various locations throughout the state. Traditionally, Memorial Day also kicks off summer, and families head to the beaches, parks and backyards to picnic and barbecue.

State, Farm and County Fairs

School's out for summer, and that heralds the start of a series of fairs, starting in May with the 50th State Fair on O'ahu, followed by the State Farm Fair in July. County fairs are big events, especially on the Neighbor Islands. Kaua'i usually holds its county fair in August, while Hawai'i County and Maui County usually have theirs in September. Popular fairground munchies such as cotton candy, candy apples and corn on the cob are sold alongside local-style plate lunches, hot dogs and hamburgers.

Feast of the Holy Ghost

Portuguese immigrants brought the Feast of the Holy Ghost to Hawai'i with them when they arrived in the late 1800s. The event is highlighted by a three-day festival that begins on the Friday night just before the Seventh Dominga, the seventh Saturday before the feast, when the "Blessing of the Meat and Bread" takes place. A portion of beef and bread is blessed by a priest and distributed to each member present. A bowl of soup or stew is also served to everyone, recalling the importance of charity to the poor.

Today, many Feast of the Holy Ghost affairs take on a distinctly local flavor, with plate lunches and Hawaiian and Filipino food being sold in addition to hamburgers and hot dogs. One Neighbor Island festival proudly touts its pasteles, chow fun, fruit smoothies, homemade jams and baked goods, in addition to its Portuguese bean soup and malasadas.

Japanese lanterns, Obon season

Obon

Starting in June and running through August is "Bon Dance Season" in Hawai'i. To avoid conflicting with neighboring institutions, Buddhist temples on each island carefully schedule their Obon observances so that there is nearly one per weekend spread out over this time of year. While Obon is a time to show respect to the dead, it is also treated as a colorful and spirited community event that is open to everyone. Food booths sell favorites such as saimin with teri sticks, hot dogs, andagi, shave ice, corn on the cob, fried noodles, SPAM™ musubi and sushi.

Flavors of Honolulu

The Flavors of Honolulu, held on the last weekend in June, is billed as Hawai'i's largest outdoor food, wine and entertainment festival. Formerly known as the Taste of Honolulu, this event fills the Honolulu Civic Center grounds adjacent to Honolulu Hale, drawing more than 50,000 people each year. The festival combines sample-sized servings of gourmet entrées, local favorites and ethnic delicacies with live entertainment, wine and

beer tastings, cooking demonstrations and children's activities. It has established a template for many smaller "Taste of ..." functions and events throughout the state.

Kapalua Wine & Food Festival

Started more than 20 years ago, the Kapalua Wine & Food Festival has evolved into an extravaganza that draws thousands of visitors to the luxurious West Maui resort each year. The four-day event, held in late June or early July, is the longest-running festival of its kind in Hawai'i and features master sommeliers, renowned chefs and numerous celebrities.

Kenjinkai and Kumiai Picnics

One of the traditional links with the past are summer picnics held by kenjinkai and kumiai groups in Hawai'i. Kenjinkai are associations based on the Prefectural origins of one's immigrant ancestors, while kumiai are organizations of families from a particular local area or neighborhood, if you will. They include picnic food (shave ice, watermelon), as well as ethnic food and games.

Fourth of July

Picnics, parades, picnics, fireworks displays … picnics.

Makawao Rodeo and Parade

On Maui, the Fourth of July means it is time for the annual Makawao Rodeo and Parade. For more than 40 years, this event hosted by the Maui Roping Club has featured paniolo (cowboy) competition between more than 300 competitors from around the world. The festivities also include live entertainment, country-western dancing and lots of food booths for participants to enjoy.

Independence Day Rodeo and Horse Races

Held at the Parker Ranch Rodeo Arena in Waimea on the island of Hawai'i, this event began as the Parker Ranch Rodeo over 45 years ago. Seven area ranches send their best cowboys to compete in events ranging from horse racing to team ranch mugging. The event features food booths, shopping and activities for children.

Rodeo season

Korean Festival

The annual Korean Festival at Kapi'olani Park includes cultural activities and demonstrations, such as a tea ceremony, youth singing contest, Korean cultural exhibits and various product vendors. Cooking demonstrations and performances of Korean dance and taekwondo are also popular. The event is best known, however, for its food, including popular specialties from over 20 restaurants and community groups. There is also a fiery kim chee-eating contest.

Greek Festival

The annual Greek Festival is traditionally held at McCoy Pavilion, Ala Moana Park, in August. The festival is famous for its authentic Greek food, such as gyros, souvlaki, moussaka, spanakopita, baklava and kataifi, along with wine, beer and ouzo shipped in from Greece.

Chinese Moon Festival

The Chinese Moon Festival is observed in mid-August to celebrate a successful harvest. It is a time for thanksgiving and feasting. True to its name, the moon itself and moon-inspired moon cakes are the stars of this festival. Moon cakes are round cakes filled with sweet red bean paste, lotus paste, date paste, dried fruits or other sweetmeats.

Tet Trung Thu

The Vietnamese Children's Moon Festival is held in mid-August to early September. It is similar to the Chinese Moon Festival.

Big Island Festival

The Big Island Festival took a one-year hiatus in 2007, vowing to return in late August or early September 2008. In five previous years, this Festival drew up to 2,000 food and wine connoisseurs to the South Kōhala coast of the island of Hawai'i and featured wine tasting, exhibits and educational displays.

A Taste of the Hawaiian Range

Established in 1996, A Taste of the Hawaiian Range has grown from a modest affair featuring a dozen restaurants, six food vendors and approximately 350 guests to one of the premiere food extravaganzas in Hawai'i. The event is the brainchild of the Mealani Research Station on the Big Island, which is associated

Moon cake, Chinese Moon Festival

with the University of Hawai'i's College of Tropical Agriculture and Human Resources. It now attracts some 2,000 excited foodies to the Hilton Waikoloa Village's Grand Ballroom each September. The event has grown to include approximately 50 chefs and restaurants and over 60 exhibitors.

Labor Day Weekend

Some of Hawai'i's larger labor unions sponsor traditional Labor Day outings for their members. Otherwise, as on Memorial Day and the Fourth of July, families pull out all the stops in enjoying outdoor picnics, potlucks and backyard barbecues.

Okinawan Festival

Started over 25 years ago, the Okinawan Festival is one of the largest ethnic festivals in Hawai'i. Over the Labor Day weekend, tens of thousands of people descend on Kapi'olani

Park to enjoy two days of Okinawan and Hawaiian entertainment, cultural displays and lots of food. Favorites include pig feet's soup, andagi, Okinawan soba, anda-dogs (like corn dogs, only with andagi batter), barbecue chicken, yakisoba, chili and rice, kālua pork Hawaiian plate, shoyu pork, hamburger, hot dogs, soda and shave ice.

Andagi, dense deep-fried Okinawan doughnuts, are becoming more popular, and thus easier to find, but it's always good to be able to make your own when the craving hits:

Andagi
Makes 4 dozen doughnuts

4	eggs
¾ c.	milk
¾ tsp.	vanilla
2 c.	sugar
4 c.	flour
3½ Tbsp.	baking powder
¼ tsp.	salt
	Vegetable oil, for deep-frying

In a large bowl, beat eggs, milk and vanilla together; mix in sugar. In a separate bowl, sift flour, baking powder and salt together; add to egg mixture. Stir until dry ingredients are moistened, but do not over-mix after combining with liquid ingredients.

In a deep frying pan, heat oil to 350°F. Drop dough, in half-fist-sized portions, into hot oil; fry until doughnuts are golden brown and rise to the surface. To do this the Okinawan way, fill your right hand with dough, then squeeze it out by moving your thumb toward your index finger and drop it gently into the hot oil.

Aloha Festivals

The Aloha Festivals start in August and run through October, with events on all islands. The Aloha Festivals showcase Hawai'i's music, dance and history. The Waikīkī Ho'olaule'a, held in September, is one of the highlights of the Aloha Festival. Kalākaua Avenue between Lewers Street and Kapahulu Avenue is alive with entertainment stages and lots of food booths.

Tailgate party, Aloha Stadium

UH Football Season

Kicking off in September and culminating in December, the University of Hawai'i Warrior football team's play season is the talk of the town. The aroma of tailgate parties wafts from the Aloha Stadium parking lot, while other football fans gather at pay-per-view football parties at friends' homes. Inside the stadium, recently expanded food concessions serve up a variety of local favorites alongside stadium standbys.

Hispanic Heritage Festival

The Hawaii Hispanic Chamber of Commerce presents the annual Hispanic Heritage Festival at Kapi'olani Park Bandstand. The all-day festival features ethnic food and entertainment.

Halloween

Candy *is* a food, no?

Kona Coffee Cultural Festival

The Kona Coffee Cultural Festival takes place in Kailua-Kona on the Big Island each year from late October to early November. The 10-day festival includes more than 30 community events, including coffee tastings, art exhibits, recipe contests and more. The Festival, the oldest product festival in Hawai'i, honors the multi-ethnic heritage of Kona coffee pioneers.

Thanksgiving

It's all about the turkey, of course, but here you may not get a traditional roast turkey. In Hawai'i, you're just as likely to have your bird deep-fried, smoked, kamado'd or kālua'd these days—with all the trimmings, including rice, of course. Gotta get poke.

Christmas

Family gatherings, office parties, out-of-town guests, crawling the malls, surfing the swap meets ... I'm going to burst. Gotta diet—New Year's is right around the corner!

No one indulges in all of these events and activities, of course, and there are other events and activities not mentioned here, but this listing of significant food-related holidays and festivals does underscore the notion that we in Hawai'i do sort of eat and drink our way through the year. Welcome to paradise.

Coffee cherry-picking contest, Kona Coffee Cultural Festival

EPILOGUE: BURNT RICE

In the old days, my grandmother cooked rice in a heavy pot on a kerosene stove. Before that, she cooked rice over an open fire on an outdoor stove fashioned out of a big metal drum cut in half. The bottom of the pot would often become coated with a layer of burnt (koge) rice. Rather than mix the burnt bits in with the rest of the white rice, my grandmother would first stir, or "turn," the rice so it would steam properly, and then serve it to her family without disturbing the dark crust on the bottom.

Nothing was wasted, so after everyone had eaten, my grandmother—like many women of her time—would scrape up the burnt portion, season it with a little salt and eat it. Or else she would pour tea into the pot to loosen the hardened layer and eat the resulting rice gruel with tsukemono (pickled vegetables).

You don't see burnt rice anymore. Starting with the introduction of the first automatic rice cookers in the late 1950s, fast-forwarding to the amazing, do-everything "fuzzy logic" machines of today, burnt rice has been skillfully and systematically micro-processed into oblivion. This must be very important, considering how Japan unleashed its formidable postwar technological tsunami in the quest to create perfect, unburnt rice.

Why, then, do I find myself haunted by the flavor, aroma and texture of burnt rice? Could there possibly be something of value—kernels of wisdom perhaps—in those darkened grains? They remind me of my grandmother's humility, her willingness to give what was best to others and keep what was left for herself. She did so every day of her life—not just with rice, but in everything she did. She was the embodiment of humility in her simple gray dresses, her hair pulled smartly back in a bun.

I know she would have wanted her children's, grandchildren's and great grandchildren's lives to be better than hers—and for the most part that's so. We have raised our standard of living. We are free to pursue our dreams. We wear what we want to wear, say what we want to say and eat what we want to eat—while freely disposing of the burnt and imperfect parts of our lives.

But I remember, too, that my grandmother not only ate the burnt rice—she made it look delicious. Today, I know that it was. Now we can go to fancy Japanese izaka-ya restaurants and pay a nice sum for yaki-onigiri, rice balls that have been salted, brushed with a

light shoyu or miso glaze and lightly charred over a hibachi. They are delicious eaten with tsukemono—just like my grandmother ate.

Sometimes I think my grandmother was so far ahead of us that we are only now appreciating what she always knew. Many great chefs around the world recognize umami, the so-called fifth taste sensation defined as a "savoriness" or "delicious flavor," which is best exemplified by dashi, a flavorful soup stock drawn from certain meats and seafood and seaweed. Today, I realize that my grandmother demonstrated a masterful grasp of umami in her incomparable oden and nishime. There was great sophistication and complexity in such outwardly simple dishes—just as there was great strength and infinite dignity in her humble life.

It is often said that we are what we eat. In compiling this book I have come to appreciate how important it is to also know *why* we eat what we eat, for food represents an important link, both physical and spiritual, to our past—and to the values that define who we are.

KAU KAU
CONNECTION

YAKI-ONIGIRI: GRILLED RICE BALLS

We began these Kau Kau Connections with those two universals, rice and salt, and it's fitting that we end with them as well. For a reasonable facsimile of burnt (koge) rice, assemble the following:

Rice—one cup for every 2-3 musubi (rice balls) you desire
Salt
Soy sauce or miso paste
Various fillings and side dishes (be creative): umeboshi (pickled plums), katsuoboshi (shaved bonito), canned tuna mixed with shoyu, teriyaki chicken, takuan (yellow pickled radish), other tsukemono (pickled vegetables).

Cook the rice, reducing the amount of water slightly to avoid making it overly mushy.

When the rice is cool enough to touch, wet your hands and sprinkle salt on them. Shape the rice with pressing and rolling motions until your rice ball is firm. Poke a hole in the rice ball and insert your desired fillings.

Next, toast the rice balls on a grill over a slow flame. A stovetop fish grill is ideal, but a barbecue grill could suffice as long as the grill's bars are not too far apart. As the edges start to turn brown, baste the rice with shoyu or miso. Turn and toast the rice balls some more. Baste both sides, being careful not to burn them. Turn over again if necessary. When both sides are golden brown, they are ready to serve.

Garnish the plate with tsukemono, takuan pickles and/or a small mound of bonito flakes topped with a splash of soy sauce.

For a really special treat, try yaki-onigiri ochazuke: Place one of the yaki-onigiri rice balls in a bowl and cover with hot green tea. Serve with pickles.

Just like grandma used to eat—but different, too: a new look at an old tradition.

BIBLIOGRAPHY

A DASH of Aloha: Healthy Hawai'i Cuisine and Lifestyle, Kapi'olani Community College, University of Hawai'i, Watermark Publishing, 2007.

A Puerto Rican Poet on the Sugar Plantations of Hawai'i, Blase Camacho Souza and Austin Dias, Puerto Rican Heritage Society of Hawai'i, Honolulu, 1997.

"A two-scoop challenge," Catherine E. Toth, *Honolulu Advertiser*, April 24, 2005.

"Add a twist to Chinese New Year favorites," Wanda Adams, *Honolulu Advertiser*, February 2, 2005.

"Aloha Andy's," Burl Burlingame, *Honolulu Star-Bulletin*, May 31, 1999.

"Beyond Kalbi," Jackie Young, special to the *Honolulu Star-Bulletin*, November 7, 2007.

Boy from Kahaluu: An Autobiography, Tom Ige, Kin Cho Jin Kai, Honolulu, 1989.

"By Request: … and what's a picnic without a starchy salad?" Betty Shimabukuro, *Honolulu Star-Bulletin*, May 26, 2004.

"Chefs Share Their Stories of Mom," *Honolulu Advertiser,* May 2, 2008.

"Christmas Past in Waimea," *Waimea Gazette*, Nancy Piianaia, December 1997.

"Clearing up Miso Butterfish and Black Cod," Susan Scott, *Ocean Watch*, susanscott.net, February 28, 2003.

Cooking from the Heart, Sam Choy, Mutual Publishing, Honolulu, 1995.

Cuisine Hawaii: Featuring the Premier Chefs of the Aloha State, Sam Choy, Pleasant Hawaii, Inc., Honolulu, 1990.

Dear Okaasan … It's Pick Coffee Time Again, Jean Misaki (Yoshida) Matsuo, Hawai'i, 2003.
Ethnic Foods of Hawai'i, Ann Kondo Corum, Bess Press, Honolulu, 1983.

Favorite Island Cookery (series), Honpa Hongwanji Buddhist Temple, Honolulu.

"Foraging from the Land," *Paddling Hawaii*, Audrey Sutherland, Latitude 20 Books, 1998.

From Then to Now: A Manual for Doing Things Hawaiian Style, The 'Opelu Project 'Ohana, 1996.

"Gen Y: How Boomer Babies are Changing the Workplace," Cathy S. Cruz, *Hawaii Business*, May 2007.

"Getting to the Roots of Hawaii Regional Cuisine," Betty Fullard-Leo, *Coffee Times*, May 1997.

"Go with your gut: L&L Drive-Inn's rapid-fire expansion …" Jacy L. Youn, *Hawaii Business*, December 1, 2002.

"Growing a new industry in the back yard," Lyn Danninger, *Honolulu Star-Bulletin*, July 8, 2001.

Hans L'Orange Field: Common Ground, Uncommon Glory 1924-1999, Hans L'Orange Field Baseball Park Council, 1999.

Hawaii Pono: A Social History, Lawrence Fuchs, Harcourt, Brace & World, Inc., New York, 1961.

Hawai'i Homefront: Life in the Islands during World War II, MacKinnon Simpson, Bess Press, Honolulu, 2008.

Hawai'i's Home Cooking, Elizabeth Meahl, Alu Like, Mutual Publishing, Honolulu, 2004.

Hawaii's 2nd SPAM™ Cookbook, Ann Kondo Corum, Bess Press, Honolulu, 2001.

Hawaiian and Pacific Foods, Katherine Bazore, M. Barrow's and Co., New York, NY, 1940.

Hawaiian Cookbook, Ladies' Society of Central Union Church, Honolulu, 1896.
"Here Come the MILLENNIALS! (Generation Y consumers)," Leslie Skarra, Carol Cronk, Audrey Nelson, *Prepared Foods*, May 2001.

"Here's the scoop on mac salad," Kekoa Catherine Enomoto, *Honolulu Star-Bulletin*, June 17, 1998.

"In A Nutshell, Boiled Peanuts Better For You," Kent Faulk, *Free Republic*, October 28, 2007.

"Jackie's Provides Authentic Puerto Rican Pastele," Lisa Sekiya, *Honolulu Advertiser*, May 11, 2007.

Journey to the Sandalwood Island: A Family Saga, J.W. Lau (undated).

"Just Down the Street: Sidestreet Inn," Betty Shimabukuro, *Honolulu Star Bulletin*, August 25, 1999.

Just Hungry, a food blog established in 2003, Maki, January 29, 2007.

Kipu–Huleia: The Social History of a Plantation Community, 1910-1950, William K. Yamanaka, Seattle, Washington, 1996.

Kokoro: Cherished Japanese Traditions in Hawaii, Japanese Women's Society of Honolulu, Island Heritage, Honolulu, 2004.

"Life Aboard a Canoe," Polynesian Voyaging Society website, pvs.kcc.hawaii.edu

Local Food: What to Eat in Hawaii? Joan Clarke, Namkoong Publishing, Honolulu, 1997.

"Local Grinds: Food and Resistance in Hawai'i," Megan Lee Kawatachi, Brown University (Thesis), 1997.
Local Homemaking Recipes, Hawaii Division of Vocational Education, Department of Public Instruction, Honolulu, 1932.

"More venues offer diners a taste of Hawaii," Vanessa Hua, *San Francisco Chronicle*, July 3, 2006.

"Mr. Zip: The Higa brothers, founders of Zippy's …" Betty Shimabukuro, *Honolulu Star-Bulletin*, April 14, 2004.

My Mom's Favorite Recipes from Hawaii, by Eric Costanios and Annette Galeon (undated).

Okinawan Mixed Plate, Hui O Laulima, Honolulu, 2000.

'Ōlelo No'eau: Hawaiian Proverbs and Poetical Sayings, Mary Kawena Pukui, Bishop Museum Press, Honolulu, 1983.

On the Rise, Russell Siu, L.A.K. Enterprises, Honolulu, 1996.

Pahoa Yesterday, Hiroo Sato, Hilo, Hawai'i, 2002.

Paper Trails: Cultural Imperialism from the late 19th Century as seen through Documents, Literature and Photographs, Marc Jason Gilbert, North Georgia College and State University.

Parker Ranch Paniolo: Yutaka Kimura, Jiro Nakano, United Japanese Society of Hawaii, Honolulu, 1992.

Pau Hana: Plantation Life and Labor in Hawaii 1835-1920, Ronald Takaki, University of Hawai'i Press, Honolulu, 1983.

Poi, paiai, University of Hawai'i Ethnic Studies, 1978.
"Portrait of a Mystery: What Makes Macaroni Salad a Local Treat?" Cynthia Oi, *Honolulu Star-Bulletin*, March 17, 1999.

"Shave ice through the ages," Catherine Toth, *Honolulu Advertiser*, September 24, 2006.

"Shave ice," Mike Gordon, *Honolulu Advertiser*, July 2, 2006.

"Sofrito: The heart of a Puerto Rican Meal," Nadine Kam, *Honolulu Star-Bulletin*, April 15, 1998.

Sugar Town: Hawaii Plantation Days Remembered, Yasushi "Scotch" Kurisu, Watermark Publishing, Honolulu, 1995.

Sukiyaki: The Art of Japanese Cooking and Hospitality, Fumiko, South Sea Sales, Honolulu (undated).

The Columbia Guide to Asian American History, Gary Y. Okihiro, Columbia University Press, New York, NY, 2001.

The Companies We Keep, Bob Sigall and students at Hawai'i Pacific University, Small Business Hawai'i, Honolulu, 2004.

The Epicure in Hawaii, Barbara Thompson, Polynesian Food Specialties, Honolulu, 1938.

The First Strange Place: The Alchemy of Race and Sex in World War II Hawaii, Beth Bailey and David Farber, The Free Press, New York, NY, 1992.

The Food of Paradise: Exploring Hawaii's Culinary Heritage, Rachel Laudan, University of Hawai'i Press, Honolulu, 1996.

The Hawai'i Coffee Book, Shawn Steiman, Watermark Publishing, Honolulu, 2008.

The Hawai'i Farmers Market Cookbook, Hawaii Farm Bureau Federation, Watermark Publishing, Honolulu, 2006.

The Island Plate, Wanda Adams, Island Heritage, Honolulu, 2006.

The Lymans of Hawai'i Island: A Pioneering Family, MacKinnon Simpson, Lyman House Memorial Museum, 1993.

The Maui Book of Lavender, Alii Chang, Lani Medina Weigert, Jill Engledow, Watermark Publishing, Honolulu, 2008.

"The Musubi Mystique," Betty Shimabukuro, *Honolulu Star-Bulletin*, June 19, 2002.

The New Cuisine of Hawaii, Janice Wald Henderson, Villard Books, New York, NY, 1994.

The Omiyage Guide: Island Gifts to Go, Donovan M. Dela Cruz and Jodi Endo Chai, Watermark Publishing, Honolulu, 2002.

The Shoreline Chef: Creative Cuisine for Hawaiian Reef Fish, Elmer Guzman, Watermark Publishing, Honolulu, 2003.

We Go Eat, A Mixed Plate from Hawai'i's Food Culture, Susan Yim, editor, Hawaii Council for the Humanities, 2008.

Weenie Royale: Food and the Japanese Internment, National Public Radio, http://www.npr.org/templates/story/story.php?storyId=17335538&sc=emaf

"You Are What You Eat," Nadine Kam, *Honolulu Star-Bulletin*, April 1, 1998.

"You may be the guest, but don't go empty-handed," *Topeka Capital-Journal*, December 1, 2002.

W. T. Haraguchi Farm,
Hanalei, Kaua'i.

PHOTO CREDITS

Shuzo Uemoto 11, 12, 16 bottom, 21, 45 left, 50, 52, 53, 55, 57, 59, 61, 63, 67, 69, 71, 73, 75, 77, 98, 106, 107, 116, 120, 121, 140, 145, 149 top, 152, 153, 154, 170, 178

Hawai'i State Archives 4, 5, 6, 7 bottom, 10, 13, 16 top, 17, 20, 22, 23, 26, 28, 29, 30, 31, 32 top, 33, 37, 39 right, 42, 44, 46, 47 left, 48, 54, 56, 60, 83, 96, 101, 105, 108, 146 right

Adriana Torres Chong (photography and styling) ii, iv, vi, 1 top, 15, 34, 35, 36, 47 right, 49, 51, 103, 119, 139 right, 171, 172, 173

Aimee Harris 146 left

Ali'i Kula Lavender 148

Arthur Suehiro 88 bottom

Barbara Long 70

Big Island Candies 149 bottom

Coffees of Hawai'i 147 right

Dawn Sakamoto iii, 2, 3, 18, 133, 138, 142, 143, 155, 158, 166

DeSoto Brown 81 left, 84, 85, 86, 90 top, 91, 93

Dietrich Varez 8

Doug Young 111, 114, 132,

Eloise Nakama 41

Frederika Bain 1 center, 144

George Engebretson 81 right, 87, 92, 94, 95

George Kaya 72

Hawai'i Farm Bureau Federation 141

Hawaiian Electric Co. 88 top

Hormel Foods 1 bottom, 97

iStock vi, 19, 43, 45 right, 76, 99, 100, 104, 109, 151, 160, 161, 162, 163, 164, 167

Jo McGarry 157, 165 left

Joe Carini 113

Kaua'i Coffee Co. 147 left

Kawaguchi Family 74

Kona Coffee Cultural Festival 165 right

Lew Harrington 134 right, 135

MacKinnon Simpson 82

Maui Land & Pineapple Co. 64

Nagasako Family 62

Olivier Koning 139 left

Punalu'u Bake Shop 150

Rae Huo 110, 123, 125, 127, 129, 136, 137, 159

Roy Tokujo 130

Samantha Guzman 134 left

Sandy Yoshimori 66

Sugino Family 68

Sullivan Family of Companies 118

The Don Ho Trust 117

The *Honolulu Advertiser* 89

U.S. Army Museum 79, 80

'Ulupalakua Ranch 58

RECIPE CREDITS

All recipes from the author unless credited in the text or listed below.

Lomilomi Salmon, p. 18
More of Our Favorite Recipes, Maui Home Demonstration Council, 1968

Kahuā Ranch Beef Stew, p. 19
Kahuā Ranch

Haupia for a Crowd, p. 25
Adapted from *Ohana Style Cookbook II*, Friends from Hilo High School, 2005

Kulolo, p. 25
Hawaiian Cookbook, Ladies' Society of Central Union Church, 1898

"Lawalu" Fish, p. 25
The Epicure in Hawaii, Barbara Thompson, 1938

Poi Cocktail, p. 25
Local Homemaking Recipes, Hawaii Division of Vocational Education, Department of Public Instruction, 1932

Manapua (Char Siu Bao), p. 40
Hawaiian Electric Co.

Miso Soup, p. 45
Hisako Higa, co-founder with husband William Higa and George Higa of Hawaiian Miso & Soy Co.

Vinha D'Alhos, p. 47
Hawaiian Electric Co.

Preserved Starfruit, p. 64
Church of the Holy Cross Cookbook, Hilo, 1981

Old-Fashioned Shave Ice Syrup, p. 100
Tracy Miyashiro and Florence Ajimine

Miyashiro, in *Oldies But Goodies*, Kamehameha Schools Alumni Association, 1983

Basic Macaroni Salad, p. 102
Betty Shimabukuro,
Honolulu Star-Bulletin

Macaroni-Potato Salad, p. 103
Hawaiian Electric Co.

Comfort Foods, p. 130
As told to Arthur Kaneshiro

Saimin Broth, p. 131
Helen Shiroma Kaneshiro,
Honolulu Star-Bulletin

INDEX OF RECIPES

INDEX

INDEX *(continued)*

About the Author

Arnold Hiura is an independent writer, editor and media consultant based in Honolulu, Hawai'i. He is a partner in MBFT Media, which provides a variety of communications and creative services to businesses and community organizations. He previously served as editor of the *Hawaii Herald* and curator for the Japanese American National Museum. He was born and raised in the sugar plantation town of Pāpa'ikou, about five miles north of Hilo, on the Big Island of Hawai'i.

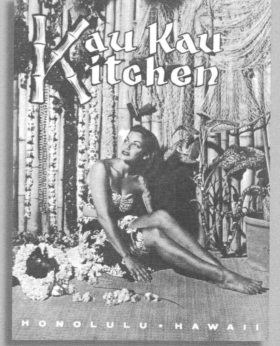